T0270524

"With [...] you around the C[...] ingredients and differing ways of using them. I grew up in Saint Lucia and have enjoyed a lifetime of learning the ways other nations treated the same ingredients of my youth. Lesley highlights eleven important staples of the region's cuisine and invites you to island-hop in your own kitchen with wonderfully selected dishes. Bon app!"

—NINA COMPTON,
James Beard Award–winning chef

"In this rich and inviting text, Lesley Enston shows the world that the Caribbean—a region fractured by colonialism and for too long defined by its economic role as a tourist paradise—is a place of abundance and unique culinary cultures. There is so much love and deep research in how Enston presents the commonalities and differences."

—ALICIA KENNEDY,
author of *No Meat Required: The Cultural History and Culinary Future of Plant-Based Eating*

"In *Belly Fully*, Lesley Enston shares the stories and flavors that have shaped her lifelong love affair with Caribbean food. From her mother's effortless cooking style, infused with love and tradition, to her father's culinary experiments with Trinidadian staples like curried chicken and souse, Lesley's recipes inspire in the ways they approach, transcend, and unify cultural boundaries on page after delicious page."

—HAWA HASSAN,
author of *In Bibi's Kitchen*

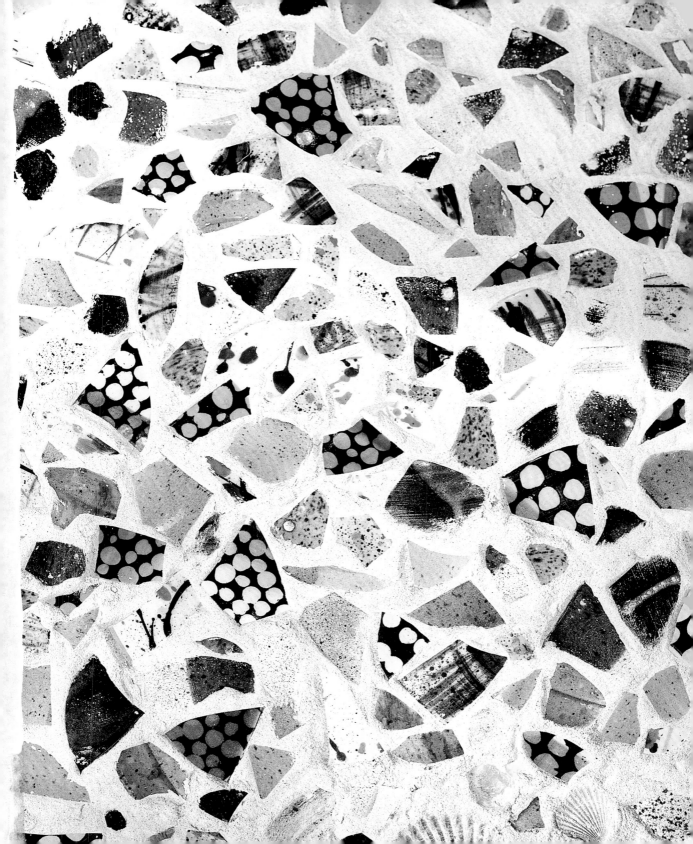

BELLY FULL

EXPLORING CARIBBEAN CUISINE
THROUGH 11 FUNDAMENTAL
INGREDIENTS AND OVER 100 RECIPES

LESLEY ENSTON

10
TEN SPEED PRESS
California | New York

FOR MY **MOTHER**, MERLE ENSTON, WHO TAUGHT ME TO PRIORITIZE JOY AND THAT LOVE IS THE MAIN INGREDIENT TO ANY DISH, AND MY **FATHER**, KEN ENSTON, WHO SHOWED ME THE POWER OF THE WRITTEN WORD AND HOW TO MAKE A SALAD.

CONTENTS

O INTRODUCTION 1   O OTHER INGREDIENTS OUTSIDE THE KEY ELEVEN 10
O EQUIPMENT 18   O SEASONING BASES AND BLENDS 21

BEANS 24
CALABAZA 42
CASSAVA 60
CHAYOTE 78
COCONUT 92
CORNMEAL 114
OKRA 130
PLANTAINS 150
RICE 174
SALTED COD 194
SCOTCH BONNET PEPPERS 210

O ACKNOWLEDGMENTS 230   O ABOUT THE AUTHOR 232
O FURTHER READING 234   O FURTHER COOKING 235   O INDEX 237

RECIPES

SEASONING BASES AND BLENDS

EPIS 21
HAITI

GREEN SEASONING 22
TRINIDAD AND TOBAGO

RECAÍTO 22
Green Sofrito
PUERTO RICO

SAZÓN 23
DOMINICAN REPUBLIC

SAZÓN 23
PUERTO RICO

BEANS

DIRI AK PWA 28
Rice and Beans
HAITI

CALA 29
Black-Eyed Pea Fritters
ARUBA

CURRIED CHANA AND ALOO 30
Curried Chickpeas and Potatoes
TRINIDAD AND TOBAGO

STEW PEAS 33
JAMAICA

JUG JUG 34
Pigeon Pea Mash
BARBADOS

SÒS PWA BLAN 35
White Bean Sauce
HAITI

FRIJOLES NEGROS 36
Stewed Black Beans
CUBA

PHOLOURIE 39
Split Pea Fritters
TRINIDAD AND TOBAGO

HABICHUELAS GUISADAS 41
Stewed Red Beans
PUERTO RICO

CALABAZA

SOUP JOUMOU 47
Freedom Soup
HAITI

CALABAZA CON AJO 50
Steamed Calabaza with Garlic
CUBA

PUMPKIN SOUP 51
SAINT LUCIA

PUMPKIN RICE 52
SAINT VINCENT AND THE GRENADINES

PUMPKIN CHOKA AND SALTFISH 53
Stewed Calabaza and Salted Cod
TRINIDAD AND TOBAGO

CALABAZA PUREE 54

PUMPKIN FRITTERS 55
BARBADOS

AREPA DI PAMPUNA 57
Calabaza Pancakes
CURAÇAO

CALABAZA PIE 58

CASSAVA

METEMGEE 64
Provision Stew
GUYANA

AREPITAS DE YUCA 66
Cassava Fritters
DOMINICAN REPUBLIC

BOIL AND FRY CASSAVA 67
Cassava Hash
TRINIDAD AND TOBAGO

CASABE/KASAV/ KASSAVE 69
Cassava Flatbread
ACROSS THE CARIBBEAN

CASSAVA PONE 71
Cassava and Coconut Pudding
TRINIDAD AND TOBAGO

BAMMY 72
Cassava Bread Soaked in Coconut Milk
JAMAICA

PEPPERPOT 73
Meat Stew
GUYANA

YUCA CON MOJO 76
Boiled Cassava with Mojo Sauce
CUBA

CHAYOTE

CHAYOTE AND WATERCRESS SALAD WITH SOUR ORANGE VINAIGRETTE 81

LEGIM 82
Vegetable Stew
HAITI

CHAYOTES RELLENOS 83
Chayotes Stuffed with Picadillo
PUERTO RICO

GRATIN AU CHRISTOPHINE 84
Cheese-Stuffed Chayotes
MARTINIQUE

STUFFED CHO CHO 86
JAMAICA

CREAM OF CHAYOTE SOUP 87

TRINI CHOW MEIN 89
TRINIDAD AND TOBAGO

CHAYOTE SLAW 90

COCONUT

COCONUT MILK 97

OIL DOWN 98
Vegetables Stewed in Coconut Milk
GRENADA

CHICKEN COLOMBO 101
Curried Chicken
MARTINIQUE/ GUADELOUPE

COCONUT BAKE 103
Coconut Flatbread
TRINIDAD AND TOBAGO

WILTED DASHEEN LEAVES WITH COCONUT MILK 104

RUNDOWN 106
Mackerel with Reduced Coconut Milk
JAMAICA

SUGAR CAKE 107
Coconut Candy
BARBADOS

KÒK GRAJE 109
Coconut Candy
HAITI

TEMBLEQUE 110
Coconut Pudding
PUERTO RICO

PIÑA COLADA ICE CREAM 111

CORNMEAL

MAYI MOULEN AK ARANSÒ 118
Cornmeal with Smoked Herring
HAITI

SORULLITOS DE MAÍZ 119
Cornmeal Fritters
PUERTO RICO

FESTIVALS 120
Cornmeal Fritters
JAMAICA

TAMAL EN CAZUELA 122
Cornmeal and Pork Shoulder Casserole
CUBA

PEN MAYI 123
Sweet Cornbread
HAITI

AREPA 125
Cornmeal Cake
DOMINICAN REPUBLIC

CORNMEAL PORRIDGE 126
JAMAICA

CONKIES 127
Steamed Sweet Cornmeal Dumplings
BARBADOS

OKRA

ARROZ CON QUIMBOMBÓ 133
Rice and Okra
CUBA

CALLALOO 135
Okra and Dasheen Greens Soup
TRINIDAD AND TOBAGO

FRIED OKRO 136
Stir-Fried Okra
TRINIDAD AND TOBAGO

OKRA AND SALTFISH 137
GUYANA

FUNGEE 138
Cornmeal and Okra
ANTIGUA

GRILLED OKRA WITH CHARRED SCALLION VINAIGRETTE 141

MOLONDRONES GUISADOS 142
Stewed Okra
DOMINICAN REPUBLIC

TONMTONM AK KALALOU 145
Mashed Breadfruit with Okra
HAITI

CHOP UP 148
Vegetable Mash
ANTIGUA

PLANTAINS

LABOUYI BANNANN 155
Plantain Porridge
HAITI

TORTILLA DE PLÁTANO MADURO 157
Sweet Plantain Omelet
CUBA

MANGÚ 158
Mashed Green Plantains with Quick-Pickled Onions
DOMINICAN REPUBLIC

MOFONGO 160
Fried Mashed Plantains with Chicharrónes
PUERTO RICO

PASTELÓN 163
Plantain "Casserole"
DOMINICAN REPUBLIC

PIÑON 165
Plantain "Casserole"
PUERTO RICO

FRIED SWEET PLANTAINS 166
ACROSS THE CARIBBEAN

FRIED GREEN PLANTAINS 168
ACROSS THE CARIBBEAN

PLANTAIN TARTE TATIN 170

RICE

"PERFECT" WHITE RICE 180

CRAB AND RICE 181
TURKS AND CAICOS

DIRI AK DJON DJON 185
Rice with Mushrooms
HAITI

PEAS AND RICE 186
BAHAMAS

ARROZ CON POLLO 188
Chicken and Rice
PUERTO RICO

PELAU 189
Chicken and Rice
DOMINICA

ASOPAO DE POLLO 192
Chicken and Rice Stew
PUERTO RICO

ARROZ CON DULCE 193
Rice Pudding
PUERTO RICO

SALTED COD

ACCRAS DE MORUE 198
Salt Cod Fritters
MARTINIQUE

BACALAITOS 200
Salt Cod Fritters
PUERTO RICO

APORREADO DE BACALAO 201
Scrambled Eggs with Salted Cod
CUBA

ACKEE AND SALTFISH 203
JAMAICA

BOULÈT LAM VERITAB AK LANMORI 204
Fried Breadfruit and Salt Cod Balls
HAITI

BREADFRUIT PIE 205

BULJOL 206
Stewed Salted Cod
TRINIDAD AND TOBAGO

SÒS MORI 208
Stewed Salted Cod
HAITI

SERENATA DE BACALAO 209
Salted Cod Salad
PUERTO RICO

SCOTCH BONNET PEPPERS

PIKLIZ 214
Spicy Pickled Cabbage
HAITI

PEPPER SAUCE 215
Hot Sauce
TRINIDAD AND TOBAGO

FÉROCE D'AVOCAT 216
Spicy Salted Cod and Avocado Pâté
MARTINIQUE

CHIKTAY 217
Spicy Smoked Herring Salad
HAITI

MANGO CHOW 219
Spicy Mango Salad
TRINIDAD AND TOBAGO

JERK CHICKEN 222
JAMAICA

SÒS TI-MALICE WITH SHRIMP 225
Shrimp with Hot Sauce
HAITI

PEPPER SHRIMP 227
Spicy Whole Shrimp
JAMAICA

SNAPPER ESCOVITCH-ISH 228
Grilled Snapper with Spicy Shallot Vinaigrette
JAMAICA

INTRODUCTION

All my life, I have been surrounded by Caribbean people and our food. I grew up in a half Trinidadian, half Canadian household in Toronto. My mother, born in Princes Town, a small town in the south of Trinidad, was known in the family for her cooking. She had an easy, unfussy way in the kitchen, but everything always came out delicious and it was clear she cooked with love. While my father was not the main cook of the house, he cared very much about food and where it came from, and had a few staples—mostly salads—we could count on him to add to almost every meal. He also had two Trinidadian dishes in his repertoire: curried chicken (which would make my mom's face twist up every time she ate it, though she never intervened in the process) and souse, a chilled soup made with lots of limes and pig's feet. My mother refused to have anything to do with this dish—she didn't eat pork growing up and couldn't wrap her head around cold, congealed pig's feet—and would generally leave the kitchen if it was in the works. My dad would stand at the stove looking like a mad scientist, stirring the pig's feet around in a big bowl, grinning with delight all the while.

As a child, I went to countless Trinidadian family functions and they always featured tables laden with food: dishes I hated as a child (callaloo), things I loved (stewed kingfish), and everything in between. We never talked much about the origins of these dishes, but the pride that went into preparing and serving them was clear.

I visited Trinidad many times in my youth, mostly staying in the house in Princes Town where my mother grew up. There I discovered what fruit was actually supposed to taste like, and that though I hated eggs at home in Toronto, I loved the ones from the chicken there in the yard. I became familiar with the smell of burning sugarcane. I learned to embrace stews that combined unidentifiable ingredients with easily identifiable animal parts, a mix that I would have refused at any other time, but somehow, on the island, was pure delight.

As I got older and became more aware of my cultural identity, I found myself drawn to other people of the Caribbean islands. It was easy to find Trinidadian and Jamaican pockets in Toronto, and when I started coming to New York City in the '90s, I encountered Puerto Rican and Dominican cultures. Though our languages and cooking spices aren't the same, I felt comfortable and understood. Later, in Brooklyn, I was introduced to Haitian culture. In many ways their culture is wildly different from that of Trinidad. For instance, Trinidadians always sound like they're laughing, and Haitians always sound like they're yelling. And yet I felt at home in their food, their music, and that unmistakable vibe of a person (or the child of one) who grew up with the sun in their face, surrounded by the Caribbean Sea.

As I've learned more about the history of my mother's native island and all the other nations that dot the warm waters around it, I continue to be struck by the layers and complexities of our culture and cuisine. The Caribbean is the original melting pot, and as a result, our food has a rich, though at times harrowing, narrative.

The Atlantic slave trade was one of the most profoundly world-altering events in all of human history. As early as the sixteenth century, boats carried weapons and other commodities from European nations to Africa, where they were exchanged for enslaved Africans. The enslaved were then sent to the Americas—including the islands of the Caribbean—as unpaid laborers to grow sugarcane, coffee, and cotton. These crops were shipped back to Europe and made into goods that would start the cycle all over again. Boats carried people, livestock, and produce not just back and forth across the Atlantic, but around and throughout the entire world in the name of capitalism. Cassava, indigenous to the Americas, was embraced by enslaved Africans as similar to the root vegetables they ate at home, and was eventually taken to Africa, where it now grows as if it were native. Plantains were brought from New Guinea on Portuguese ships and have become not only a staple in the Caribbean but also in West Africa as a result of the trade.

The dishes found in the Caribbean region today come from all those who make up our history. Our food culture started with the Arawak, Carib, and Taíno, who sailed their boats from the mainland to the islands two thousand years before Columbus set foot there. It is rooted in Central and West African culinary traditions and modified for the new world that was forced upon them. It has aspects of all the colonial powers that orchestrated the Atlantic slave trade— England, France, Portugal, and Spain. It was later peppered with food practices from indentured servants pulled from colonies in China and India. Over time, all these influences have created a cuisine that is dynamic, diverse, and unique.

I have spent many years studying the ways in which this motley crew of cultures came together to create my favorite cuisine. While the story of the region is overall the same—Columbus showed up, "discovered" the lands and the people already living there, exploited them to the point of near extinction, then brought in enslaved Africans, kicking off a horrific generations-long practice of using people as free labor to further the expansion and wealth of the colonial powers— each island has a singular version of this history, which translates into their food. For instance, because the Haitian Revolution against the French and subsequent

freedom of the enslaved Africans happened so much earlier than any other successful revolt against the colonialists, Haiti has retained more African food practices than some other islands. In countries like Guadeloupe, Guyana, Jamaica, and Trinidad, indentured servants brought from China or India in the nineteenth century, as the answer to the abolition of slavery, have had a huge impact on their cuisine, bringing with them their cooking methods such as stir-frying and seasonings like ginger and star anise.

Unfortunately, as so often happens in the shadow of colonialism, the region is in many ways culturally fractured. Rather than celebrating our differences as Caribbean people, we dig into them, refusing to recognize the beauty in both our diversity as well as what we all share. Jamaicans and Haitians regularly fight about the "correct" way to prepare rice. Trinidadians sneer at Jamaicans' preparation of roti, saying their hands are too "African," and therefore are heavy-handed. It's (problematically) implied that they don't have the light touch the Indian immigrants, so prolific in Trinidad, are thought to. Dominicans and Puerto Ricans routinely argue about mofongo—who created the dish, and who does it best—ignoring the fact that the dish originated in Africa. All these distinctions are reflected in larger cultural battles, with each country believing it is somehow better than the others.

The truth is, we are all cooking from the same place with many of the same ingredients, and the differences and nuances between us—the ways in which each nation navigated its history—are a thing of beauty. We all eat the soupy stews of our African ancestors and use corn and cassava in place of wheat like the Taíno. We all use ingredients that were introduced by Indigenous peoples, came from Africa on the same ships that brought the enslaved, or traveled from far-off lands in the hands of European colonizers. We are all children of those who had to learn to adapt to new surroundings, trying to hold on to tradition while forging a new path with limited means.

All across the Caribbean, whole foods are essential. In recent years, some processed foods and premade spice blends from companies such as Goya and Grace have made their way into Caribbean kitchens, but many of our mothers and grandmothers continue to exclusively use fresh, whole foods. This is coming back into favor with younger generations. The cuisines of several countries feature many plant-based dishes, because land is at a premium and animals take up a lot of space. Many people are too poor to afford the luxury of meat, which is how my mother grew up. As a result, I grew up eating a multitude of vegan meals, never knowing it was a huge culinary movement or trend. There are several recipes in this book that would traditionally be made with small amounts of salted meat, which is the most many could afford for flavoring. For those recipes, I have chosen to make the meat optional, as my mother and her family rarely—if ever—cooked that way, and while I can't ignore the depth of flavor some meat can provide, I find most dishes perfectly satisfying without it.

This book does not aim to be an encyclopedia of Caribbean food, as that could take a lifetime to compile. Instead, I am using eleven common and key ingredients we all use to explore our cuisine: **beans**, **calabaza**, **cassava**, **chayote**,

coconut, **cornmeal**, **okra**, **plantains**, **rice**, **salted cod**, and **Scotch bonnet peppers**. Through these ingredients, I hope you will discover commonalities you didn't know existed, foods you've never tried, or a new way to enjoy an old favorite. Some of these items might be familiar to you and others may be entirely new. Have you ever seen a chayote in a grocery store, looking like a puckered green Muppet face, and wondered "What the hell is that, and what do I do with it?" Or perhaps you'd love to incorporate nutritious okra into your diet but can't get past the slime. Or maybe you signed up for a bean subscription and need to find a new way to prepare them before your family revolts. Each chapter includes foundational information about the ingredient: historical facts, cultural uses, tips for picking the best specimens, and basics on how to prepare them.

I want it to be clear as someone who grew up eating and cooking Trinidadian food that while I believe our food has many inherent similarities, I understand across the board that I am not an expert in the cuisine of other nations. I am, in a way, still coming at most of these dishes as an outsider, or at least as someone who's been invited over but doesn't live there. I care deeply about showcasing every recipe in a way that will make each nation proud. I love us and want this book to represent us in the most magnificent light. I have been sure to research these recipes, and the cuisines of each country, in depth. To get these recipes on paper, I have talked to and cooked with friends, aunties, aunties of friends, chefs, and recipe developers, all of varying Caribbean descent.

The recipes in this book range from traditional to creative adaptations. The traditional recipes are especially meaningful to me, as I feel these recipes often get overlooked in today's cookbook canon but are no less worthy than any fanciful modern twists. However, what I hope this book underscores is the Caribbean way of making do, the spirit of creative license, and the basic idea that you can work with what you've got. You can make substitutions based on what your kitchen holds at any given time, or what your family will or will not tolerate. Even if it's not deemed "traditional," you're still making the dish you set out to make. These dishes all vary from house to house and table to table so much, and it's okay to put your own spin on it.

As these eleven ingredients are so fundamental in Caribbean cooking, you will discover many recipes that use more than one, which I hope will encourage you to keep these ingredients on hand. Some, like rice and cornmeal, are used all over the world and are readily available anywhere. Others are more specific, but because so many different ingredients made their way around the world during the Columbian Exchange, you may be able to find them in different cultural markets. In addition to Caribbean markets, African, Latin American, Indian, and Chinese marketplaces often stock many of these ingredients. Many of these pantry items are also available online.

The Caribbean is a delightful, complicated, layered place where pain and joy live side by side. The violent way our culture was forged gave birth to a people full of life. We come from this divided and multicultural heritage and have mixed and matched our histories to create something truly unique. A win for anyone from

any of these islands feels like a win for me, my family, and my ancestors. And one thing is true for all of us: We all cook with love, and we all eat with joy. "Me belly full" is a phrase you'll hear throughout the English-speaking Caribbean. It has an obvious meaning—a full and satisfied stomach—but can also mean a full and satisfied heart and soul. My aim is that this book will have that effect on you.

I believe this book will help everyone, Caribbean and non-Caribbean alike, find a deeper appreciation and understanding of the complexities that make up our vibrant cuisine. You will, in these pages, also be introduced to my daughter, Desalin, who has been my right hand through this whole process at the ripe age of four, and her father, Atibon, the unofficial mayor of Haitian Brooklyn, who somehow seems to know every single person of Haitian descent in the tristate area. It has been a joy to cook through these recipes at home with both of them helping at every turn. I hope this book continues the movement to showcase our cuisine and raises awareness that our food is beautiful. That one-pot, work-with-what-you've-got dishes are artful. That feeding your family from the land and your heart is magical. I am confident that *Belly Full* will unite readers of Caribbean descent under the banner of food, that we may push forward to a future that celebrates our culture together.

OTHER INGREDIENTS OUTSIDE THE KEY ELEVEN

ALLSPICE

Europeans gave this berry its name because it tasted like a combination of cinnamon, nutmeg, and cloves. It's also known as pimento (not to be confused with the fresh Trinidad pimento peppers listed later) or Jamaica pepper. Native to the Caribbean, it still grows wild in Jamaica and Central America. Allspice is something that makes West Indian curry distinct from Indian or British curry, and true Jamaican jerk chicken is made with the branches of this tree. I like to have both whole allspice berries (which will keep longer) and ground allspice (which better integrates into baked goods) on hand.

BELL PEPPERS

Regardless of their color, these peppers are found a lot across the region. Green bell peppers are most often used as a seasoning, but red bell peppers work their way into the dish itself or are used in seasoning bases like Haitian Epis (page 21). They are native to the Caribbean and Central and South America, so it's likely that the Indigenous peoples of these regions introduced Europeans and enslaved Africans to this fruit.

CHICKEN

In the Caribbean, people eat all sorts of meat, but chicken holds a special place for a few reasons. Chickens are small and can easily be raised anywhere, even on small islands. And they are everywhere! From the countryside of Trinidad to the city of San Juan, I have been woken up by roosters everywhere I go in the region and have watched hens saunter in the streets. If possible, it's ideal to use meat from chickens that were raised as humanely as possible, and who got to roam around outside and be chickens while they were alive. I say this not to be an obnoxious nouveau hippie (which I kind of am), but because this is the closest you're going to get to a chicken from the islands, who largely get to just *be chickens*.

Most of the recipes featuring chicken in this book require you to cut bone-in chicken thighs into pieces. This means cutting through the bones, which is not as intimidating as it sounds. You will, however, want to be sure your knife is very sharp. To cut through a chicken bone, place the chicken thigh skin-side down in the middle of your cutting board. With a very sharp chef's knife, make a mark where you're going to cut, then pull your arm back and bring the knife down squarely and with force, whacking it hard enough to cut into the bone. This usually takes two or three hits, but you'll be surprised at how often your knife lands in the same place it hit before and how easily it can cut through the bone. With practice, this will become very intuitive, and you may find some satisfaction in it. The noise of cutting chicken into pieces very much takes me back to my childhood kitchen! When I want to cut a chicken thigh into three pieces, I usually cut off the fleshy flap on the side, then cut through the middle of the bone, resulting in two bone-in pieces and one boneless piece.

CINNAMON

This spice shows up in dishes from every nation. In several English-speaking islands, you may find cinnamon simply called "spice" or "hard spice." True cinnamon, *Cinnamomum verum*, originates from Sri Lanka and Indonesia, while its cousin, *Cinnamomum cassia*, which is often also referred to as cinnamon but is actually cassia, hails from China. Both plants can be found growing in the Caribbean. I keep the rolled-up quills of bark, which we refer to as cinnamon sticks, and ground cinnamon on hand in my kitchen. In recipes where you infuse liquid with the flavor of cinnamon, using the bark is best. For ease, I prefer pre-ground cinnamon for most baking, as grinding the bark into a powder can be laborious and my little electric spice grinder protests. I use pre-ground cinnamon so often that I don't have to worry about it losing its potency.

CLOVES

Cloves were one of the spices that Columbus set out from Spain to find. They originate from Indonesia and likely came to the Caribbean by way of the Atlantic slave trade. Clove is an essential flavor profile for some islands, especially Haiti. They do equally well in savory or sweet preparations and are always added to our teas at home for their medicinal benefits.

CULANTRO

Native to the Caribbean and Central and South America, culantro is a distant, more pungent cousin of cilantro. While they look nothing alike, they do share a distinct flavor profile, though culantro takes it up 100. Interestingly, I have found that cilantro haters tend to be less upset about culantro, and can sometimes even tolerate it. It goes by many names around the islands, including bhandhania, chadon beni, cilantro ancho, recao, and recaíto. In this book, I will refer to it as "culantro," as that's how it's most often labeled in grocery stores in the US; if you're shopping elsewhere, be aware that it could be called any of the above. It is now grown in tropical regions around the world, and is likely to be found in Asian markets in addition to Caribbean and Latin American markets.

While culantro is hardier and can hold its own in slow-cooked dishes better than its cousin, you can easily substitute cilantro; just use about twice as much as the recipe calls for.

EVAPORATED MILK

The widespread use of evaporated milk in the Caribbean is almost definitely due to a lack of cattle in the region. Milk is hard to come by, so preserved dairy is much more likely to be in someone's kitchen. My aunt's pantry in Princes Town was always stocked with it. While it isn't something I use often, there's no denying it imparts a level of richness that regular milk doesn't have, and I do love it in certain baked goods. These days, there are many great organic options from grass-fed cows. Evaporated milk should not be confused for condensed milk, which is heavily sweetened.

GARLIC

One could easily argue that garlic is *the* single most important ingredient in Caribbean cooking. You won't see any of us cook anything savory without copious amounts of garlic. You'll notice that all the seasoning blends in this book include a lot of garlic, and the recipes these blends appear in have . . . more garlic. In my own kitchen, my personal measurement for the garlic is something like "a boatload." Garlic originated somewhere around South Asia or the Middle East and was used by the ancient Egyptians. It has traveled all around the world and probably came to the Caribbean with the Europeans. Whenever I speak of a clove of garlic, I'm talking about a nice plump, juicy one. If you end up with one of those heads that have many little cloves, feel free to double the quantity. If you're using something like elephant garlic, you can cut the amount in half. As always, feel free to trust your own judgment—as my daughter says, "You can just freestyle." One last note: In many contemporary recipes, garlic is only cooked for a brief time, and people will tell you to never,

ever burn garlic. In Caribbean culture, we aren't afraid of a little color on the garlic and the flavor that brings. I call for adding the garlic with the onion, as all the cooks in my family have always done and every other cook of Caribbean descent I've watched in their homes have, too, but if you prefer, you can absolutely wait until the onions are ready, then add the garlic and cook for 30 seconds to 1 minute.

GINGER

When I was growing up, my mother would put ginger in almost everything she cooked, and if left to my own devices, I could easily do the same. This rhizome originated in Asia, and probably came to the Caribbean with either Indian or Chinese indentured servants. It grows particularly well in Jamaica, which is thought to have some of the best ginger. In this book, I only ever call for fresh ginger, even in baked

goods. Ground ginger doesn't have the same zing that fresh does, and zing is what our food is all about. Store it in an airtight container or zip-top bag in the crisper drawer of your refrigerator. If you can get your hands on just-picked very fresh ginger, you should use it, as it is delightfully juicy. Ginger is also very easy to grow at home: Just stick a rhizome in some soil with the pokey things pointing up, make sure it gets light, and give it nice amounts of water. Before you know it, you'll see green sprouts coming up.

LIMES

Limes are an important part of Caribbean cuisine. They are used to wash meat and add flavor to both sweet and savory dishes. Limes in the Caribbean are different from the ones found in the US. There are some that look more like green lemons, and then there are others, such as the key lime, that are small but mighty. However, the limes we get here in the US, mostly from Mexico, are a more than appropriate substitute. Always look for the heaviest ones; they should give a little when you squeeze them.

NUTMEG

Originally from Indonesia, this spice made its way to Grenada very early on, after the English briefly took over the Banda Islands from the Dutch in the nineteenth century and transplanted nutmeg all across their colonies. Since then, this magical fruit has settled in on the island so well that it appears on their flag. I have never in my life lived in the same house as ground nutmeg, and to this day, grating it fresh makes me think of my mother. Please buy whole nutmeg and grate it on a Microplane or the finest holes of a box grater as you need it. Many recipes here will call for more nutmeg than you may be used to using. Don't be scared—it's delicious.

OIL

Generally, I don't get too hung up on what kind of oil I use. Most of the recipes here call for olive oil, and I always use extra virgin. In the tropics, coconut oil is often used, which adds a delicious, slightly nutty taste. The many fried dishes need a neutral oil with a high smoke point, but which type you use is really up to you. I generally use grapeseed, safflower, or canola oil for frying, but when in doubt, good old-fashioned "vegetable" oil works, too. If you're trying to keep it on the healthier side—which may sound like an oxymoron, but some oils are certainly better for you than others—avocado is supposed to be the best. Unfortunately, it's also one of the priciest oils around.

PROVISIONS

I debated featuring "provisions" as one of the main ingredients in this book, but we would have run out of space! Also called viandas in Cuba, the Dominican Republic, and Puerto Rico, provisions are truly at the root of all Caribbean cuisine. These are foods that the enslaved were given as rations, and were sometimes allowed to grow on small plots of land known as provision grounds. This category includes cassava, yam, sweet potato (sometimes called boniato or batata—not the orange kind we use in the US), malanga, plantain, and taro. They are all starchy and high in carbohydrates, a necessary thing for getting through hours upon hours of intense labor. Provisions are still very much a part of Caribbean cuisine today and are often paired with small amounts of meat or beans as they would have been in the past.

SCALLIONS

Though they're sometimes called chives in the English-speaking Caribbean, scallions should never be confused with what we know as chives in the US. Originating in Asia, they are now used profusely throughout most of the world. Scallions are essential to dishes on islands English and French are spoken and are almost always used in addition to, not instead of, mature onions. Scallions can range from very slender to very robust; when I call for a scallion, I'm talking about one that's middle of the road, so feel free to adjust your amounts to fit your scallion size. And while we might trim a little off the top if it's looking sad, Caribbean cooks always use the whole scallion, all the way through the dark green parts.

SEASONING/TRINIDAD PIMENTO PEPPERS

These are a bit of a mystery to me. They are clearly related to the Scotch bonnet, as they look like an elongated sibling. They also have the same smell and taste as a Scotch bonnet, but without the heat (*most* of the time; every now and then you'll come across one with some bite!). Though they are mandatory on many islands, such as Grenada, Trinidad, and Saint Lucia, to name a few, they are not that easy to come by stateside, unless you live in an area with a large Caribbean population. As such, I've made them optional in this book, though it pains me to do so, because I could add them to just about anything. Dried seasoning peppers can be purchased online; if you have a green thumb, the seeds are also easy to find online, and they aren't hard to grow.

SOUR ORANGE

Also known as bitter orange or Seville orange, these citrus fruits are originally from Asia. They found their way to Europe somewhere around the twelfth century, then made their way on ships to the Caribbean and Central and South America. Sour oranges are often used to season meat and show up in Cuba's famous Mojo Sauce (page 76). They have a unique flavor, but can be replaced with a 50/50 mix of lime juice and sweet orange juice as a reasonable substitute. Sour oranges can be found in Asian, Caribbean, and Latin American markets.

STAR ANISE

Originally from southern China, this potent spice that smells like licorice has found a home in the Caribbean. It is used across many different islands, often in beverages. It features most prominently in Haitian cuisine, where liquid is often infused with star anise flavor for baking or to use in porridges.

THYME

This member of the mint family is ubiquitous in the cuisine on islands English and French are spoken. Also native to the Mediterranean, thyme is believed to have spread around the world because of the Romans, who used it to purify rooms, and most likely came to the Caribbean with the European colonists. In this book, I call for measured quantities of thyme leaves, but honestly, this is unheard of in Caribbean cooking—we just throw big sprigs in whole, letting the leaves fall off during cooking and fishing out the stems before serving. If this sounds good to you, by all means, do it! It's what I do myself. Know, however, that there are huge differences in what constitutes a "sprig" (is it a big woody one with five different stems on it, or one of those soft, wispy ones, or somewhere in between?), so measuring the leaves is the only way to truly be consistent. To remove them, hold the top of the stem with one hand and run your other hand down the length of the stem to strip off the leaves. As you get more used to removing them (a task Desalin loves to do, thank goodness), it will become very easy to eyeball the resulting pile of leaves without measuring, and even to size up a sprig and guess the quantity of leaves it holds. Fresh thyme is preferred in Caribbean cooking and is available almost everywhere, but if necessary, one-third of dried thyme can be used instead.

TOMATOES

Not one single island would ever cook without tomatoes. Whether used fresh, in a sauce, or as a paste, this fruit finds its way into all sorts of dishes. Originally from Peru, tomatoes surely made their way to the islands with one of the first waves of immigrants from the mainland. The Indigenous peoples of the region then probably introduced the enslaved Africans to them, and from there, magic was born. For fresh tomatoes, I usually call for Romas (plum tomatoes), not because I love them, but because I find they are one of the more reliable varieties out of season. Please always feel free to substitute whatever tomato you like, just keeping in mind size. One big beefsteak could sub for two Romas.

TURMERIC

Originating in India, this relative of ginger has been used medicinally throughout Asia for many centuries, and likely found its way to the Caribbean with Indian indentured servants. In the Caribbean, it is often called saffron (but should not be confused with actual saffron threads), and can show up in all kinds of places, such as Grenada's Oil Down (page 98). It's what gives curry its distinctive color; I once had Buljol (page 206) in Saint Lucia that was vivid with turmeric, which was a game changer for me!

VANILLA

Used in sweet preparations all over the world, this seedpod was originally found growing wild in Mexico and other parts of Central America and the Caribbean. Though large-scale production of vanilla is now largely located in Madagascar and Tahiti, it is still grown in Mexico and the Caribbean. I'm never without the biggest bottle of vanilla extract I can get my hands on, and my own personal measurement always includes an extra splash over the teaspoon listed in most recipes.

VINEGAR

The use of vinegar in Caribbean cuisine likely goes back far before anyone else even got to the islands. It is thought that the Indigenous people probably preserved food with it, from meat to fruit, and that it was made out of anything one could make vinegar from. Today, it is still important for cleaning and seasoning meat and as part of different spice blends and hot sauces. In my home, I most often use apple cider vinegar, but to be quite honest, you can use whatever your favorite is, as long as it's not balsamic!

EQUIPMENT

Though Caribbean food can have a lot of ingredients, the preparation itself is quite easy, and it doesn't require a lot of fancy equipment. Here is a list of a few items that will come in handy for making the recipes in this book (or really any recipe at all).

BLENDER OR FOOD PROCESSOR

A good blender or food processor comes in very handy. It helps you avoid the tedious grating of cassava or coconut and makes short work of things that must be pureed. If you don't have either of these (and I highly recommend you get at least one, if not both), you can grate certain ingredients on a box grater. To mash ingredients into a paste, as you do for the seasoning blends on pages 21–23, you can use a mortar and pestle, or pilon, as they call it in Cuba, the Dominican Republic, Haiti, and Puerto Rico. For soupy recipes, you can use an immersion blender to puree the ingredients directly in the pot they cooked in, or carefully transfer the contents of the pot to a standing blender and blend it in batches.

HANDS

Your hands are your number one tool in cooking, always. From shaping dough to peeling plantains to mixing, a pair of clean hands is the most intuitive tool you've got. Specifically, I find mixing a marinade into meat is easiest and most efficiently done with my hands. Just be sure to wash your hands thoroughly before and after.

LARGE, HEAVY-BOTTOMED POTS

Caribbean food is all about long-cooking dishes, and for that, you need solid heavy-bottomed pots. Dutch ovens are great, and the calderons (heavy aluminum pans) found in many Caribbean kitchens are of course the OG Caribbean pot. It doesn't really matter what kind it is, as long as it's thick and heats slowly and evenly. Thin metal pots that heat up fast will 100% burn your food.

PILON

A pilon (mortar and pestle) is key to Caribbean cooking. As Haitian Kreyòl is the unofficial second language of my household, I spell it with no accent, however in Spanish it would be a *pilón*. It's a fantastic tool for preparing garlic for cooking or mashing it into a paste with salt and other herbs. (Though I will often mince a clove of garlic, if my ancestors saw me, they would probably roll over in their graves.) It can also be used for grinding spices. (My pepper mill has been broken for months now; we just grind up our peppercorns in a stone pilon.) If you don't have a pilon, that won't prevent you from making the recipes in this book, but they're handy to have around and are an attractive addition to your kitchen.

SHARP KNIVES

I know this should be a given, but I just want to include a PSA here about sharp knives: A dull knife is both dangerous and frustratingly ineffective. I lived in London for two years and not once did I meet a sharp knife in anyone's home. It was a challenge. You'll chop and peel a lot of things with knives in this book, as well as cut through bones in meat, so a sharp knife is key! Though the days when someone would come through your neighborhood ringing a bell to advertise their knife-sharpening services are gone (I just dated myself there), there are loads of tools available to help keep your knife sharp, ranging from simple rods to whetstones to fancy electric devices you can buy to sharpen at a moment's notice. You can also sometimes find knife sharpeners at your local farmers' market or kitchen store.

WOK

A wok is not essential, but it is my preferred vessel for frying. Its very high sides prevent splatters, and its bowl shape allows you to slide things down into the hot oil, if you want, rather than dropping them from above and being splashed.

SEASONING BASES AND BLENDS

The number one key to Caribbean cooking is the seasonings. Our food is *highly* seasoned, which I think can come as a bit of a surprise to people who aren't used to it. When the enslaved Africans arrived in the Caribbean, they could not get their heads around the bland food eaten by the European colonists and added their own methods for flavoring food, as well as learning those of the region's Indigenous peoples. There was no lack of herbs and spices around them, and the inferior-quality food given to the enslaved had to be made palatable somehow. In addition to simply making things taste good, many kinds of seasoning helped to preserve food, which was necessary in the hot, humid climate.

Seasoning bases give the cuisine of each region a distinctive flavor and form the backbone of most dishes. Making them in bulk—as we do in this section—is a fairly recent thing, as prior to blenders and refrigeration, it just wasn't possible. Previously, seasoning bases would have been made at the time of cooking, usually in a pilon, a job that was (and is still) often given to children. While there are as many versions of these seasonings as there are islands, the five recipes here are a good place to start. Note that these bases are not generally used in lieu of chopped-up aromatics and herbs, but in addition to them, which creates a dynamic layer of flavor.

This is the way I like to make these bases, but everyone makes them their own way. Feel free to experiment with the ingredients. I never include salt or hot pepper in any of my bases, which allows me to decide what direction I'm going with the dish and how much salt or heat it needs. One thing you'll notice they all have in common is garlic—lots of garlic!

EPIS

HAITI

Though I love each and every one of these flavor bases, I probably use epis the most. You'll find it in most of the traditional Haitian recipes, such as Sòs Pwa Blan (page 35) and Soup Joumou (page 47), but it can be used all sorts of other ways, including as the vinaigrette for grilled okra (page 141). I find it's the most versatile seasoning base and have used it in and on just about everything you can think of. As always, consider this less of a recipe and more of a guide. Adjust the amounts as you see fit, and add whatever you have lurking in the fridge that seems like a good idea. Chef Nadege Fleurimond adds basil to hers, and it's fantastic! If you have sour orange left over from another recipe, squeeze that on in there. Some shallots? Yes please!

MAKES 3 CUPS

1 red bell pepper, roughly chopped
1 green bell pepper, roughly chopped
1 medium yellow onion, roughly chopped
4 scallions, roughly chopped
1 cup fresh parsley leaves
1 head garlic, cloves smashed and peeled
1 tablespoon fresh thyme leaves
¼ cup extra-virgin olive oil
¼ cup apple cider vinegar
2 tablespoons fresh lime juice
A few good grinds of black pepper

Combine all the ingredients in a food processor or blender and puree until smooth. Store in an airtight glass jar in the fridge for up to 1 month.

GREEN SEASONING

TRINIDAD AND TOBAGO

A version of green seasoning can be found on many of the islands that were formerly under British rule. Though it isn't something I remember my mother (or anyone else in the family) having on hand when I was growing up, the smell brings back so many memories of my mother cooking that I'm sure she was making it on a one-off basis rather than in large batches. I am now never without a jar of green seasoning in my fridge. In addition to all the recipes in this book that call for it, such as the Trini Chow Mein (page 89), Callaloo (page 135), and Pelau (page 189), it's a great way to season any kind of meat, and fish in particular, as well as a nice way to jazz up plain rice. If you can't find culantro, substitute a bunch of cilantro. This is, once again, just a guideline.

MAKES 2 CUPS

1 bunch culantro (about 8 leaves)
½ cup fresh cilantro
½ cup fresh parsley leaves
1 head garlic, cloves peeled
1 medium yellow onion, roughly chopped
1 shallot, chopped
5 scallions, roughly chopped
¼ cup fresh thyme leaves
1 celery stalk, roughly chopped
1 (1-inch) piece fresh ginger, peeled and roughly chopped
1 seasoning pepper, seeded and roughly chopped (optional; see page 14)
¼ cup fresh lime juice

Combine all the ingredients in a food processor or blender and puree until smooth. Store in an airtight glass jar in the fridge for up to 1 month.

RECAÍTO

GREEN SOFRITO
PUERTO RICO

Talking about recaíto and sofrito can be tricky territory. In some camps, this version is the only version, and the word *recaíto* is interchangeable with *sofrito*. In others, sofrito is more like the Dominican sazón on page 23, which would make this recipe distinctly recaíto, which comes from the word *recao*, the Puerto Rican name for culantro. Are you confused yet? According to Nuyorican chef and food historian César Pérez, the word *sofrito* actually refers to the act of cooking a combination of oil, jamón de cocinar (salted ham), Spanish olives, tomato of some kind (fresh, paste, or sauce), *and* recaíto. Regardless of where you stand, I love this stuff, especially because I could probably just season everything in the world with culantro and never look back. If you can't get ají dulce peppers, you can omit them, or add a little extra green bell pepper, if you like. Getting them where I live in Brooklyn can be hit or miss, so when I find them, I like to buy a lot and stick them in my freezer, where they'll keep for 3 to 4 months.

MAKES 2 CUPS

1 green bell pepper, roughly chopped
1 bunch culantro (about 8 leaves), or 2 cups fresh cilantro
2 medium yellow onions, chopped
6 ají dulce peppers, seeded
1 head garlic, cloves peeled

Combine all the ingredients in a food processor or blender and puree until smooth. Store in an airtight glass jar in the fridge for up to 1 month.

SAZÓN

DOMINICAN REPUBLIC

Despite all the arguing between them, it can get very tricky sometimes to differentiate between food from the Dominican Republic and Puerto Rico for an outsider. In fact, my friend Geko Jones, who is half Puerto Rican and half Colombian, has admitted he finds there's very little difference between the two territories (our mutual friend Sarah, who is Dominican and helped me with several recipes in this book, has smoke coming out of her ears *right now*). This blend is one of those instances where, for all intents and purposes, Dominican sazón is like the "regular" sofrito from PR discussed in the recipe for Recaíto. You could argue the sour orange juice makes it distinct, but I suspect there are plenty of Puerto Rican families adding sour orange to theirs as well. The only thing I can offer is that this base in particular is based on Sarah's mami's, who in turn learned it from her own mother, which makes it inherently Dominican. If you can't find culantro, which Dominicans call cilantro ancho, add another bunch of cilantro.

MAKES 2 CUPS

½ green bell pepper, roughly chopped
½ red bell pepper, roughly chopped
1 small red onion, roughly chopped
1 Roma (plum) tomato, chopped
3 scallions, roughly chopped

1 bunch cilantro, leaves and stems chopped
1 bunch culantro, chopped
5 garlic cloves, peeled
1 tablespoon dried oregano
¼ cup sour orange juice (see page 14)

Combine all the ingredients in a food processor or blender and puree until smooth. Store in an airtight glass jar in the fridge for up to 1 month.

SAZÓN

PUERTO RICO

Though the name is the same, this dried blend is nothing like Dominican sazón. My first encounter with sazón was in my ex's kitchen as he taught me to make Habichuelas Guisadas (page 41). This was way back when it never dawned on me that you could make your own spice blends, and I took Goya as the bible. However, with ingredients that are easy to find, it couldn't be simpler to make your own, and it will last forever. But if you're not a DIY everything kind of person, there are some great options for premade versions these days that have simple ingredients from small makers you can trust, such as Ilyana Maisonet's collaboration with Burlap and Barrel, or Loisa.

MAKES A SCANT ¼ CUP

1 teaspoon ground coriander
1 teaspoon ground cumin
1 teaspoon ground achiote
1 teaspoon garlic powder

1 teaspoon kosher salt (optional)
½ teaspoon dried oregano
¼ teaspoon freshly ground black pepper

Mix all the seasonings well and store in an airtight container in a cool location. It will keep indefinitely, though as with all ground spices, it will lose its potency over time.

BEANS

Other names: FRIJOLES, HABICHUELAS, PWA

I GREW UP EATING LEGUMES of some kind on a regular basis. Often, they were the main source of protein in our meals. Being vegan wasn't a popular thing then, and—as I didn't know another way—the fact that we only ate meat sometimes wasn't a big deal to me. In high school, I was exposed to other ways of eating: My best friend, who was half Croatian and half Czech, invited me to meals at her house that were always centered around massive amounts of meat from a variety of animals. That way of eating was so unfamiliar to me, I was actually shocked.

I greatly appreciate the fact that my mother, who grew up eating mostly meatless dishes largely due to poverty, fed us like this. While I am no longer afraid of meat-laden tables, I can easily do without it and feel totally satisfied by a plant-based meal. The Caribbean is a land of hearty bean dishes. And while many of them, such as the stewed kidney beans from Jamaica (see page 33) and Puerto Rico (see page 41), traditionally include some animal part (pork snout, cow foot, salt beef, salt pork, or pork ear), I have elected to prepare the bulk of these dishes in this book without meat. This is in part to honor my mother, who was not interested in having any of these things in her pot, and also in part because I have cultivated a joy in eating these kinds of foods meat-free. They are just a bit lighter and leave you feeling with just a bit more energy.

Providing key amounts of protein and fiber, beans are a staple food all over the world. The favorite beans in Caribbean kitchens have their roots in both Indigenous and African culture: *Phaseolus vulgaris*, the "common bean," encompasses many varieties, including green, black, kidney, and pinto beans; these are native to the Americas and are used in every Caribbean kitchen. *Cajanus cajan,* or pigeon peas (also known as congo or gungo beans) and *Vigna unguiculata,* known as black-eyed peas, were brought to the Caribbean via Africa during the slave trade and are also very popular around the islands.

Before anyone else arrived, the islands' Indigenous peoples (the Arawak, Carib, and Taíno) were cultivating beans. They were an ideal crop for several reasons. If you've ever tried growing them yourself, you'd see why. They sprout easily and quickly, producing bean pods rather fast and very prolifically. In addition, they are part of what are known as the "three sisters" in native farming—beans, corn, and calabaza (or squash). These three plants help each other thrive when grown together. Beans enrich the soil by pulling in nitrogen, which is essential for growing just about anything.

However, when the Europeans showed up, the farming of beans stalled as native people left their land to mine for the colonizers. It wasn't until enslaved Africans, who had been eating beans for at least three thousand years, showed up with their own knowledge, preferences, and—some believe—seeds that the bean game really took off in the Caribbean. The Africans were in close contact with the native people of the island from the very beginning, as they lived in close proximity. Surely in this contact, the two groups traded agricultural knowledge. The Indigenous peoples may have told the Africans about their own bean species (the "common bean" mentioned above), where to grow them, and the best times of year to plant them. Likely both groups knew of the positive effect the plants had on the soil.

As you'll learn later in the rice chapter (page 174), in addition to beans in their diet, the enslaved Africans were also used to rice from their homelands. In fact, rice and beans had been part of their dietary lexicon for hundreds of years. Adapted with a twist that came from the herbs found on the islands, rice and beans in some form has become ubiquitous with Caribbean food and is the national dish of more than one island.

In this book, I almost exclusively call for dried beans. Though they take much more time to cook than canned, the difference in flavor and texture is well worth it. They also cost much less than canned beans, even if you're buying fancy organic ones. Black beans, kidney or other red beans, and pigeon peas are probably the most common legumes to find on tables around the Caribbean, but many more, including black-eyed peas, chickpeas, and a variety of white beans, make appearances. In this chapter, you'll find several types of beans to explore.

NUTRITION*: Nutrition levels vary greatly from bean to bean. All beans, however, are high in fiber and low in fat and cholesterol.

HOW TO BUY*: There's no hard-and-fast rule. The best advice I can give is to buy your beans from a source that's likely to have high turnover. Old beans take longer to cook, and ain't nobody got time for that. I love the beans from Rancho Gordo; all the cultivars they sell have been almost surreal. But honestly, you can make perfectly fantastic dishes with any brand of bean.

DIRI AK PWA

RICE AND BEANS ○ HAITI

1 cup dried kidney
    beans
8 cups water
3 tablespoons extra-
    virgin olive oil
1 yellow onion,
    chopped
4 garlic cloves, minced
1 cup Coconut
    Milk, homemade
    (page 97) or
    store-bought
1 Scotch bonnet
    pepper
5 whole cloves
1 teaspoon fresh
    thyme leaves
2 cups long-grain rice,
    such as jasmine or
    basmati
1½ teaspoons
    kosher salt

SERVES 6 TO 8

Rice and beans is a ubiquitous dish in Caribbean cuisine, and every island will claim theirs is the best. That sort of claim is, of course, completely subjective, but as a person who grew up eating Cuban, Jamaican, Puerto Rican, and Trinidadian versions, I am possibly willing to give the heavyweight title to Haiti. What makes Haiti's take on rice and beans so special is the use of cloves, as well as the method of boiling the rice until most of the liquid has been absorbed before turning down the heat. This makes the rice somewhat grainy and more structured. Coconut milk, largely found in preparations in the south of the island, adds flavor and a subtle creaminess; in the north, the dish is more often made with water.

Diri ak pwa is made with bean varieties that include black beans (pwa nwa), pinto beans (pwa bè), and pigeon peas (pwa congo). However, small red beans or kidney beans (pwa wouj) are my personal favorite. They give the rice a beautiful reddish hue and have a buttery taste.

In a large, heavy-bottomed pot, combine the beans, water, and 1 tablespoon of the olive oil. Bring to a boil over high heat. Boil for 15 minutes, then reduce the heat to medium-low, cover, and cook for 1 hour or so, until the beans are tender; check occasionally to make sure they're submerged and add water if necessary. A properly cooked bean should squish between your fingers but still be firm enough not to fall apart.

Drain the cooked beans, reserving the cooking water. You should have 2½ cups of liquid—add additional water if needed.

Rinse the pot, then set it over medium heat. Add 1 tablespoon of the oil, the onion, and the garlic. Cook, stirring occasionally, until the onion begins to brown, 5 to 8 minutes. Stir in the beans and cook for 2 minutes, then add the coconut milk. Stir to combine and bring to a simmer.

Stud the pepper with the cloves (as if it's an orange and you're making a Christmas decoration), then add it to the pot, along with the thyme and the reserved bean cooking water. Raise the heat to medium-high and bring the mixture to a boil. Add the rice and salt and boil until most of the liquid has been absorbed, 15 to 20 minutes. (If you're worried that the rice is about to burn, that means you're doing it right. This is what makes it particular to Haiti.)

Add the remaining 1 tablespoon oil, reduce the heat to low, and cover. Cook for 10 to 15 minutes more, until the rest of the liquid has been absorbed. Discard the pepper (and the cloves, which usually float to the top if they fall out of the pepper). Fluff the rice with a fork and serve. The diri ak pwa will keep in an airtight container in the fridge for 2 to 3 days. The beans can also be cooked up to 3 days in advance, and stored in their cooking liquid in the refrigerator. Bring them to room temperature before straining and cooking.

CALA

BLACK-EYED PEA FRITTERS ○ ARUBA

1 cup dried black-eyed
  peas
¼ cup water
2 garlic cloves,
  chopped
½ Scotch bonnet
  pepper
1 teaspoon kosher salt
Neutral oil, for frying

SERVES 6 TO 8

These fritters originated in West Africa, like the black-eyed peas themselves. You can also find them in Jamaica, where they are called by their African name, accras, and are more highly spiced. But this simpler version from Aruba is deeply satisfying. While I am a big proponent of not soaking beans, you absolutely cannot skip it here. The beans won't cook fast enough otherwise, and their skins can only be removed if they've been soaked. You can leave the skins on, but they have an earthy taste that can be a bit overpowering. I like to remove about half of them, because even half is enough to make a difference (and frankly, removing all of them is extremely tedious). The batter can be made several hours in advance, refrigerated, and brought to room temperature before frying. The Scotch bonnet here is just for a light kick and some flavor; heat is not meant to be the dominant experience. Though it isn't traditional, these are really delicious with Mayoketchup (page 119), Tamarind Sauce (page 40), or Pikliz (page 214).

Place the black-eyed peas in a large bowl or pot, add cold water to cover, and set aside to soak overnight. Drain the peas and rub them together with your hands to remove at least some of their skins, discarding any that come off.

Transfer the black-eyed peas to a food processor and add the water, garlic, Scotch bonnet, and salt. Process for a few minutes, until the mixture is completely smooth.

In a wok or deep skillet, heat about 1 inch of oil over medium-high heat until it reaches 350°F. If you don't have a thermometer (I don't!), you'll know the oil is ready if a bit of batter bubbles deeply when dropped in.

Form the black-eyed pea mixture into balls, using a heaping tablespoon for each. Carefully place them in the hot oil, being sure not to crowd the pot, and fry until golden brown, 4 to 5 minutes per side. If they start to brown too quickly, reduce the heat and wait a few moments before adding more. Remove the fritters with a slotted spoon or tongs and place on paper towels to drain. Serve immediately.

CURRIED CHANA AND ALOO

CURRIED CHICKPEAS AND POTATOES
○ TRINIDAD AND TOBAGO

3 tablespoons
coconut oil

1 small yellow onion,
diced

5 garlic cloves, minced

1 Scotch bonnet
pepper, minced

2 tablespoons Trinidad
curry powder

¼ teaspoon ground
turmeric

½ teaspoon ground
cumin

6 culantro leaves,
minced

2 teaspoons fresh
thyme leaves

1 large potato, peeled
and chopped into
1-inch cubes

2 (15.5-ounce) cans
chickpeas, drained
and rinsed

3 scallions, thinly sliced

3 cups water

2 teaspoons
kosher salt

"Perfect" White Rice
(page 180), for
serving

SERVES 6 TO 8

This dish was in regular rotation in my house growing up. It was the reason the house constantly smelled like curry and all our spoons were stained yellow. Reflecting the huge impact East Indians have had on Trinidadian cooking, this vegan recipe can be found in households across the island, served over rice or inside roti. Trinidad curry powder is key. I like the brand Chief, but there are others available, and all are easily found online. In addition to making delicious curry, it's also one of my go-to seasonings in general, and I particularly like using it on roasted vegetables.

While I almost always opt for dried beans over canned, I have discovered that canned chickpeas work perfectly fine here, which makes this dish a weeknight-meal contender. If you'd like to use dried chickpeas, be sure to soak them overnight, then cook them in fresh water for at least an hour, or until tender, and save their cooking water to be used in step 3. If you can't find culantro (also called chadon beni, shado beni, or bhandhania in Trinidad), you can substitute 1 cup fresh cilantro leaves. Make it a complete meal by stirring in baby spinach at the end and serving the curry over rice.

In a large, heavy-bottomed pot, heat the coconut oil over medium-high heat. Add the onion, garlic, and Scotch bonnet and cook, stirring occasionally, until they begin to brown, 5 to 8 minutes. Add the curry powder, turmeric, cumin, culantro, and thyme. Cook, stirring frequently, until fragrant and grainy, about 1 minute. The mixture will look dry and like it's sticking to the bottom of the pot.

Add the potato and stir to coat. Add the chickpeas and scallions and cook for 2 minutes more. Again, it might look like things are about to burn. Don't worry—they won't.

Stir in the water, enough to just barely cover the ingredients, and bring to a boil. Add the salt, then reduce the heat to medium-low. Simmer, uncovered, occasionally stirring and smashing some of the potatoes against the side of the pot with a wooden spoon to release their starch, until the curry is thick and the potatoes are nearly melting into the sauce, about 40 minutes. Don't worry if the curry looks too watery at first; the liquid will evaporate and the potato starch will thicken it up nicely. Remove from the heat and serve with the rice. This dish keeps well in an air-tight container in the refrigerator for up to 5 days or in the freezer for up to 4 months.

STEW PEAS

JAMAICA

BEANS

1 pound dried kidney beans or other red beans
6 cups water
1 (13.5-ounce) can coconut milk, or 2 cups homemade Coconut Milk (page 97)
6 garlic cloves: 3 smashed and peeled, 3 minced
1 teaspoon allspice berries, crushed
1 yellow onion, diced
5 scallions, thinly sliced
2 teaspoons fresh thyme leaves
1 Scotch bonnet pepper
2 teaspoons kosher salt, plus more as needed

SPINNERS (OPTIONAL)

1 cup all-purpose flour
½ teaspoon kosher salt
¼ to ½ cup water

"Perfect" White Rice (page 180), for serving (optional)

SERVES 6 TO 8

The name for this dish might be confusing as these are kidney beans, despite being called peas in Jamaica. My half-Jamaican cousin once walked into a Trinidadian restaurant and ordered stew peas. The woman behind the counter stared at her and responded, "You mean stew *beans*?" Kidney beans are one of the most preferred beans across the islands. There could be several reasons for this. They cook relatively quickly without soaking and that ability to break down easily also leads to less gas (bonus!). They add their sugars to the cooking liquid, which makes it thick and tasty. On the flip side, they are one of the least nutritious of the commonly used legumes and are relatively difficult to grow. Flavor wins, I suppose.

This dish often includes meat such as salt beef, salt pork, pig tail, or other offal. And yes, that is delicious. But I grew up eating so little meat, I find a great deal of comfort and joy in just the beans and the decadent creaminess of the coconut milk, which is just how my Jamaican auntie Rosie Mae made it. This is a dish that really gives you a look into someone's kitchen, and you'll find it simmering on Jamaican stoves from Kingston, Jamaica, to Flatbush, Brooklyn. The spinners, flour dumplings given the name because they spin and sink as they cook, are optional (unless you're Jamaican), but they do help thicken the stew. This dish freezes beautifully and is an exciting thing to find when you're desperately searching the freezer for a meal.

Make the beans: In a large, heavy-bottomed pot, combine the beans, water, coconut milk, smashed garlic cloves, and the allspice berries and bring to a boil over medium-high heat. Reduce the heat to low, cover, and simmer, undisturbed, for 1 to 1½ hours, until the beans are nearly tender.

Add the minced garlic, the onion, scallions, thyme, Scotch bonnet, and salt. Stir to combine, cover, and simmer for 20 minutes more, until the stew begins to thicken.

Meanwhile, make the spinners, if desired: In a medium bowl, mix the flour and salt together. Add the water, 1 tablespoon at a time, mixing until a stiff dough forms. Let the dough rest for 10 minutes. Pinch off a scant tablespoon of dough and roll it between your hands, creating a cigar shape. Place the spinner on a plate, and repeat with the remaining dough.

Add the spinners to the pot with the beans and gently push them under the surface of the liquid. Cover the pot and cook for an additional 15 minutes to steam the spinners; cut one open to make sure it's cooked through if you aren't sure. Remove the pot from the heat.

Taste for salt (beans can handle a lot of seasoning, so you may want to add up to a full teaspoon more). Serve alone or over rice. Store leftovers in an airtight container in the fridge for 3 to 4 days or in the freezer for up to 4 months.

JUG JUG

PIGEON PEA MASH ○ BARBADOS

2 cups pigeon peas
   (fresh, thawed
   frozen, or canned)
1 teaspoon kosher salt
2 cups water
5 slices bacon, diced
1 small yellow onion,
   diced
3 garlic cloves, minced
2 scallions, thinly sliced
1 teaspoon Green
   Seasoning,
   homemade
   (page 22) or
   store-bought
2 tablespoons fresh
   parsley leaves,
   minced
1 teaspoon fresh
   thyme leaves
¼ cup guinea flour
   (sorghum flour)
1 tablespoon unsalted
   butter (optional)

SERVES 4 TO 6

This dish is traditionally served around Christmas in Barbados, probably because December is peak season for pigeon peas. Jug jug is thought to have descended from the Scottish dish haggis, which was brought to the island when Oliver Cromwell sent prisoners of war, criminals, and political rebels to Barbados in the 1600s. It feels like a bit of a leap, as haggis features offal and this dish stars pigeon peas, but we can roll with it. Traditionally, one would use salt pork or beef, but I really enjoy the bit of smokiness and umami that you get from just a little bit of bacon, without having to commit to full bites of meat. The guinea flour called for in the ingredient list could easily confound you, but in tracing the lineage, one discovers it's another name for sorghum flour, and it's easily found online or in stores like Whole Foods. This recipe is traditionally made with fresh peas, so dried pigeon peas are not ideal. Luckily, canned ones are easy to find, and you can often find them frozen as well. Fair warning: This dish isn't the most attractive when finished, and when I first offered it to Desalin, she looked at me like I was crazy. But after she took a (very tentative) bite, she gave it her highest rating: "Yum!"

In a medium pot, combine the pigeon peas, salt, and water. Bring to a boil over medium heat, and cook for 15 minutes, until the peas are very tender. Drain the peas, reserving the cooking water.

In the same pot, cook the bacon over medium heat until crispy, about 8 minutes. Spoon off 2 tablespoons of the rendered fat from the pot and discard it (or save it for another use, if bacon fat is your thing!). Add the onion, garlic, and scallions to the pot and cook in the remaining bacon fat until the onion begins to brown, 5 to 8 minutes. Stir in the green seasoning, parsley, and thyme and remove from the heat.

With a spatula, scrape the bacon mixture from the pot into a food processor. Add the cooked peas and process on low until a rough paste forms. Set aside.

In the same pot, bring the reserved pea cooking water to a boil over medium-high heat. Add the pea mixture, then the guinea flour, stirring continuously. Reduce the heat to medium-low and simmer for 15 minutes, making sure to stir often to break up any lumps of flour, until it's thickened. Stir in the butter, if desired, then remove from the heat and serve. The jug jug can be stored in an airtight container in the fridge for up to 3 days.

SÒS PWA BLAN

WHITE BEAN SAUCE ○ HAITI

1 pound dried
   white beans
9 cups water
6 garlic cloves:
   3 smashed and
   peeled, 3 minced
3 scallions, roughly
   chopped
4 whole cloves
3 tablespoons extra-
   virgin olive oil
1 large shallot, minced
2 tablespoons Epis
   (page 21)
2 tablespoons
   chopped fresh
   parsley leaves
2 teaspoons fresh
   thyme leaves
1 Scotch bonnet
   pepper, pricked all
   over with a fork
2 to 3 teaspoons
   kosher salt
Freshly ground
   black pepper
"Perfect" White Rice
   (page 180), for
   serving

SERVES 6 TO 8

Sòs pwa is something between a sauce and a stew and is often served with rice or Mayi Moulen (page 118). It's even given to you in a little coffee cup to go at Haitian restaurants with almost every order. Sòs pwa is sometimes served as a completely smooth sauce, but I like to keep some texture and only blend half to three-quarters of the beans. While I generally prefer sòs pwa nwa, the black bean version, which I make with coconut milk, sometimes the urge for the taste of white beans (pwa blan) just hits me. I find white beans need a lot of water and more seasoning than other beans, but after that they will give you their best. Any kind of white bean will do here; navy, cannellini, or great northern beans all work great. While sòs pwa may be considered a side or even a condiment, in my household, when paired with mayi moulen and some veggies, it makes a complete and filling meal.

In a large stockpot or Dutch oven, combine the beans, water, smashed garlic cloves, scallions, whole cloves, and 1 tablespoon of the olive oil and bring to a boil over medium-high heat. Reduce the heat to low, cover, and simmer until the beans are tender, 1 to 1½ hours. A bean is done when it squishes firmly but completely between your two fingers. It shouldn't disintegrate and should hold some shape.

At the tail end of cooking the beans, in a small saucepan, heat the remaining 2 tablespoons oil over medium heat. Add the minced garlic, shallot, and epis and sauté until the shallot begins to brown slightly, 5 to 8 minutes. Remove from the heat.

Allow the beans to cool slightly. Using an immersion blender, blend the beans directly in the pot until they reach your desired texture (or transfer some—or all, if you want—of the beans to a standing blender, in batches if necessary, and blend to your desired texture, then return them to the pot). Bring the beans back to a simmer over medium-high heat. Using a spatula, scrape the shallot mixture into the beans, along with the parsley, thyme, and Scotch bonnet pepper. Check the texture of the sauce; if it's gotten too thick, add a little extra water ¼ cup at a time. Add 2 teaspoons of salt and season liberally with black pepper. Cook over low heat for 30 minutes more, until the beans are silky and full of flavor. Check for seasonings, and add up to 1 teaspoon more of salt.

Serve over rice. Leftovers keep well in an airtight container in the fridge for about 3 days, though you may have to add a little water when you reheat them to loosen them up.

FRIJOLES NEGROS

STEWED BLACK BEANS ○ CUBA

1 pound dried black
   beans
8 cups water
1 green bell pepper,
   halved: ½ sliced,
   ½ diced
6 garlic cloves:
   2 smashed and
   peeled, 4 minced
1 bay leaf
4 tablespoons extra-
   virgin olive oil
1 yellow onion, diced
½ Scotch bonnet
   pepper, seeded
   and diced
1 teaspoon ground
   cumin
1 teaspoon fresh
   oregano leaves
2 teaspoons
   kosher salt, plus
   more as needed
Freshly ground
   black pepper
2 tablespoons apple
   cider vinegar
"Perfect" White Rice
   (page 180), for
   serving

SERVES 6 TO 8

A version of this classic Cuban dish can also be found in Puerto Rico and parts of Central and South America. It is also a cousin to Haitian sòs pwa nwa. Black beans are highly nutritious, with large amounts of folate, and I think they are beautiful. I also happen to love them because they don't require soaking, which appeals to my last-minute meal tendencies. The Cuban take on this dish uses a sofrito (a base of fried aromatics), a generous amount of olive oil, and a splash of vinegar to create a deep and flavorful dish. Most recipes call for dried oregano; I always prefer fresh, but feel free to halve the listed amount and use dried. And though hot pepper isn't traditionally used, you'll find Scotch bonnet in the ingredient list here—I can't help myself! Serve with some rice and a salad.

In a large heavy-bottomed pot, combine the beans, water, sliced bell pepper, smashed garlic cloves, bay leaf, and 1 tablespoon of the olive oil. Bring to a boil over medium-high heat. Boil, uncovered, for 15 minutes, then reduce the heat to medium-low, cover, and cook for 1 to 1½ hours, until the beans are tender but not mushy. (The cooking time will vary depending on the age of your beans; old beans take longer.)

In a small skillet, heat the remaining 3 tablespoons oil over medium heat. Add the onion, diced bell pepper, and minced garlic and cook until the bell pepper is soft and the onion begins to brown, 8 to 10 minutes. Add the Scotch bonnet, cumin, and oregano and stir to combine. Scrape the sofrito into the pot with the beans, season with the salt and black pepper to taste, and stir to combine. Reduce the heat to medium-low, cover, and cook for 30 to 40 minutes more, until the beans start to break down. Remove from the heat, and stir in the vinegar and taste for salt (beans can really take a lot of seasoning, so you may want to add up to a full teaspoon more). Remove the bay leaf and serve over rice.

PHOLOURIE

SPLIT PEA FRITTERS ○ TRINIDAD AND TOBAGO

¾ cup split pea flour
¾ cup all-purpose
  flour
1 teaspoon kosher salt
1 teaspoon active
  dry yeast
¼ teaspoon ground
  turmeric
½ teaspoon baking
  soda
¼ teaspoon ground
  cumin
1 cup plus up to
  2 tablespoons
  warm water
2 garlic cloves, minced
1 teaspoon Green
  Seasoning,
  homemade
  (page 22) or
  store-bought
Neutral oil, for frying
Tamarind Sauce
  (recipe follows)
  and/or Mango
  Chutney (recipe
  follows), for serving

SERVES 6 TO 8

Pholourie is one of my all-time favorite snacks. I think that's partly due to the split pea flour they're made with—I have never met a split pea I didn't like. These fritters also make me think of my childhood, and were 100% one of my favorite things about visiting Trinidad, especially when they were served covered in a mango chutney. In my memories, the taste of the split pea flour is very prominent, but today it seems people in Trinidad are using a higher ratio of wheat flour in the mix. In Guyana, they often make these with nothing but split pea flour, which I love, but the fritters come out much denser. Pholourie were brought to the Caribbean by indentured servants from India and are a descendant of fuluri, chickpea flour fritters that also include split pea paste. Split pea flour is very easy to find in Caribbean and Indian groceries but also abounds on the internet. Be warned: These fritters are highly addictive. Serve them with tamarind sauce, mango chutney, or both!

In a medium bowl, mix both flours, the salt, yeast, turmeric, baking soda, and cumin. Add 1 cup of warm water slowly, whisking with a fork until a loose batter (like pancake batter) forms. If it's still too thick, add more water 1 tablespoon at a time. Mix in the garlic and green seasoning. Cover and let the batter sit for about 1 hour, or until it doubles in size.

In a wok or deep skillet, heat about 2 inches of oil over medium-high heat until it reaches 350°F. If you don't have a thermometer, you'll know the oil is ready if a bit of batter bubbles deeply when dropped in.

Carefully drop balls of dough into the hot oil, using a tablespoon to portion out the dough and another small spoon to scoop it out of the tablespoon. Cook, using a wooden spoon to gently roll the pholourie around in the oil to make sure they are cooking evenly on all sides and encourage them to form a ball shape, until they are golden and puffy, about 8 minutes. Drain on paper towels and serve immediately, with tamarind sauce and/or mango chutney.

TAMARIND SAUCE

In Trinidad, this sauce is most often made with actual tamarind pods, which is delicious, but removing the fruit from the pods is time-consuming. Tamarind paste is better, but a life hack I learned from Ramin Ganeshram's *Sweet Hands* is the best of all: Dissolve tamarind concentrate with some hot water, mix in the seasonings, and call it a day. The end result is thinner than the traditional sauce, but no less tasty. Tamarind concentrate can be found in West and East Indian groceries, as well as online.

MAKES A SCANT 1 CUP

2 tablespoons tamarind concentrate
2 teaspoons brown sugar
¾ cup hot water (at least 110°F)
½ Scotch bonnet pepper, seeds removed for less heat, minced
2 garlic cloves, grated
1 culantro leaf, minced (optional)
1 teaspoon kosher salt
¼ teaspoon ground cumin

In a small bowl, combine the tamarind concentrate and brown sugar. Add the hot water and stir until the tamarind and sugar have completely dissolved. Add the Scotch bonnet, garlic, culantro (if using), salt, and cumin and stir to combine. You can serve the sauce right away, but it does benefit from sitting for an hour or two to allow the flavors to marry. It can be spooned on top of the fritters or used as a dip. It keeps well in an airtight container in the fridge for up to 2 weeks.

MANGO CHUTNEY

There are as many versions of mango chutney as there are Trinidadians, and all of them are good. This one is served raw, which makes a nice fresh contrast to the fried decadence of a fritter. You don't want a completely green mango, nor do you want a ripe one. You want one that's firm but has developed some sugars—what Trinidadians will call "force ripe." Look for mangoes that are firm, with just a bit of give when you squeeze it, and not yet fragrant.

MAKES 1 CUP

1 half-ripe mango (any variety), peeled, pitted, and roughly chopped
6 culantro leaves, roughly torn
2 garlic cloves, smashed and peeled
½ Scotch bonnet pepper (optional)
1 teaspoon kosher salt
1 teaspoon fresh lime juice
Up to ¼ cup water, as needed

In a food processor, combine the mango, culantro, garlic, Scotch bonnet, salt, and lime juice and pulse until the mixture forms a thick paste that drips very slowly off your spoon. If the chutney is too thick, with the processor running on low, slowly add up to ¼ cup water. The chutney will keep in an airtight container in the fridge for 2 to 3 days.

HABICHUELAS GUISADAS

STEWED RED BEANS ○ PUERTO RICO

1 pound dried kidney beans or other red beans
8 cups water
1 large yellow onion, halved: ½ left whole, ½ diced
6 garlic cloves: 2 smashed and peeled, 4 minced
2 bay leaves
3 tablespoons extra-virgin olive oil
½ green bell pepper, diced
½ cup Recaíto (page 22)
2 teaspoons Puerto Rican Sazón, homemade (page 23) or store-bought
1 cup tomato sauce
1 cup peeled and diced calabaza (about 5 ounces)
2 to 3 teaspoons kosher salt
"Perfect" White Rice (page 180), for serving (optional)

SERVES 6 TO 8

Anyone who has had any kind of culinary interaction with Puerto Rico or its people has had habichuelas guisadas. A meal is barely considered complete without it. Every restaurant brings out a bowl of it with your food no matter what you order, whether you're in San Juan or Brooklyn. My very first boyfriend basically told me if I didn't learn to make habichuelas guisadas, we were done. Problematic ultimatum aside, I learned. Since then, I have ditched the Goya brand seasonings he insisted were necessary, but the smell and the taste of this dish still take me back to Brooklyn in the '90s and his Bushwick kitchen. The connection to Jamaican Stew Peas (page 33) is very obvious, but the seasonings are purely Puerto Rican. If you can't find calabaza squash (West Indian pumpkin), substitute butternut or kabocha.

In a large, heavy-bottomed pot or Dutch oven, combine the beans, water, onion half, smashed garlic cloves, bay leaves, and 1 tablespoon of the olive oil and bring to a boil over medium-high heat. Reduce the heat to low and simmer, undisturbed, for 1 to 1½ hours, until the beans are tender.

Near the end of the beans' cooking time, in a skillet or wide saucepan, heat the remaining 2 tablespoons oil over medium heat. Add the diced onion, minced garlic, and bell pepper and sauté for 3 to 5 minutes, until the onion and pepper are soft. Add the recaíto and cook until it's fragrant, about 3 minutes. Add the sazón and tomato sauce and cook for 3 to 5 minutes more, until the tomato sauce has become one with all the other ingredients.

Scrape the onion-pepper mixture into the pot with the beans, then add the squash and about 2 teaspoons of the salt. Cook for 30 to 40 minutes more, until the beans look like they want to break down and have made the cooking liquid velvety. Remove the pot from the heat.

Taste for salt (beans can handle a lot of seasoning, so you may want to add up to a full teaspoon more). Remove the bay leaves, and serve over rice as a main or on its own as a side. Store leftovers in an airtight container in the fridge for 3 to 4 days or in the freezer for up to 4 months.

CALABAZA

CUCURBITA MOSCHATA

Other names: JOUMOU,
WEST INDIAN PUMPKIN

THIS IS A SQUASH THAT CAN confuse many non-Caribbean people. Trinidad and other English-speaking nations call it pumpkin; Haitians call it joumou; Cubans, Dominicans, and Puerto Ricans call it calabaza. All these terms refer to "squash" in general; however, across the region (and in this book), it's a variety of the *Cucurbita moschata* squash, known in English as West Indian pumpkin, that is used. In this book I refer to it as calabaza as it will often appear in grocery stores under that name, and to avoid confusion with a sugar pumpkin. Shaped much like the pumpkin we in the US and Canada know from Halloween, this squash has pale skin that varies in color from white to green. Its flesh is mild and sweet, and though aesthetically it most closely resembles a kabocha squash, I'd say its flesh is closer to butternut in both texture and flavor; either make a fine substitute for calabaza.

This cultivar is native to Central and South America, as well as the Caribbean, and was found growing alongside corn and beans (the "three sisters," as Native Americans refer to them) upon Columbus's arrival in the Caribbean. Today, you can find this squash in Caribbean and Latin American markets, as it is still very much grown and eaten in the places of its origin. In this chapter, calabaza is the star of the show, but much like coconut, it can show up just about anywhere, and you'll find it in other recipes peppered throughout the book. It adds a bit of sweet silkiness to soups and stews, as well as some color and nutrition. The practice of adding it to bean dishes and stews likely comes from the Taíno. Its most famous use is probably in Haitian Soup Joumou (page 47) or Freedom Soup, which has been eaten every January 1 since 1804 to celebrate Haitian Independence Day.

NUTRITION: Much like its other squash relatives, calabaza is an excellent source of beta-carotene and vitamins A and C.

HOW TO BUY: If you're able to find one at a Caribbean market, it will likely only be sold in pieces, as the squash grows to be quite large (though on occasion I've seen some the size of basketballs being sold whole). It could be called calabaza, joumou, or West Indian pumpkin, depending on which Caribbean population is largest in the area. The color of the skin doesn't matter, but if it's cut, look for clean, unblemished flesh. When sold precut, they don't last too long in the fridge, so either use it within a few days, cut it up into cubes to freeze, or make it into puree (page 54) to freeze.

HOW TO PREPARE: As this squash has a hard skin, I find a sharp knife is a better tool for peeling than a vegetable peeler. If the squash is whole, cut off the bottom of the squash so it sits flat on your cutting board. Cut it in half, then scoop out the seeds with a spoon. Hold a piece of squash firmly in place with one hand, and cut downward to remove the skin, working in sections all around the fruit. Because of all the crevices, the skin will not come off evenly, and that's okay.

HISTORY OF SOUP JOUMOU

When the French colonists settled on the island they called Saint-Domingue, they tasked the enslaved Africans with cultivating and cooking calabaza, known as joumou in the region. However, the French wouldn't allow the enslaved to eat the fruit, as they considered it a delicacy. This was part of a long list of ways the colonizers created a divide between themselves and the enslaved and tried to enforce a social hierarchy.

The Haitian Revolution, led by people such as Henri Christophe, Toussaint Louverture, and Jean-Jacques Dessalines (Desalin's namesake and the first emperor of a free Black republic in the world), lasted for thirteen years. On November 18, 1803, the freedom fighters were finally able to take control of the territory and their lives, defeating the French once and for all in the Battle of Vertières. On January 1, 1804, they celebrated, and Jean-Jacques Dessalines declared it a free nation, reclaiming the island's original name, Ayiti, in honor of its Indigenous inhabitants. According to some accounts, as part of the celebration, Marie-Claire Heureuse Félicité Bonheur Dessalines, Dessalines's wife and the first empress of Haiti, distributed soup joumou to the freed Africans who would go on to become the first Haitians.

The significance of this soup has never wavered, and it remains a hugely important part of Haitian culture today. For more than two hundred years, every January 1, Haitians across the globe celebrate Independence Day and their ancestors' hard-won freedom with bowls of soup joumou. Large pots are made to share, and family and friends bring their own versions. So much soup is made and passed around that anyone growing up in a Haitian household knows the first week of the year will be filled with leftovers. Everyone has their own take on the soup, what can go in and what can't, but the key ingredient is always, of course, the joumou, for what it symbolizes. This soup represents Black revolution, freedom, and equity, not just for Haitians, but for all of us of the African diaspora. The Haitian Revolution was the only successful slave revolt in the entire world. It set off a chain reaction that resulted in freedom for the enslaved across the Caribbean and eventually in the United States, where slave owners tried to hide the news of this revolution from their slaves for as long as possible. It has inspired people across the globe living under oppression to rise up. This soup is the physical manifestation of all that. In our house, we come together to make it every year, and though I am not Haitian, I feel proud to carry on this tradition to celebrate what the nation did for us all, and what we can do when we work together.

SOUP JOUMOU

FREEDOM SOUP ○ HAITI

KREYÒL SPICE SACHET

6 whole cloves, toasted
5 allspice berries, toasted
5 whole black peppercorns, toasted
5 whole white peppercorns, toasted
2 bunches thyme
3 scallions
5 parsley sprigs
4 bay leaves
5 culantro leaves

SOUP

1 pound oxtail
1½ pounds beef neck bones or chuck beef stew meat
½ cup plus 2 tablespoons Epis (page 21)
6 cups water
4 pounds calabaza, peeled, seeded, and cut into 2-inch chunks (see page 45)
4 tablespoons kosher salt
2 carrots, diced
2 turnips, peeled and diced
1 chayote, peeled and diced (see page 80)
2 malanga, peeled and diced (see Note)
3 tablespoons extra-virgin olive oil

As much soup joumou as I've eaten and helped make in my life (which is a lot!), it was important to me to have someone of Haitian descent share their version of this soup due to this dish's deep significance to Haitian culture. The first person I thought of was chef Cybille St.Aude-Tate, who, with over sixteen years of experience in restaurants, has made it her mission to celebrate her Haitian roots as well as Black and Afrocentric food traditions and community.

To create this recipe, Cybille dug deep into history. Haitian historian Bayyinah Bello has shared the first recorded recipe for soup joumou. Cybille was amazed to discover that it was hardly different from the version made today; the main exceptions were that the first versions were meat-free with no pasta. While pasta has become a common ingredient, it's unclear when it made its way to Haiti or how.

While the soup has fundamentally stayed the same, it is important to remember that this soup, just like all the other traditional recipes in this book and beyond, is something that is forever changing in nuanced ways. What the soup is depends entirely on who is making it and what their circumstances are at that moment. Cybille says people should make the soup their own but be wary of changing its integrity. Leave out ingredients you wouldn't find in Haiti or the Caribbean or that would change the flavor profile of the soup entirely. When Atibon first saw these ingredients, he started raising Haitian red flags at the culantro and was quick to say it was *not* used by his people. Cybille used it in lieu of sorrel leaves, which are a traditional ingredient and grow prolifically throughout the Caribbean, but are very hard to find stateside. I've tried so many versions of this soup, and I like them all (though, like Cybille, I am defiantly Team No Pasta), but I have to say this may be the best I've ever had. All soup joumou recipes require a lot of work. While it's a simple soup in some ways, there are a lot of ingredients and a lot of steps. But think of this as a ritual. With each step, with each layer, you are paying homage to a legacy of revolution, freedom, and Black excellence.

Cybille is in awe of what she calls the mystic aspect of the soup. She thinks about how long her people have been making it and how it has stayed nearly the same: "We're *still* making it with the same intention and the same kind of fire behind it . . . and millions of people are participating in this! This is the biggest conjuring I've ever been able to partake in. We're intentionally making this spell, and we've been doing it as a people, every year on this one day, en masse for over two hundred years. I've never seen anything like it. It's so mystical, it's so magical, it's so quintessentially Haitian."

RECIPE CONTINUES

1 leek, roots and dark green tops trimmed, diced

1 yellow onion, cut into small dice

4 garlic cloves, smashed and peeled

2 celery stalks, cut into small dice

1 Scotch bonnet pepper

¼ head cabbage, shredded

¼ cup Pikliz vinegar (page 214) or fresh lime juice

Hard dough or coco bread, for serving

SERVES 8 TO 10

Note: If you can't find malanga, which is a long, hairy, sort of cone-shaped root, sometimes mistakenly called taro, substitute another ground provision such as batata, eddo, or yam.

Note: To toast spices, heat a small skillet over medium heat. When it's hot, add the spices, swirling them in the pan occasionally until they are fragrant, 2 to 4 minutes. Remove them from the pan immediately or they will continue to toast in the residual heat.

Combine all the ingredients for the spice sachet in a spice bag or in a piece of cheesecloth tied with twine.

In a container with an airtight lid, season the oxtail and beef neck bones with ½ cup of the epis. Cover and refrigerate for at least 3 hours, but preferably overnight.

In a large pot, combine 5 cups of the water and the calabaza and bring to a boil over medium-high heat. Cook for about 25 minutes, until the squash is fork-tender. Using an immersion blender, blend the squash and its cooking liquid directly in the pot until smooth (or carefully transfer them to a standing blender, in batches if necessary, and puree until smooth). Set aside.

Fill a separate large pot with water and add 2 tablespoons of salt. Bring to a boil over high heat. Add the carrots, turnips, chayote, and malanga and boil until just cooked through, 7 to 10 minutes. Drain and set the veggies aside.

In a very large stockpot, heat the olive oil over medium-high heat. Add the beef and oxtail and sear until browned, 5 to 8 minutes on each side, then transfer to a plate. Add the leek, onion, garlic, and celery to the pot and cook until soft, 3 to 5 minutes. Add the remaining 2 tablespoons epis and cook until very aromatic and incorporated into the vegetables, about 3 minutes. Add the remaining 1 cup water, the Scotch bonnet, the spice sachet, the seared beef and oxtail, and the cabbage. Cover and cook over medium-low heat for about 20 minutes, until the oxtail begins to soften.

Add the pureed squash and remaining 2 tablespoons salt. Stir until well combined, cover, and cook for 25 minutes. Add the cooked vegetables and simmer for 10 minutes more, then check the oxtail; it should be falling off the bone.

Turn off the heat, remove the spice sachet, and add the vinegar. Serve hot! This is best enjoyed with a side of hard dough or coco bread.

CALABAZA CON AJO

STEAMED CALABAZA WITH GARLIC ○ CUBA

2 pounds calabaza,
   butternut squash,
   or kabocha squash,
   peeled, seeded,
   and cut into 2-inch
   cubes (see page 45)
Kosher salt
3 tablespoons extra-
   virgin olive oil
5 garlic cloves, minced
Minced fresh parsley,
   for garnish

SERVES 4 TO 6

This incredibly simple dish feels representative of much of Cuban cuisine—so much can be done with so little, and with the right combination of ingredients in just the right ratios, a dish can truly sing. Though I'm usually a fan of roasted squash, steaming it allows the true, clean flavors to come through and retains that beautiful color. I encourage you to try this recipe as written at least once! Once you've done that, I do welcome you to try any additions, as Caribbean cooking is all about adapting to your environment and your taste buds. The simplicity of the dish belies the savory decadence that generous amounts of garlic and olive oil bring.

Place the calabaza in a medium sauce-pan and add water to cover, then add 2 teaspoons salt. Bring to a simmer over medium heat, then cook until the calabaza is tender, 10 to 15 minutes.

Meanwhile, in a small skillet, heat the olive oil over medium-high heat until fragrant and shimmering. Add the garlic and cook for just 10 seconds, then remove the pan from the heat and let the garlic infuse the oil.

Drain the calabaza and place it in a large bowl. Immediately scrape the garlic oil into the bowl and toss gently. Taste for salt. Sprinkle with parsley and serve warm or at room temperature.

PUMPKIN SOUP

SAINT LUCIA

2 tablespoons extra-virgin olive oil
1 small yellow onion, diced
5 garlic cloves, minced
1 seasoning pepper, minced (optional; see page 14)
4 scallions, sliced
2 teaspoons fresh thyme leaves
3 pounds calabaza, peeled, seeded, and cut into 2-inch cubes (see page 45)
4 cups water or vegetable stock
1 to 2 teaspoons kosher salt
Freshly ground black pepper

SERVES 6 TO 8

In Saint Lucia, a man once told me his mother was the best cook he had ever known. When I asked what dish he thought was her finest, he told me about her pumpkin soup. It was simple, he explained, and he walked me through the ingredients and steps. He said something about that soup warmed his soul, and when he was going through a particularly tough time in his life, his mother would bring him batches of it, which truly lifted his spirits. He said he'd tried and tried to replicate it, and while his versions were perfectly good, they could never fully compare to hers. While I suspect the secret ingredient was, as it always is, love, I have tried my best to make a version that does hers justice.

Pumpkin soup shows up on all the islands, the most famous version probably being Soup Joumou (page 47) from Haiti, followed closely by Jamaican pumpkin soup. Those soups have many ingredients and usually include meat, and while the squash is blended, the other ingredients remain whole. Saint Lucia has a tradition of this super simple pumpkin soup, and it shows up on the menu of nearly every restaurant on the island. It would also be great with coconut milk, but here it is in its simplest state, just like Mom made.

In a large Dutch oven or other heavy-bottomed pot, heat the olive oil over medium heat. Add the onion and garlic and sauté until the onion begins to brown, 5 to 8 minutes. Add the seasoning pepper (if using), scallions, and thyme and cook for 3 minutes, until the pepper begins to soften. Add the calabaza, stir to coat, and cook for 3 to 5 minutes, until the squash begins to break down.

Pour in the water and bring to a boil over high heat. Add 1 teaspoon of the salt and black pepper to taste, then reduce the heat to medium-low, cover, and cook until the calabaza is soft, 20 to 25 minutes.

Using an immersion blender, blend the soup directly in the pot until completely smooth (or carefully transfer the soup to a standing blender, in batches if necessary, and blend until smooth). Taste for salt and serve hot. Leftovers will keep in an airtight container in the fridge for up to 3 days or in the freezer for up to 3 months.

PUMPKIN RICE

SAINT VINCENT AND THE GRENADINES

1 tablespoon
    coconut oil
1 small yellow onion,
    diced
2 scallions, thinly sliced
3 garlic cloves, minced
1 teaspoon fresh
    thyme leaves
1 cup cubed calabaza,
    peeled, or
    butternut squash
1 cup Coconut
    Milk, homemade
    (page 97) or
    store-bought
1 cup water
Kosher salt
1 cup long-grain rice
1 tablespoon unsalted
    butter

SERVES 4 TO 6

While this recipe is not necessarily what these small islands are famous for (they are huge on breadfruit there, and they are also known for their buljol and ducana), the assistant principal at Desalin's school said that of all her Vincy mother-in-law's dishes, this is her absolute favorite. Mommy G, as she's known to the family, was surprised to be asked for this recipe, but it's a great alternative to plain rice if you want to serve a side with some impact. It also adds some nutrition to a meal. The calabaza gives it a bit of sweetness and is complemented by the savory spices. Coconut milk and a bit of butter add a hint of luxury to an otherwise simple dish.

In a medium saucepan, heat the coconut oil over medium heat. Add the onion, scallions, garlic, and thyme and sauté until the onion is soft, 3 to 5 minutes.

Add the calabaza, stir to coat, and cook for 3 minutes, until the squash just starts to soften.

Add the coconut milk, water, and salt to taste. Bring to a boil, add in the rice and butter, then reduce the heat to low, cover, and cook for 30 minutes, until all the liquid has been absorbed. Fluff before serving.

PUMPKIN CHOKA AND SALTFISH

STEWED CALABAZA AND SALTED COD
○ TRINIDAD AND TOBAGO

1 tablespoon coconut oil or neutral oil

1 small yellow onion, diced

4 garlic cloves, minced

1 seasoning pepper, seeded and minced (optional; see page 14)

4 culantro leaves, or ¼ cup fresh cilantro, chopped

3 scallions, thinly sliced

2 pounds calabaza, peeled, seeded, and cut into 1-inch cubes (see page 45)

¼ cup water, plus more if needed

8 ounces salted cod, desalted (see page 197)

"Perfect" White Rice (page 180) or Coconut Bake (page 103), for serving

SERVES 4 TO 6

This dish is one of the few that I forced my mother to teach me properly to make. It was a quintessentially Merle Enston dish, but she didn't make it as often as her Buljol (page 206). This probably made it more of a treat. I very vividly remember her explaining that the kind of "punkin" (as a Trini would say) you got was key—some are filled with water and some are not, so it was important to keep an eye on that. In her version, the ingredient list was much smaller: Along with the calabaza and salted cod, she simply sautéed onions and garlic. I marveled with wonder and disbelief every time I watched over her shoulder that those ingredients were all it took to create this lush dish. I've added other standard Trinidadian seasonings because I just love them so, but every time I make it, I can feel my mom rolling her eyes behind me, muttering how I don't need that stuff under her breath, especially the culantro. I grew up eating this dish, and always assumed it was standard Trinidadian fare as is, but have come to realize adding saltfish was Mom's own riff.

In a heavy-bottomed pot or Dutch oven, heat the coconut oil over medium heat. Add the onion, garlic, and seasoning pepper (if using) and sauté until the onion starts to brown, 5 to 8 minutes. Add the culantro and scallions and cook for 2 minutes, until the scallions begin to brown.

Add the calabaza and stir to coat. Add the water, then reduce the heat to medium-low, cover, and cook for 25 to 30 minutes, stirring occasionally and mashing the squash here and there as it begins to soften. If the water evaporates but the squash still isn't breaking down, add more water 1 tablespoon at a time.

Once the squash is broken down into a relatively even mush, add the fish and cook for 5 minutes more, until warmed through. Serve over rice or with coconut bake.

CALABAZA PUREE

2 pounds calabaza
 or other winter
 squash of your
 choice, halved,
 seeded, and peeled
 (see page 45)

MAKES 2 CUPS

Long ago I said goodbye to canned pumpkin in favor of freshly made puree. At the end of the day, it doesn't take that long to come together, and a big batch requires no more effort than a small one. The color alone—a bright and happy yellow-orange, compared to the moody, gray-tinged hue of canned pumpkin— should be enough to convert you. Several recipes in this book, including the Arepa di Pampuna (page 57), Cassava Pone (page 71), and Calabaza Pie (page 58), call for it. I like to buy a bigger piece of squash (or a whole one, depending on what kind I'm using), and measure 1-cup portions of the extra puree into zip-top bags to freeze; laying the bags flat makes for easy freezer storage. One never knows when Pumpkin Fritters (page 55) will be requested (spoiler alert: In my home, that's all the time).

Cut the calabaza into roughly 2-inch cubes (you should have about 3 cups). In a saucepan large enough to fit the cubes in no more than two layers, combine the squash and enough water to barely cover it. Cover and cook over medium-high heat until the squash is very tender, 20 to 25 minutes. Drain and let it cool a bit.

You can either mash the squash with a fork or a potato masher, or, for a smoother texture, you can process it in a food processor or blender. The puree will keep in an airtight container in the fridge for several days or in the freezer for about 3 months.

PUMPKIN FRITTERS

BARBADOS

1½ cups all-purpose
  flour
1 teaspoon baking
  powder
½ teaspoon ground
  cinnamon
¼ teaspoon freshly
  grated nutmeg
¼ teaspoon kosher salt
1 cup Calabaza Puree
  (page 54)
⅓ cup Coconut
  Milk, homemade
  (page 97) or
  store-bought
⅓ cup packed
  brown sugar
½ teaspoon grated
  fresh ginger
1 teaspoon vanilla
  extract
¼ teaspoon almond
  extract
Neutral oil, for frying
Powdered sugar, for
  dusting

SERVES 6 TO 8

Fritters like this show up all over the islands. We all know pumpkin and these spices are a match made in heaven, and when you fry all that . . . well, it's like little fried pumpkin angels landed on earth. While the recipe for pumpkin fritters doesn't differ much from island to island, I particularly like the combination of spices and the flour ratio found in most recipes from Barbados. There are some weeks that if I open my mouth to say "I'm going to cook . . . ," Desalin will finish the sentence with "Pumpkin fritters?" This is a suggestion, a hope, and, ever so slightly, an order. They aren't too sweet even after dusting them with sugar and make a great treat for a brunch spread.

In a medium bowl, whisk together the flour, baking powder, cinnamon, nutmeg, and salt. In another medium bowl, whisk together the calabaza puree, coconut milk, brown sugar, ginger, vanilla, and almond extract until smooth. Mix the wet ingredients into the dry ingredients with a fork or a wooden spoon, until all the flour has been mixed in and a stiff dough has formed.

In a wok or deep skillet, heat about 2 inches of oil over medium-high heat until it reaches 350°F. If you don't have a thermometer, you'll know the oil is ready if a bit of dough bubbles deeply when dropped in.

Using a heaping tablespoon, carefully place balls of dough in the hot oil (you may need to use another spoon to scrape the dough out of the table-spoon). Be sure not to crowd them; work in batches, if needed. Fry until golden brown on all sides, 8 to 10 minutes total. Using a slotted spoon or tongs, transfer the fritters to paper towel–lined plates to drain. Let cool a bit, then dust with powdered sugar and serve immediately.

AREPA DI PAMPUNA

CALABAZA PANCAKES ○ CURAÇAO

1 cup all-purpose flour

3 tablespoons granulated sugar

2 teaspoons baking soda

1 teaspoon ground cinnamon

½ teaspoon freshly grated nutmeg

¼ teaspoon kosher salt

2 eggs

1 cup Calabaza Puree (page 54)

½ cup whole milk

1 teaspoon vanilla extract

¼ cup raisins (optional)

Coconut oil, for the pan

Powdered sugar, for dusting (optional)

MAKES ABOUT EIGHT 4-INCH PANCAKES

Part of the Dutch Caribbean, Curaçao has a somewhat unusual cuisine for the islands. In addition to the African and Indigenous influences on the food, the Dutch colonists seem to have left a large mark (you can see it in dishes with names like stroopwafel and oliebollen), more so than the European influence on many other islands. These pancakes feel like a Dutch treatment of a native ingredient. These are not just any old pumpkin pancakes. They are unique, largely because of the amount of egg—it makes for a denser pancake with that distinct eggy taste—and are thicker than your average pancake. While they aren't my everyday pancake, they are filling and satisfying. Traditionally, they are served sprinkled with powdered sugar, but I am not ashamed to say I like them doused in maple syrup. The raisins are also traditional, but certainly optional. Don't be afraid of the amount of spice. Caribbean people do nothing halfway, and the squash can stand up to it. I often double the recipe so there are enough pancakes left over to freeze, as they reheat easily in the oven, on the stovetop, or in the toaster, and are a compelling way to get my child out of bed on a school day.

In a small bowl, mix together the flour, granulated sugar, baking soda, cinnamon, nutmeg, and salt; set aside. In a medium bowl, beat the eggs until fluffy. Add the calabaza puree, milk, and vanilla and mix with a fork until fully blended, then whisk the dry ingredients into the wet ingredients until combined. Fold in the raisins, if using.

Heat a large skillet over medium heat. When the skillet is hot, drizzle it with a small amount of oil (I love coconut oil, but anything will do here), then ladle ¼ cup of the batter onto the skillet for each pancake, forming a 4-inch round. If you pour it in slowly, close to the pan, the batter will round out on its own.

Cook on the first side for 3 to 5 minutes, until bubbles begin to form on the surface and you see the edges turning brown. Using a wide spatula, flip the pancake and cook on the second side for a few minutes, until golden brown. Repeat the process with the remaining batter.

Serve immediately, dusted with powdered sugar or another topping of your choice. You can also let the pancakes cool, then store them in an airtight container in the freezer for up to a month.

CALABAZA PIE

1 recipe for Pie Crust
(page 170)
Butter for greasing
the pan

FILLING

2 cups Calabaza Puree
(page 54)
3 eggs, beaten
½ cup packed
brown sugar
¼ cup grated fresh
coconut (optional)
1 teaspoon grated
fresh ginger
1 teaspoon ground
cinnamon
½ teaspoon freshly
grated nutmeg
½ teaspoon ground
allspice
1 cup Coconut
Milk, homemade
(page 97) or
store-bought
Coconut Whipped
Cream (page 171)
or ice cream, for
serving

SERVES 8 TO 10

I just love this recipe. The West Indian pumpkin feels a bit lighter and fresher here than the traditional sugar pumpkin (butternut squash will also do in a pinch). The coconut milk in the recipe is surprisingly subtle. Rather than bopping you over the head with coconut flavor, it just gives a light silkiness to the calabaza, as opposed to the decadence heavy cream would add. But since there's little in life I love more than being bopped over the head with coconut flavor, I like to add a bit of grated fresh coconut. For people sensitive to texture, I feel you. I promise that it doesn't feel as weird as you're thinking, but if it freaks you out, the grated coconut is definitely optional. I have made this pie for many dinner parties, and always with great success.

Preheat the oven to 350°F. Grease a 9-inch pie dish.

Remove the dough for the crust from the fridge and let it warm up just a bit so you're able to manipulate it, then flour a flat surface. Using a floured rolling pin, roll out the dough into a round a bit wider in circumference than your pie dish. Start from the middle and roll outward, rotating the dough as you go. Transfer the dough to your pie dish, make sure the edge is about even, and then form it however you like. When I feel fancy, I try pinching the edge all the way around, or sometimes I just crimp it with a fork. Line the dough with aluminum foil and place either pie weights or dried beans on top, enough to weigh the foil down. Bake the crust for about 20 minutes, until it's a light golden color. Remove the foil and the weights, and allow the crust to cool completely. Reduce the oven temperature to 325°F.

Make the filling: In a large bowl, mix the calabaza puree, eggs, brown sugar, coconut, if using, and ginger. Add the cinnamon, nutmeg, allspice, and coconut milk and mix slowly so as not to splash anything around. Pour the filling into the crust and bake for about 1 hour, until the middle is mostly firm. If the edges of the crust start to brown too deeply, cover them with foil.

Remove from the oven and let the pie cool completely before slicing and serving. Serve with coconut whipped cream or ice cream.

CASSAVA

MANIHOT ESCULENTA

Other names: MANYÒK, MANIOC, YUCA

IN SOME WAYS, THERE is no other ingredient here more representative of the Caribbean than cassava. Called yuca by the Taíno, this staple food was brought to the Caribbean thousands of years ago when Indigenous peoples first made the trip by canoe from South America, where cassava had been cultivated for over ten thousand years. It was a staple food in the pre-Columbus Americas and was often depicted in Indigenous art. The native peoples of the islands learned all the tricks of this tuber, the bitter varieties of which contain lethal amounts of cyanide. By removing all the liquid from the grated flesh, even bitter cassava was rendered safe to eat. It was most often dried and roasted to become a bread, known then—and today—as casabe or kasav, which has been in existence since about 2000 BCE.

The cassava root was so important to the Taíno that it factored heavily in their religious ceremonies, and its planting was of religious importance. As with many of the foods that would come to be known as provisions or viandas, it is very easy to grow and can prosper in all kinds of conditions.

In the inland jungles of Guyana, where there is still a large Indigenous population, the Macushi tribe grows up to twenty-six different cultivars of bitter cassava. Cassava is so treasured that cassava stalks will be given as a gift to anyone starting (or restarting) a farm. Not only is this an act of kindness, but it also ensures an exchange of varieties, which helps prevent entire crops from being wiped out.

Enslaved Africans learned how to prepare this tuber from their native sisters and brothers. Pepperpot (page 73) is very much a result of the two worlds colliding. Casabe (page 69) and Bammy (page 72) are both foodstuffs that the Taíno taught the Africans how to make, especially the Maroons (see page 220), who needed portable food that wouldn't spoil as they trekked through the mountains in search of freedom. They also learned about its poisonous qualities, and bitter cassava was used by both natives and enslaved Africans as a means of suicide, which was considered better than living under the conditions they were subjected to by their European enslavers, and to poison those same enslavers.

This versatile root journeyed from Brazil to Africa with the Portuguese in the sixteenth century and has since become a primary food staple in many countries across the continent. Here in the United States, the most common variety on the market is sweet cassava, which can be eaten without concern. Cassava is often added to soups and stews, deep-fried, or boiled and sautéed. It has a somewhat gummy texture that I love and makes me think of trips to Trinidad in my youth. A friend of the family's mother who we always visited on every trip to the island would make a soup with fish heads and cassava. As a child, I was not into those fish heads, but the cassava more than made up for it.

NUTRITION: Cassava is high in carbohydrates, which would have been important for giving people energy on limited means. It also contains resistant starch, which takes longer to pass through a person's body and breaks down more on the way. It's a much healthier alternative to, for instance, white bread. It is also a good source of vitamin C.

HOW TO CHOOSE: The skin of the cassava we get here in the United States is covered in wax to help preserve it. Look for roots that are firm, with no dark or soft spots. Break off the very tip of the root; the flesh should be white and smell fresh. Rotting cassava smells particularly putrid, so it's not hard to detect! Any roots with soft spots are not long for this world and should be passed over.

HOW TO PREPARE: Don't try to use a vegetable peeler to remove the tough skin on this root. It will end in frustration or pain. Cut the root horizontally in half or thirds, depending on its size. With a sharp paring knife, slice the skin lengthwise on each piece. Work the tip of the knife under the skin and gently pull at it; it will come off surprisingly easily. Do this all the way around the root; the skin will come off in large pieces. When the skin has been removed, cut each piece in half lengthwise and, using the same sharp paring knife, remove the thin core that runs down the middle by cutting along either side of it at an angle, forming a V; the core will pop right out. Grate or chop the cassava as needed. If you're prepping your cassava in advance, put it in a bowl of cold water until you're ready to cook it, or it will discolor quickly.

METEMGEE

PROVISION STEW ○ GUYANA

STEW

1 to 1½ pounds
   cassava, peeled and
   cored (see page 63)
1 pound Caribbean
   sweet potato
   (see Note)
2 ripe plantains,
   peeled
1 pound yellow yam
1 tablespoon
   coconut oil
1 small yellow onion,
   diced
5 garlic cloves, minced
1 Roma (plum) tomato,
   diced
1 celery stalk, diced
3 scallions, thinly sliced
1 tablespoon fresh
   thyme leaves
4 cups homemade
   Coconut Milk
   (page 97), or
   1 (13.5-ounce) can
   coconut milk mixed
   with 2 cups water

DUFF (DUMPLINGS)

1 cup all-purpose flour
1 teaspoon kosher salt
½ teaspoon baking
   powder
Pinch of sugar
1 cup plus
   2 tablespoons water

1 teaspoon kosher salt

SERVES 4 TO 6

Note: Caribbean sweet
potatoes may also be
called batatas, boniatos,
or white yams.

This dish has cooking roots in Central and West Africa, where the food was largely based on wet stews, and across much of the continent, Africans had been using coconut in their cooking for centuries before crossing the Atlantic. The cassava is likely an Indigenous touch.

This recipe is adapted from my neighbor Miss Bibi, as we know her, who moved to Bed-Stuy from Guyana with her husband in 1995. You can add any other ground provision you like, or even use American sweet potatoes, but cassava is a must. Its texture is a key part of the dish. Even though it is called a stew, this dish should be much thicker than your average stew (and will thicken even more as it cools). This is one instance where homemade coconut milk is superior to canned. The concentrated thickness of canned coconut milk doesn't cook down as well. But if you must use canned, be sure to thin it as described in the ingredient list. Most provisions will start to change color as they oxidize, but you can prevent this by putting them in a bowl with cold water to cover until you're ready to add them to the pot.

This, as with so many Caribbean dishes, is a choose-your-own-adventure kind of thing. Miss Bibi adds carrots, okra, and spinach to hers, noting that you don't have to cut any of the vegetables very small, as everything will cook down. Many people use salted meat or salted fish in this recipe, but I choose to go Miss Bibi's route, keeping it veggie and serving it with fish on the side. The duff dumplings take a bit of practice, but just remember that they only need a light touch.

Make the stew: Fill a large bowl and a separate smaller bowl with cold water. Cut the cassava, sweet potato, plantains, and yellow yam into roughly 2-inch chunks, dropping them into the water as you work to prevent them from discoloring (drop the yellow yam into the smaller bowl to keep it separate from the other provisions).

In a large stockpot or Dutch oven, heat the coconut oil over medium heat. Add the onion, garlic, tomato, celery, scallions, and thyme and sauté until the veggies start to get soft, 3 to 5 minutes. Drain the yellow yam, add it to the pot, and give everything a good stir to coat. Add the coconut milk. (Ultimately, you want the liquid to just reach the top of the provisions, but we still have a lot to add.) Cover and cook until the yams begin to soften, about 15 minutes.

Meanwhile, make the duff: In a medium bowl, stir together the flour, salt, baking powder, and sugar. Add the water a bit at a time, stirring until the dough comes together. It should be cohesive but not wet. Gently and briefly knead the dough and shape it

into a ball with your hands. Don't be overzealous; if you work it too much, the dough will get tough, and duff should be airy. It's okay if it's not totally smooth. Set the dough aside.

Drain the cassava, sweet potatoes, and plantains and add them to the stockpot along with the salt. It might seem like there's not quite enough liquid, but don't worry—there is! Cook, uncovered, for 10 minutes.

Meanwhile, separate the dough for the duff into 6 even balls and lightly shape them into ovals.

Add the duff to the pot, nestling them among the provisions. They shouldn't be submerged. Using a spoon, bathe the duff with a bit of the coconut milk, then cover the pot and cook for 15 minutes, or until the duff are cooked through. Immediately remove the duff from the pot.

Serve the duff alongside the metemgee. This is best eaten the same day, as the provisions will continue to absorb the liquid and get a bit mushy, but is still very tasty on day 2; store in an airtight container in the fridge.

AREPITAS DE YUCA

CASSAVA FRITTERS ○ DOMINICAN REPUBLIC

1 pound cassava,
    peeled, cored,
    and grated or
    shredded with a
    food processor
    (see page 63)
1 large egg, beaten
1 teaspoon kosher salt
1 teaspoon aniseed
½ teaspoon sugar
Neutral oil, for frying

SERVES 6 TO 8

Yuca, the Taíno term for cassava, is still used on the Spanish-speaking islands, and the simplicity of these fritters makes the taste and texture of the tuber shine. The anise is the secret sauce, adding its hint of licorice to create just a bit of mystery. I once scoured grocery stores for anise with my Dominican friend Sarah while on a trip to Connecticut so we could make these. When we had no luck, she pronounced the project a flop—that's how important the anise is. These are great on their own but are also delicious dipped in Mayoketchup (page 119) or Tamarind Sauce (page 40).

In a medium bowl, combine the cassava, egg, salt, aniseed, and sugar and stir until evenly incorporated.

In a wok or deep skillet, heat 2 inches of oil over medium-high heat until it reaches 350°F. If you don't have a thermometer, you'll know the oil is ready if a bit of the cassava mixture bubbles deeply when dropped in.

Using a tablespoon, drop balls of the cassava mixture into the hot oil and cook until they're a deep golden brown, 4 to 5 minutes on each side. If they're browning too fast, reduce the heat and wait a bit before adding more. Drain on paper towels and serve immediately.

BOIL AND FRY CASSAVA

CASSAVA HASH ○ TRINIDAD AND TOBAGO

1 pound cassava, peeled, cored, and cut into 1-inch cubes (see page 63)

1 tablespoon kosher salt, plus more as needed

2 tablespoons extra-virgin olive oil

1 small yellow onion, thinly sliced

2 garlic cloves, minced

½ seasoning pepper, minced (optional; see page 14)

1 teaspoon fresh thyme leaves

2 Roma (plum) tomatoes, diced (about 2 cups)

2 scallions, thinly sliced

SERVES 4 TO 6

In Trinidad, "fry" really means "cook in a skillet with a bit of oil." This dish is reminiscent of home fries, but with a Caribbean twist. Boiling then searing is one of my favorite treatments for cassava: You get a bit of golden crisp on the outside, but the inside remains delightfully chewy.

Place the cassava in a large pot and add the salt and water to cover by 1 inch. Bring to a simmer over medium-low heat and cook until tender, 10 to 15 minutes. Drain and set aside.

In a wide skillet, heat the olive oil over medium heat. Add the onion and garlic and cook until the onion is soft, 3 to 5 minutes. Add the seasoning pepper (if using) and the thyme and cook for another minute.

Add the tomatoes and cook until they're beginning to break down, about 5 minutes. Add the cassava and cook, stirring just occasionally, until it begins to brown, 8 to 10 minutes. Toss in the scallions and remove from the heat. Taste for salt and serve immediately.

CASABE/KASAV/KASSAVE

CASSAVA FLATBREAD ○ ACROSS THE CARIBBEAN

2 pounds cassava,
    peeled and cored
    (see page 63)
1 teaspoon kosher salt

SERVES 4 TO 6

I'd originally assigned this recipe to Haiti, as the Haitian version is the one I'm most familiar with, but there isn't an island in the Caribbean that doesn't make this flatbread, so ultimately, it belongs to us all. This is truly a legacy of the Indigenous peoples of the islands (the Taíno, Carib, and Arawak all made this bread), and when it's being made on a large scale, the method is the same as it has been for centuries. While all three Indigenous groups called the tuber yuca, it was the Taíno that named the bread *casabe*.

As mentioned at the beginning of this chapter, this dish has been around since about 2000 BCE (see page 62). It was one of the first foods Columbus and his people were given upon arriving in the region, and it hasn't changed since. One thing that made it so appealing is its shelf life: I've read historical reports of casabe keeping for *years*! It was a perfect food for long travel and was a staple for captives and captors alike on the ships that carried human cargo back and forth across the Atlantic, as well for the Maroons (see page 220) on their long hikes into the hills in search of freedom.

This bread is a true labor of love, as grating and squeezing the cassava is really no joke. If you're going to use a food processor, make sure you let it run for a while. There are delicious variations of this dish that include a layer of grated coconut and a bit of sugar in the middle, but I love the simplicity and adaptability of straight-up cassava. Casabe is wonderful with peanut butter, cheese, Chiktay (page 217), on its own, or—Atibon's favorite—as wayal topped with peanut butter and Pikliz (page 214). When eaten immediately, it is still pliable; once cooled, it becomes much harder, with a satisfying crunch.

Using the smallest holes of a box grater, grate the cassava as finely as possible. Alternatively, chop the cassava into roughly 2-inch chunks and use a food processor, letting it run until the cassava is like a paste, periodically stopping and scraping down the sides.

Working in manageable batches, transfer the cassava to a piece of cheesecloth or a clean kitchen towel. Gather the sides and, holding the bundle over a bowl (with a wide bottom, if possible), twist to squeeze out every drop of liquid you possibly can from the cassava, letting it fall into the bowl. If you can, enlist someone else to help you with this process, as your hands and arms will get tired and there's always more liquid to be squeezed. You're essentially trying to make cassava flour (also known as farine), so it needs to be as dry as possible. Put the squeezed cassava in a medium-size bowl before moving on to the next batch. Set aside the bowl with the cassava juice—we'll get to that in a bit.

RECIPE CONTINUES

A few handfuls at a time, put the cassava between your hands and rub them together over a medium bowl, then break up any leftover chunks with your fingers. It should look fluffy and pretty dry. Mix in the salt with your fingers.

Pour out the liquid from the bowl of cassava juice, leaving behind the thick white film at the bottom. This is starch, which you'll use to help the cassava flour hold together. If you have a decently wide-bottomed bowl with a lot of surface area, you can leave the starch in there to dry out a bit, or you can transfer it to a plate to dry for 10 minutes or so. It doesn't need to be bone-dry, but you don't want it to be soaking wet.

Heat a skillet over medium-high heat (the size of the skillet will depend on how big you want to make your casabe; I like mine about 6 inches in diameter). A nonstick skillet is a beautiful thing here, but not mandatory.

While the skillet heats, break up the starch and add it to the bowl of cassava. Mix it in with your fingers. Don't worry too much if it's still a bit wet and seems like it's not spreading evenly; it will work its magic regardless.

Sprinkle some of the cassava into the hot pan, forming a roughly ¼-inch-thick layer with your desired circumference. Use a spatula to neaten the edges and press it down a bit. If you're steady-handed, your hand is actually the best tool to do this, but don't hurt yourself! Place a clean kitchen towel over the cassava round, making sure it's completely covered, and press down again. This will allow the cassava to steam a bit and cook more thoroughly, without getting as wet as it would if you covered the pan with a lid. Cook for 5 to 7 minutes, until the bottom is golden brown, then use a spatula (the wider the better) to lift the round off the pan and flip it over. Repeat the process on the second side. Transfer the casabe to a plate and repeat with the remaining cassava.

While casabe will allegedly keep at room temperature for more than a year, I'd recommend storing it in an airtight container and eating it within a week.

CASSAVA PONE

CASSAVA AND COCONUT PUDDING ○ TRINIDAD AND TOBAGO

3 cups grated
    peeled cassava
    (see page 63)
1 cup grated fresh
    coconut (or frozen)
½ cup Calabaza Puree
    (page 54)
1 cup packed
    brown sugar
1 teaspoon grated
    fresh ginger
1 teaspoon ground
    cinnamon
¼ teaspoon freshly
    grated nutmeg
½ teaspoon
    freshly ground
    black pepper
¼ teaspoon kosher salt
2 tablespoons
    coconut oil
1 teaspoon vanilla
    extract
¼ teaspoon almond
    extract
1 cup Coconut
    Milk, homemade
    (page 97) or
    store-bought

SERVES 10 TO 12

Pone is a dessert I've had countless times—at aunties' houses in Toronto and Trinidad, or from the Caribbean grocery my mom would drag me to when I was younger. But it wasn't until later in life that I discovered it's mostly made of cassava and was likely a dessert created out of necessity. In the early days of slavery, the colonists bemoaned the lack of wheat throughout the islands and finally accepted cassava as a reasonable substitute. Breads and sweets were created with the root in the absence of wheat flour. The texture of this dessert is a bit hard to describe. The starch from the cassava makes it sort of gummy, bordering on a pudding, but not all the way there. It's also gluten-free. The black pepper is mandatory—it adds a bite that's key to the flavor of pone.

Preheat the oven to 350°F. Grease an 8-inch square baking dish.

In a large bowl, mix together the cassava, grated coconut, calabaza puree, brown sugar, ginger, cinnamon, nutmeg, pepper, salt, coconut oil, vanilla, and almond extract until well blended. Add the coconut milk and stir until the mixture is uniform. Pour the mixture into the prepared baking dish and bake, rotating the dish halfway through the cooking time, for 80 to 90 minutes, until the top is golden and the edges pull away from the sides of the baking dish. The middle will still be a little mushy; this is okay. Remove from the oven and let cool completely before cutting into squares (the edge pieces are particularly covetable). The pone will keep in an airtight container at room temperature for 2 to 3 days.

BAMMY

CASSAVA BREAD SOAKED IN COCONUT MILK ○ JAMAICA

2 pounds cassava,
    peeled and cored
    (see page 63)
1 teaspoon kosher salt
1 (13.5-ounce) can
    coconut milk, or
    2 cups homemade
    Coconut Milk
    (page 97)
Coconut oil, for
    greasing

SERVES 4 TO 6

This side dish or snack has a history connected to both the native peoples of the Caribbean and the Maroons (see page 220), Africans who escaped slavery and lived in independent settlements. These groups lived closely alongside Indigenous peoples and picked up culinary skills from them along the way. As the Maroons were constantly on the move, hiding from colonial slave owners, they had to develop food that was portable, and the flatbread made from cassava by Jamaica's Indigenous inhabitants was ideal. Today, you can find premade bammies in Caribbean groceries, but as with most things, making them from scratch is worth the trouble. The initial preparation is much the same as for Casabe (page 69). The main differences between casabe and bammy are their thickness—bammies are much thicker and chewier—and the added step of soaking bammies in coconut milk, which probably served as a way to both rehydrate the dried food and add nutrients. They are commonly served with Ackee and Saltfish (page 203) or Rundown (page 106), but are also great as an accompaniment to anything saucy, or as a snack on their own, as Desalin can testify!

Chop the cassava into roughly 2-inch chunks and place it in the bowl of a food processor. Let it run until the cassava is like a paste, periodically stopping and scraping down the sides.

Working in manageable batches, transfer the cassava to a piece of cheesecloth or a clean kitchen towel. Gather the sides and twist to squeeze the liquid out of the cassava. It's okay if the cassava remains a tiny bit wet.

A few handfuls at a time, put the squeezed cassava between your hands, rubbing them together over a medium bowl, then break up any leftover chunks with your fingers. Mix in the salt with your fingers.

Form 1 cup of the cassava into a ball and place it on a clean flat surface. Using the bottom of a jar or glass, press down firmly on the ball of cassava, forming a disk that's about ½ inch

thick. (Many people do this directly in the pan, but I have found that the edges crumble when it's this thick.)

Heat a medium skillet over medium heat. Cook the bammies (however many will fit in the pan at once without touching) in the dry pan until lightly golden, 8 to 10 minutes per side.

Depending on the size of your bammies, you can keep them whole or cut them into 4 wedges each. Place the whole bammies (or wedges) in a medium bowl or baking dish and cover them with the coconut milk. Set aside to soak for 10 minutes.

Lightly coat the bottom of the same skillet with coconut oil and heat over medium heat. Remove the bammies from the coconut milk and fry, working in batches if needed, until deeply golden, about 5 minutes on each side. They are best served immediately.

PEPPERPOT

MEAT STEW ○ GUYANA

2 pounds beef chuck, cut into 2-inch cubes

2 pounds oxtail

½ cup distilled white vinegar

1 head garlic, cloves peeled and mashed with a mortar and pestle or minced

1 tablespoon fresh thyme leaves

2 teaspoons freshly ground black pepper

¼ cup packed brown sugar

2 cinnamon sticks

1 tablespoon whole cloves

2 (3-inch) strips of orange zest

¾ cup cassareep (see page 75)

2 cups hot water

2 teaspoons kosher salt

SERVES 8 TO 10

Pepperpot is another dish that represents Caribbean history, combining the Indigenous knowledge of the preservation qualities of cassareep with the African penchant for making wet stews. Cooks all over the islands were famous for their pepperpots, and it was one of the few "native" dishes that the Europeans seemed to agree was delicious. The secret ingredient is cassareep syrup, a by-product of grated bitter cassava. It is a preservative, and because of its strength, a cook's pepperpot could last her entire lifetime; she would just continue to add new ingredients and more cassareep as time went on—I read of one cook maintaining a pepperpot for years, until it was eventually passed on to her successor a generation later! Today, most islands have a version of pepperpot, but many are actually more like a soup, or even like callaloo. Guyana preserves the true pepperpot, with few ingredients and heavy on the cassareep. This may be because on the mainland, Guyana still has a large Indigenous population living in the *bush* (the West Indian word for the jungle or deep countryside).

This recipe is another one from our neighbor Miss Bibi, who makes a delicious pepperpot. There are a few ways to prepare this dish, but I like hers best. Unlike many others, she chooses not to marinate the meat in the cassareep, which I find lightens it up just a touch. Some people claim that pepperpot should only contain meat, hard spices, sugar, and cassareep, but thankfully, Miss Bibi belongs to the same season-the-heck-out-of-everything camp as I do. It's still a relatively simple dish and is a classic Christmas breakfast for the Guyanese, who serve it with homemade bread alongside. Miss Bibi doesn't eat pork, so she only uses beef, but pork is a welcome addition. You can really use just about anything you like, but make sure something you put in there has bones. I have not included the traditional step of cleaning meat throughout most of this book, but I chose to here, as this is Miss Bibi's way, and I do like the bit of seasoning the vinegar gives the meat. Pepperpot is meant to be made at least one day ahead of the time you plan to eat it, so be sure you factor that in. It may be hard to believe, but you really can leave this out at room temperature. Just reheat it a couple of times a day, and it can stay on your stovetop for up to a week.

Place the chuck and oxtail in a large bowl and add the vinegar. Fill the bowl to the top with warm water and let it sit for 15 minutes. Drain and rinse the meat, then transfer it to a clean large bowl.

Add the garlic, thyme, and pepper and use clean hands to mix them with the meat. Cover the bowl and place it in the fridge for at least 2 hours or up to overnight.

About 30 minutes before you plan to cook it, remove the meat from the fridge and let it come to room temperature.

RECIPE CONTINUES

Place the oxtail in a large Dutch oven or other heavy-bottomed pot, cover, and cook over low heat, undisturbed, for about 1 hour, until the meat is becoming tender to the touch. Add the beef chuck, brown sugar, cinnamon sticks, cloves, and orange zest. Raise the heat a touch to medium-low and cook, uncovered, until the meat has released its juices and they start to evaporate, 30 to 45 minutes. Give it an occasional stir to make sure nothing is sticking to the bottom and that it all cooks evenly.

Add the cassareep, hot water, and salt and mix well. Cover and cook until the oxtail meat is falling off the bone, about 1 hour more.

Turn off the heat and let the pot cool. Before serving, remove the cinnamon sticks, cloves, and orange zest. Make this at least 1 day in advance, or more. The pepperpot can be kept on your stove, covered, for up to 1 week. Twice a day bring it to a simmer over medium heat and immediately remove from the heat. If leaving it out of the fridge is non-negotiable, it can be refrigerated once cooled and reheated; the flavors just won't develop quite as deeply.

CASSAREEP

Cassareep is a syrup made from bitter cassava juice, which in its raw state contains a form of cyanide. The Indigenous peoples of Guyana taught enslaved Africans about this prize ingredient, which could preserve food, specifically meat, for a surprisingly long time, keeping it from spoiling in the hot, humid region before refrigeration was the name of the game. Making cassareep was, and still is, a laborious process and possibly a dangerous one, if not done correctly. Today, the Macushi, an Indigenous group living inland in parts of Guyana, still make cassareep the old way, using techniques and equipment that are hundreds, if not thousands, of years old.

To make cassareep, massive amounts of cassava are grated and then squeezed to extract its juice (the spent flesh is reserved and used to make Casabe, page 69). The juice is slowly cooked down until it becomes a thick syrup, a process that removes all the poison. Traditionally, cassareep would contain no other ingredients, but somewhere along the line, people got the (brilliant) idea to season it, so nowadays you'll find additions such as cinnamon, cloves, and sugar in most jars. Cassareep smells and looks a lot like molasses, but its taste is deeper, stronger, and more complex. While it is possible to make your own cassareep, bitter cassava is not always readily available outside of the islands, and most important, neither you nor I are expert enough to know when all the cyanide, which can cause dizziness, shortness of breath, and vomiting, has been cooked off. It's best to just buy it. If you don't live near a Caribbean grocery, it's very easy to source cassareep online.

YUCA CON MOJO

BOILED CASSAVA WITH MOJO SAUCE ○ CUBA

1 pound cassava, peeled, cored, and cut into 2-inch cubes (see page 63)
1 tablespoon plus ½ teaspoon kosher salt
3 garlic cloves, peeled
¼ cup sour orange juice (see page 14)
¼ cup extra-virgin olive oil
1 small red onion, thinly sliced
¼ teaspoon freshly ground black pepper

SERVES 4 TO 6

If the only kind of mojo sauce you know is from a bottle, be prepared to be amazed. Mojo is such a simple thing to put together, but the combination of spice from the almost raw garlic, the refreshing citrus, and the decadence of a lot of olive oil brings this classic Cuban sauce to the next level. When I was first introduced to Cuban food in Miami, I immediately became obsessed, which must have been fun for anyone within smelling distance. I put that garlicky liquid gold on just about anything—and still do. It's the perfect complement to the mild, chewy cassava but is also amazing with Fried Sweet Plantains (page 166); as a marinade for fish, chicken, or pork; or as a topping for grilled or fried fish, escovitch-style.

Place the cassava in a medium saucepan, add 1 tablespoon of the salt and water to cover by 1 inch, and bring to a boil over medium-high heat. Cook until the cassava is very tender, about 20 minutes.

Meanwhile, use a pilon to mash the garlic and the remaining ½ teaspoon salt into a paste. (Alternatively, use the back of a knife to mash them together on a cutting board.) Transfer the garlic paste to a small bowl and stir in the orange juice, then set aside.

When the cassava is nearly done cooking, in a small saucepan, heat the olive oil and onion over medium heat until the oil starts bubbling slightly, about 5 minutes. Carefully stir in the garlic mixture, avoiding hot oil splatters, and remove from the heat.

Drain the cassava and transfer it to a serving bowl. Pour the mojo sauce over the top, sprinkle with the black pepper, and mix everything together gently, as the cassava will break down if it's handled too much. This dish is best served immediately.

CHAYOTE

SECHIUM EDULE

Other names: CHRISTOPHENE, CHRISTOPHINE, CHO-CHO, CHOKO, MILITON, MIRLITON, TAYOTA

I CANNOT HELP BUT GIGGLE each time I see a chayote. They have been compared to a green fist, but when I look at them, I see little Muppet faces puckering their lips. I have been looking at these things all my life, and it never gets old. This fruit is a member of the gourd family and is most similar to a summer squash. It is native to Mesoamerica and spread throughout the Americas before going off on a long journey around the world as part of the Columbian Exchange.

Very mild tasting, chayote is popularly eaten as a gratin all throughout the Caribbean. You'll find three versions of this in this chapter. It is also a key ingredient in Haitian Legim (page 82) and makes a refreshing salad. In Jamaica, they pickle it with Scotch bonnet peppers.

Because of its mild flavor, chayote is more often like a backup singer than the lead in most dishes. However, much like the favored backup singers of legendary musicians, the song simply wouldn't be the same without them. In addition to the recipes here, consider using chayote anywhere zucchini or another summer squash is called for.

NUTRITION: The chayote is a very nutritious fruit and is high in vitamins A and C, as well as folic acid, a key mineral needed during pregnancy. There is some evidence it promotes heart health. In addition to the folate for birthing parents, it is known in some countries as a galactagogue, or a food that promotes lactation. In Desalin's early days, I ate a lot of chayote! Apparently, the tuber and the leaves of chayote are even more nutritious, but I have never come across them myself.

HOW TO CHOOSE: Look for those with smooth skin and closed "mouths." As they get older, they start to sprout and a little piece starts to stick out of the bottom, which to me, of course, looks like a tongue. Chayotes keep for quite a long time in the fridge. I'm not ashamed to admit that every now and then, I come across one lurking in the back that's been there for around a month, and it's still firm and good to cook.

HOW TO PREPARE: Green chayote skin is edible when cooked. The larger white varieties have tougher skin that won't break down no matter what you say. If you're using the chayote in a raw preparation, I suggest peeling it. The squash also has a pit, which is easy to remove: Simply cut the chayote in half and scoop out the pit with a small spoon. Chayote can sometimes irritate people's skin, so wash your hands thoroughly after handling, especially after peeling.

CHAYOTE AND WATERCRESS SALAD

WITH SOUR ORANGE VINAIGRETTE

VINAIGRETTE

1 garlic clove
Kosher salt
½ teaspoon fresh
thyme leaves
½ teaspoon honey
2 tablespoons sour
orange juice
(see page 14)
1 teaspoon apple
cider vinegar
Freshly ground
black pepper
3 tablespoons extra-
virgin olive oil

SALAD

1 chayote, peeled,
pitted, and
sliced into long
matchsticks
(see page 80)
1 bunch watercress,
stemmed
½ cup fresh cilantro
leaves

SERVES 4

I grew up eating green salads as an accompaniment to nearly every meal. It was my Canadian-born father's contribution to my mother's Trinidadian meals—his only culinary input that didn't make her raise an eyebrow—and his love of crisp, fresh vegetables has stayed with me to this day. Crunchy, juicy, and refreshing, chayote is delightful served raw, making it a perfect base for a summer salad. Served here with spicy watercress, another ingredient used often around the Caribbean, and cilantro, this dish is a powerhouse of nutrition and flavor.

My father was also the one who taught me to make my own vinaigrette. Though as children, my sister and I shunned his oil-and-vinegar concoctions for more exciting Kraft dressings from a bottle, it turns out we were listening. Loosely inspired by Cuban mojo sauce, the dressing for this salad features sour orange, an ingredient used often throughout the islands for marinating meat. This salad makes a perfect side dish to any meal and is particularly welcome alongside grilled fish or meat, especially Jerk Chicken (page 222).

Make the vinaigrette: Use a pilon to mash the garlic and ¼ teaspoon salt into a paste. (Alternatively, use the back of a knife to mash them together on a cutting board.) In a small bowl, combine the garlic paste, thyme, honey, orange juice, vinegar, more salt to taste, and freshly ground black pepper. Let stand for 5 minutes to allow the garlic to mellow, then slowly whisk in the olive oil.

Make the salad: In a large bowl, combine the chayote, watercress, and cilantro. Add the vinaigrette and toss to combine. Serve immediately.

LEGIM

VEGETABLE STEW ○ HAITI

2 tablespoons extra-
virgin olive oil

1 yellow onion, diced

1 head garlic, cloves
peeled and minced

3 tablespoons tomato
paste

¼ cup Epis (page 21)

1 vegetable bouillon
cube

1½ pounds eggplant,
peeled and cut into
1-inch cubes

1 chayote, peeled,
pitted, and cut
into 1-inch cubes
(see page 80)

1 teaspoon fresh
thyme leaves

¼ cup fresh parsley
leaves, chopped

2 carrots, cut into
½-inch-thick rounds

1 cup lima beans
(fresh, canned, or
frozen)

¼ large green
cabbage, sliced
(about 3 cups)

2 cups baby spinach

1 tablespoon fresh
lime juice

1 tablespoon vinegar
from a jar of Pikliz
(page 214) or apple
cider vinegar

2 teaspoons
kosher salt

SERVES 6 TO 8

I love legim and have eaten more of it than I care to admit. I chuckle sometimes, because Haitians love to talk about it as a vegetable dish, and then the first ingredient they'll tell you about is the beef. Traditional legim has quite a bit of meat in it, and frankly, it's delicious that way. I've had plenty of vegetarian versions that were perfectly fine, but none as satisfying as the ones with beef, or crab, or pork (or all of the above). However, chef Gregory Gourdet opened my eyes to a trick in his magnificent *Everyone's Table*: Get some good brown on those veggies. I know very well that getting some color on your onions, and any other vegetables you can, goes a long way to creating deeper flavor. But for this recipe, you really want to make sure the color is deep at every step, including that last part when the lid comes off. It helps to give a bit of that umami you normally get from the meat and makes the flavors a little more experienced and complex, rather than the top note you get from fresh veggies. Though I generally stay away from flavor enhancers like the ubiquitous Maggi cube, this is one place where you just can't do without it to get a layered flavor. Thankfully, today there are many organic vegetable bouillon cubes and pastes that use real ingredients. I love eating legim with just some "Perfect" White Rice (page 180), and for all my talk of making it meat-free, it also makes a great side dish for fish, chicken, or beef.

In the largest pot you've got, heat the olive oil over medium heat. Add the onion and garlic and sauté until they begin to brown, 5 to 8 minutes. Add the tomato paste and epis, and cook, stirring frequently, for 3 minutes, until the tomato paste darkens. Add the bouillon cube, breaking it up, then add the eggplant, chayote, thyme, and parsley and stir to make sure the vegetables are entirely coated in the seasonings. Reduce the heat to medium-low, cover, and cook for 20 to 25 minutes, until the eggplant and chayote are close to tender. Add the carrots and lima beans, give the pot a good stir, then spread the cabbage in an even layer over everything in the pot. Cover and cook for 30 to 45 minutes more, until all the veggies are soft enough to mash with a fork.

Raise the heat to high and add the spinach, lime juice, vinegar, and salt. Cook for 5 to 10 minutes more, until things are starting to brown and caramelize at the bottom of the pot. You want to stir it continuously and aggressively. Give it some good unearthing-the-bottom-of-the-pot stirs.

Remove from heat, and, if desired, mash the veggies with a fork or potato masher until they're relatively smooth, or leave some texture, if you prefer. The legim will keep in an airtight container in the fridge for several days or in the freezer for up to 3 months.

CHAYOTES RELLENOS

CHAYOTES STUFFED WITH PICADILLO ○ PUERTO RICO

2 or 3 large chayotes,
   halved and pitted
   (see page 80)
1 tablespoon
   kosher salt

PICADILLO

1 tablespoon extra-
   virgin olive oil
1 yellow onion, diced
6 garlic cloves, minced
¼ cup Recaíto
   (page 22)
½ green bell pepper,
   diced
1 pound ground beef
   or ground turkey
½ cup tomato sauce
¼ cup green olives,
   pitted and roughly
   chopped
¼ cup raisins (optional)
1 teaspoon kosher salt

¼ cup grated sharp
   cheddar cheese
2 tablespoons
   breadcrumbs

SERVES 4 TO 6

I really don't know whose idea it was to stuff a chayote with highly seasoned meat and stick it in the oven, but I commend them for it. The chayote skin makes a perfect neutral cup for the iconic Puerto Rican picadillo, which is also found in Cuba, and in the Dominican Republic under the name carne molida, which you will notice is heavy on the garlic. The other bonus of this edible bowl is that you get a healthy dose of vegetables (well, technically, it's a fruit, but who's counting?). The only vaguely tricky part of making this dish is scooping out the chayote flesh. It's easy to tear the skin as you're doing it, but once it's covered with meat, cheese, and breadcrumbs, who is going to notice? The more you do it, the more intuitive it becomes. It's like the chayote *wants* to be a bowl. You will likely have too much picadillo for your chayote; this is a great thing. It's also used in Piñon (page 165), and is wonderful with rice, or, with a little added tomato sauce, becomes a fantastic pasta sauce. It freezes well, and I sometimes make a double batch just for this reason.

Place the chayote in a large pot or saucepan and add the salt and water to cover by 1 inch. Turn the heat to high and cook for 20 to 30 minutes, until the chayote is very tender and easily pierced with a fork. Drain the chayote and set aside until cool enough to handle.

Scoop the chayote flesh into a bowl with a small spoon, leaving enough behind to keep the fruit intact and make a vessel. Don't worry if a bit of the skin tears in this process—the filling will hide it. Using a fork or potato masher, mash the scooped-out flesh and set it aside. Place the chayote skins in a baking dish and set them aside as well.

Preheat the oven to 350°F.

Make the picadillo: In a large skillet, heat the olive oil over medium heat. Add the onion and garlic and cook until they begin to brown, 5 to 8 minutes. Add the recaíto and cook for 2 to 3 minutes, until very fragrant, then add the bell pepper and cook for 2 minutes,

until it just begins to sweat. Add the ground beef and cook, using a wooden spoon to break up the meat into small pieces, until the meat is browned, about 10 minutes. Meanwhile, drain any liquid from the bowl of mashed chayote flesh. When the meat is browned, add the mashed chayote, tomato sauce, olives, raisins (if using), and salt to the skillet. Reduce the heat to low and simmer until the flavors have blended, 15 to 20 minutes.

Fill the chayote halves with the picadillo, then top evenly with the cheese and breadcrumbs. You're not looking for a thick cheese layer, just a hint of cheesiness. Bake until the tops are golden brown, 15 to 20 minutes. Remove from the oven and let cool just slightly before serving.

The stuffed chayote is best served immediately, but the picadillo keeps well in an airtight container in the fridge for up to 5 days or in the freezer for up to 3 months.

GRATIN AU CHRISTOPHINE

CHEESE-STUFFED CHAYOTES ○ MARTINIQUE

2 or 3 large chayotes,
   halved and pitted
   (see page 80)
1 tablespoon plus
   ½ teaspoon
   kosher salt
3 slices bacon, diced
   (optional; see Note)
1 small shallot, diced
2 garlic cloves, minced
2 tablespoons
   all-purpose flour
½ cup whole milk
1 tablespoon minced
   fresh parsley
1 teaspoon fresh
   thyme leaves,
   minced
Grating of nutmeg
Freshly ground
   black pepper
¼ cup grated sharp
   cheddar cheese
1 tablespoon
   breadcrumbs

SERVES 4 TO 6

Note: If you're not using
bacon, cook the shallots
in 2 tablespoons butter
instead of the bacon fat.

There are three recipes for stuffed chayote in this book (you'll find the others on pages 83 and 86), but this version is somewhat unusual in Caribbean cuisine. Generally, dairy is not often the star of most dishes. However, this dish is likely a nod to the French influence, with its dairy and béchamel sauce. Nevertheless, the islands manage to give a little Caribbean tilt to the culinary hat and make it our own. The bacon in this dish is kind of divine, but you can absolutely make it vegetarian—though decidedly *not* vegan—by omitting the bacon (see Note). Still delicious. Don't skip the breadcrumbs; something about the crunch helps cut all the lavish dairy.

Place the chayote in a large pot or saucepan and add 1 tablespoon of the salt and water to cover by 1 inch. Turn the heat to high and cook for 20 to 30 minutes, until the chayote is very tender and easily pierced with a fork. Drain the chayote and set aside until cool enough to handle.

Preheat the oven to 350°F.

Scoop the chayote flesh into a bowl with a small spoon, leaving enough behind to keep the fruit intact and make a vessel. If the skin tears in a few spots during this process, don't worry! The cheesy filling will hide most of the flaws. Using a fork or potato masher, mash the scooped-out flesh and set it aside. Place the chayote skins in a baking dish and set them aside as well.

In a medium saucepan, cook the bacon over medium-high heat until crispy, about 8 minutes. Spoon off about 2 tablespoons of the rendered fat from the pot and discard it (or save it for another use, if bacon fat is your thing!). Add the shallot to the pot and cook in the remaining fat until soft, 3 to 5 minutes. Add the garlic and cook for

30 seconds, then sprinkle in the flour while stirring continuously. Cook the flour, continuing to stir to prevent it from burning, until it begins to brown and smells nutty, 2 to 3 minutes.

Pour in the milk in a steady stream, continuing to stir and making sure the flour mixture has been completely incorporated with no lumps (don't let the small hunks of shallot or garlic fool you). Working quickly, as the mixture will thicken up in just a few moments, stir in the parsley, thyme, remaining ½ teaspoon salt, the nutmeg, and pepper to taste.

Remove the saucepan from the heat and stir in half the cheese until completely melted. Drain any liquid from the bowl of mashed chayote flesh, then add the flesh to the saucepan and stir to combine. Spoon the mixture into the chayote shells, using about 2 heaping tablespoons for each, then top evenly with the breadcrumbs and remaining cheese. Bake for 30 to 35 minutes, until the filling is bubbling and the tops have turned a beautiful bronze color. Remove from the oven and let cool a bit before eating.

STUFFED CHO CHO

JAMAICA

2 or 3 large chayotes,
   halved and pitted
   (see page 80)
1 tablespoon plus
   1 teaspoon
   kosher salt
1 tablespoon extra-
   virgin olive oil
1 medium yellow
   onion, diced
6 garlic cloves, minced
½ Scotch bonnet
   pepper (optional)
1 pound ground beef
   or ground turkey
2 tablespoons tomato
   paste
2 Roma (plum)
   tomatoes, diced
1 tablespoon Jamaican
   curry powder
2 teaspoons fresh
   thyme leaves
Freshly ground
   black pepper
¼ cup grated sharp
   cheddar cheese
2 tablespoons
   breadcrumbs

SERVES 4 TO 6

It's obvious that this dish is the same as the Chayotes Rellenos (page 83) from Puerto Rico, but with a Jamaican spin to the seasoning. There's no way to know who did it first or if it came about at the same time in different places. The addition of curry powder is brilliant, and though you may not think it will work with cheese, trust me, it does. Jamaican curry powder is distinct from the Trinidadian variety used in the Curried Chana and Aloo (page 30), but (and I may get in trouble for this) you can substitute one for the other in a pinch. Other than the spices, the preparation is pretty much the same as in Puerto Rico. Much like picadillo, I love having this meat filling on hand in the freezer to eat with "Perfect" White Rice (page 180) or even pasta. Who says curry and pasta can't be friends?

Place the chayote in a large pot or saucepan and add 1 tablespoon of the salt and water to cover by 1 inch. Turn the heat to high and cook for 20 to 30 minutes, until very tender and easily pierced with a fork. Drain the chayote and set aside until cool enough to handle.

Scoop the chayote flesh into a bowl with a small spoon, leaving enough behind to keep the fruit intact and make a vessel. Don't worry if a bit of the skin tears in this process; the stuffing will hide it. Using a fork or potato masher, mash the scooped-out flesh and set it aside. Place the chayote skins in a baking dish and set those aside as well.

Preheat the oven to 350°F.

In a large skillet, heat the olive oil over medium heat. Add the onion, garlic, and Scotch bonnet, if using, and cook until they begin to brown, 5 to

8 minutes. Add the ground beef and cook, using a wooden spoon to break up the meat into small pieces, until the meat is browned, about 10 minutes. Add the tomato paste, stir to thoroughly combine, and cook for a few minutes, until the tomato paste has completely dissolved.

Meanwhile, drain any liquid from the bowl of mashed chayote flesh. When the tomato paste has dissolved, add the mashed chayote, tomatoes, curry powder, thyme, remaining 1 teaspoon salt, and some good grinds of black pepper to the skillet. Reduce the heat to low and simmer until the flavors have all blended, 15 to 20 minutes.

Fill the chayote halves with the meat mixture, then top evenly with the cheese and breadcrumbs. Bake until the tops are golden brown, 15 to 20 minutes. Remove from the oven and let cool slightly just before serving.

CREAM OF CHAYOTE SOUP

1 tablespoon
   coconut oil
1 yellow onion, diced
2 celery stalks,
   chopped
3 garlic cloves,
   smashed and peeled
3 scallions, roughly
   chopped
2 chayotes, peeled,
   pitted, and diced
   (see page 80)
2 teaspoons fresh
   thyme leaves
1 (13.5-ounce) can
   coconut milk, or
   2 cups homemade
   Coconut Milk
   (page 97)
2 cups vegetable
   stock or water
   (see headnote)
1 Scotch bonnet
   pepper
Kosher salt and
   freshly ground
   black pepper

SERVES 4 TO 6

This soup is somewhat surprising, as its silky, rich feel belies the light and fresh flesh of the chayote. In New Orleans, this is accomplished by using heavy cream, but I can't think of anything less Caribbean. Of course, coconut milk is hardly light, but in comparison to cream, it manages to toe the line between decadent and refreshing. Somehow the soup doesn't taste like full-on coconut (not that I'd take issue with that), instead allowing the flavor to play a supporting role rather than taking center stage. If you choose to use homemade coconut milk, reduce the stock or water by 1 cup. This is a wondrously addictive soup that takes very little to put together and is always a crowd-pleaser.

In a large heavy-bottomed pot or Dutch oven, heat the coconut oil over medium heat. Add the onion and celery and sauté until they start to brown, 5 to 8 minutes. Add the garlic and scallions and cook for 3 minutes, until they begin to brown. Add the chayote and thyme, stirring to coat the chayote well, and cook for 5 minutes, until everything is very fragrant and the chayote is *just* beginning to soften.

Add the coconut milk and stock to the pot. Bring to a boil over high heat, then add the Scotch bonnet and season with salt to taste and a few good grinds of black pepper.

Cover the pot and reduce the heat to low. Simmer until the chayote is very tender, 20 to 25 minutes. Remove and discard the Scotch bonnet. Using an immersion blender, blend the soup directly in the pot until very smooth (or carefully transfer the soup to a standing blender, in batches if necessary, and blend until very smooth). Leftovers will keep in an airtight container in the fridge for up to 3 days or in the freezer for up to 3 months.

TRINI CHOW MEIN

TRINIDAD AND TOBAGO

SAUCE

2 tablespoons soy sauce
    or tamari
2 tablespoons oyster
    sauce
2 tablespoons fresh lime
    juice
1 tablespoon fish sauce
1 teaspoon honey
½ teaspoon Pepper
    Sauce (page 215),
    plus more for serving
½ teaspoon kosher salt

1 pound large shrimp,
    shelled
2 tablespoons Green
    Seasoning (page 22)
8 ounces lo mein
    noodles (Guyanese-
    style)
2 tablespoons neutral oil
1 star anise pod
4 garlic cloves, minced
2 teaspoons grated
    fresh ginger
3 scallions, thinly sliced
4 ounces (about 1 cup)
    brown cremini
    mushrooms, sliced
½ red bell pepper, thinly
    sliced
½ green bell pepper,
    thinly sliced
1 yellow onion, thinly
    sliced
1 small carrot, julienned
2 cups shredded green
    cabbage
½ chayote, peeled,
    pitted, and cut into
    thin matchsticks
3 culantro leaves, or
    ¼ cup fresh cilantro,
    minced

SERVES 6 TO 8

This is a clear example of the influence of the Chinese indentured servants brought to Trinidad by British colonists after the abolition of slavery in the region. Chow mein can also be found in other Caribbean nations, especially Guyana, where they manufacture a special kind of lo mein noodle for the dish. Why it's called chow mein when you use lo mein noodles is beyond me; I chalk it up to the joy we seem to get from mixing names up. Trinidadians take a classic stir-fry and add a little island flair to it with culantro, chayote (or christophene, as they call it in Trinidad), and, of course, pepper sauce. We also don't use cornstarch or any other thickening agent for the sauce. Stir-fries were my mother's go-to dinner, as they're an easy way to make sure you get the vegetables you need.

Don't be intimidated by the long list of ingredients. Once you've got everything prepped, the dish comes together quickly and makes a great healthful weeknight meal. As with any good stir-fry, use this as a base and make it your own. Whatever veggies are lurking in the crisper begging to be used make good material here, as is whatever comes back from your farmers' market haul. Use whatever protein your heart desires in place of the shrimp, or leave it out altogether.

Make the sauce: In a small bowl, stir together all the ingredients for the sauce, making sure the honey has completely dissolved. Set aside.

In a medium bowl, toss the shrimp with the green seasoning and set aside to marinate for about 30 minutes while you prep the veggies.

Cook your noodles according to the package instructions, drain, and set aside.

In a wok or large skillet, heat 1 tablespoon of the oil over medium-high heat until it shimmers. Add the shrimp and stir-fry until pink and cooked through, about 2 minutes on each side, then scrape the cooked shrimp and their juices onto a plate and set aside.

Heat the remaining 1 tablespoon oil in the same pan, still on medium-high. Add the star anise and let it sizzle for

30 seconds or so, then add the garlic, ginger, and scallions and stir-fry for 10 seconds. Add the mushrooms and cook, stirring frequently until they've released their juices and begun to brown, 2 to 3 minutes.

Add both bell peppers, the onion, carrot, cabbage, and chayote. It will seem like a lot in the pan, but everything will cook down fairly quickly. Stir-fry, tossing continuously with tongs to make sure everything cooks evenly, for about 4 minutes, until the vegetables are just starting to soften up but still retain some crunch. Add the sauce and mix thoroughly, then add the noodles and toss to combine. Cook for about 2 minutes, allowing the noodles to soak up the sauce, then add the shrimp and culantro and give it one last toss. Serve immediately, with more pepper sauce on the side, if desired.

CHAYOTE SLAW

DRESSING

1 garlic clove, peeled
½ teaspoon kosher salt
1 tablespoon fresh
   lime juice
1 tablespoon sherry
   vinegar
1 teaspoon whole-
   grain mustard
1 teaspoon grated
   fresh ginger
2 tablespoons extra-
   virgin olive oil

SLAW

1 chayote, peeled,
   pitted, and
   quartered
   (see page 80)
¼ small green cabbage
   (about 3 ounces),
   quartered
½ half-ripe mango
   (any variety),
   peeled, pitted, and
   cut into chunks
3 scallions, thinly sliced
4 culantro leaves,
   thinly sliced
½ Scotch bonnet
   pepper, minced
1 teaspoon kosher salt

SERVES 4 TO 6

When I was a child, I had a deep distrust of coleslaw. I never really liked mayonnaise, and the gloopy thing that was pretending to be a salad just never did it for me. Only in adulthood did I realize coleslaw doesn't have to have mayo, and the clouds parted and light shone down. To me, there's nothing better to serve alongside fried or spicy food than a good crispy, refreshing slaw. It's important to use a half-ripe mango here or as close to half-ripe as you can get. It adds just a hint of sweetness, rather than the cloying sugar of a fully ripe mango, and it's crunchier, too, making it the ideal partner for the extremely crunchy chayote. I really like sherry vinegar in this, but I'm not fussy; use whatever you like, as long as it's not balsamic. I once got some passion fruit vinegar from Puerto Rico and it was divine in this recipe. This salad keeps very well in the fridge and is still pretty great the next day. It's one of my favorite spring/summer potluck dishes.

Make the dressing: In a pilon, mash the garlic and salt into a paste. If you don't have one, smash the garlic on a cutting board, sprinkle it with the salt, and alternately mince the garlic and smash it against the cutting board with the side of your knife until it becomes a paste. Transfer the garlic paste to a small bowl and add the lime juice, vinegar, mustard, and ginger. Whisk in the olive oil until it's emulsified and set aside.

Make the slaw: Use a food processor fitted with the shredding disc to shred the chayote, cabbage, and mango, then transfer to a large bowl. Add the scallions, culantro, and Scotch bonnet, making sure to mix everything evenly. Add the salt and toss to combine, then add the dressing and toss again to combine. Let stand for at least 20 minutes before serving. The slaw will keep in an airtight container in the fridge for up to 2 days.

COCONUT

COCOS NUCIFERA

Other names: COCO, KOKOYE

THE COCONUT COULD EASILY BE the poster child for Caribbean ingredients. Its image, scent, and flavor can immediately conjure up a beach setting, and that wouldn't be wrong. The coconut may also be the most useful fruit on the planet. This wonderous natural package contains potable water, a high-calorie source of good fat, fuel (its shell can be used as charcoal), and fiber that can be made into rope. Its oil, in addition to its uses in cooking, can be used as a nourishing moisturizer for hair and skin. The coconut has become very trendy in recent decades with the internet touting its cosmetic and nutritional values, but those in tropical climates across the globe have known these facts for centuries or longer.

The coconut's history and subsequent journey to the Caribbean are a bit unclear. It is largely believed that coconuts were domesticated in Southeast Asia and spread around the world from there; they were likely brought to the Caribbean via the Pacific Islands by European colonists.

The name is thought to originate in part from the Portuguese and Spanish word *coco*, meaning "skull" or "grinning face" or "bogeyman." With its three indentations arranged like a spooky face, it is easy to see how this connection would be made. Despite its name, the coconut is not a nut at all, but rather a drupe, a category of fruit also known as stone fruits. The part of the coconut we use is the endosperm, which is the coconut kernel. On the outside, a fresh coconut is large, smooth, and green, but has a layer of hard brown fuzz inside. Inside this fuzzy barrier is the flesh we eat and use to make coconut milk and oil. In Caribbean recipes, this is often referred to as a "dry" coconut, as opposed to the large whole coconut you might get with its top cut off and a straw for drinking up the refreshing water inside. (If you've never done this, please find a way to do so immediately.) The water inside is something that makes coconut unique among fruit. I wish more fruits would get with the program.

In the Caribbean, as elsewhere in the tropics, coconut is used equally in sweet and savory preparations and finds its way into nearly every Caribbean dish. In addition to making everything taste better, for historical purposes, this was likely a way for the enslaved to get additional minerals, vitamins, and fat into a diet otherwise lacking in them. Africans had also been using coconut in their own food for thousands of years before the slave trade even started, so they were already familiar with it.

NUTRITION: Coconuts are high in antioxidants, which makes them anti-inflammatory. My mother suffered from rheumatoid arthritis for many years, and she always saw a difference when she used coconut oil regularly for cooking. The oil is also thought to help with Alzheimer's, though research on this is still in the works. Coconuts are also high in fiber, which we know is good for our guts.

While the fat found in coconuts is saturated, it's much better than any animal fats. And fat gets a bad rap—our bodies need this macronutrient to help us process vitamins, pad our organs, and keep our brains going strong. While one shouldn't necessarily be devouring can after can of coconut milk (as I did while working on this book), it's definitely a beneficial addition to your diet. For many people, it's also great for the hair and skin, though unfortunately, my beloved coconuts and I don't get along in this realm—coconut oil is too heavy for my low-porosity hair and causes my skin to dry out.

HOW TO CHOOSE: Always look for the heaviest coconut you can find, with a lot of water sloshing around inside. If possible, have someone at the store break it open for you before you bring it home. Though you'll miss out on the delicious coconut water, this allows you to confirm that the coconut is good. Too often I have come home with coconuts that looked fine on the outside, only to find the flesh rotting on the inside.

HOW TO PREPARE: Cracking a coconut and removing its flesh is not for the faint of heart. You might curse in the process. You might curse me, but that's okay, I can take it. I promise it's worth it! Nothing compares to fresh coconut flesh or homemade coconut milk.

If you have a whole coconut and you want to save the coconut water for drinking or to use in another recipe such as Kòk Graje (page 109), use either a hammer and a fat nail or—if you're feeling really industrious—a drill to make a hole in at least two of the eyes at the tip of the coconut. The eyes are actually germination pores, and there is one, which would be where a coconut would sprout, that will give way very easily. This will feel a little weird and invasive (I mean, who hammers a nail into someone's *eye*?), but once you've pierced it, the water will pour right out. If you don't care to save the water, you can skip straight to the next step, but be sure to put the coconut inside a sealed bag so the water doesn't splash everywhere.

There are two ways I like to crack open a coconut, and both are pretty satisfying. The easiest is to put the coconut inside a bag and smash it on the stones in my backyard. This might take two or so good throws, but it's kind of fun and always works. The more civilized way to do it is to use a hammer or the back of a heavy knife to hit the coconut hard and square around its middle, rotating the coconut as you go, until a crack appears. From there, you'll be able to pry it open.

Here comes my least favorite part: getting the flesh off the hard shell. I slide a butter knife under the flesh and slowly pry it off. Sometimes, especially if you go slowly, you'll be rewarded with a big chunk that comes off in one go. But often, you'll get little chips. The more you practice, the better you'll get at this. Just be careful, because the shell is a bit sharp, and it's easy for your hand to slip when you're trying to get that damn piece that just won't come out . . . unless that's just me!

Once it's out of the shell, your coconut meat is ready for shredding. Doing this in a food processor or blender is fine for most recipes, but there are a few recipes that really benefit from doing this by hand on a box grater; if this is the case, I have noted it in the recipe. Coconut flesh freezes beautifully, so I'll often prep more than I need. It's not my favorite activity, so once I'm doing it, I may as well go all out.

A NOTE ON
CANNED COCONUT MILK

FIRST AND FOREMOST, the only kind of canned coconut milk I am ever talking about here is full-fat. "Lite" coconut milk is an abomination and shouldn't exist. Okay, maybe those are strong words, but lite coconut milk will do you no good in this book. It's basically coconut milk–flavored water, missing its fat, which is the very key to its existence. Also, all cans are not created equal. I prefer brands that have as few ingredients as possible, though they pretty much all have guar gum or some other agent to help emulsify the milk. The fewer ingredients it contains, the more like fresh coconut milk it will act. I try to keep to organic brands as much as possible. There are some really fancy organic, natural brands out there that work amazingly. But I have found that the 365 brand coconut milk from Whole Foods is pretty reliable. I have also found (as have others, and there are articles online to prove it) that Trader Joe's brand is not great in most circumstances. It will work perfectly fine in a soup or when making rice, but pass on it (and their coconut cream) when its molecular makeup really matters, in recipes like Oil Down (page 98), Rundown (page 106), Metemgee (page 64), and Piña Colada Ice Cream (page 111).

COCONUT MILK

4 cups water
1 dry (brown)
    coconut, flesh
    removed and cut
    into rough chunks
    (see page 95)

MAKES 2 TO 3 CUPS

Making your own coconut milk is truly a labor of love, but it's really worth it. While I love me some canned coconut milk and my pantry is never without it, the difference in taste and texture is almost shocking. I see many recipes for homemade coconut milk that don't specify using warm or hot water. You do you, but I will warn you that if the water is too cold, the (beautiful, glorious) fat in the milk might separate. I've had it collect and get stuck to the side of the blender, and it's just a whole mess. Warm water will make sure the fat integrates nicely, and your coconut milk will come out luxe and creamy.

While I'd say most recipes in this book can be made with either fresh or canned coconut milk, there are two where you really should make the effort to make some yourself, if you can get your hands on the coconuts: Metemgee (page 64) and Oil Down (page 98). The leftover shredded coconut that you've squeezed freezes beautifully, ensuring that you'll have some on hand for recipes such as Coconut Bake (page 103), Cassava Pone (page 71), Pen Mayi (page 123), or any other baking you think might benefit from a little coconutty flavor. Fresh coconut milk is significantly thinner than the concentrated version in a can. In most cases, you can easily substitute 2 cups homemade coconut milk for one 13.5-ounce can (and vice versa), but there are some instances, like the Metemgee (page 64), where canned coconut milk needs to be thinned out.

In a medium saucepan, heat the water over medium-low heat until it's steaming but not boiling (about 150°F). Remove from the heat.

In a food processor or blender, pulse the coconut chunks until they are shredded into small pieces. Add the warm water and pulse again until the coconut has broken down more and the water looks white and milky. Let stand for 15 minutes to help infuse the water.

Pour the liquid through a mesh strainer or cheesecloth into a bowl or a jar and press or squeeze the coconut with all your might to extract as much milk as possible. Save the solids for another use, such as Coconut Bake (page 103) or Pen Mayi (page 123).

You have just made coconut milk! Congratulations. Fresh coconut milk is best used the same day, but can be kept in a glass jar or other airtight container in the fridge overnight.

OIL DOWN

VEGETABLES STEWED IN COCONUT MILK ○ GRENADA

1 pound salted pig tails
1 to 1½ pounds bone-in
chicken thighs,
skin removed,
cut into 3 pieces
(see page 10)
5 tablespoons Green
Seasoning (page 22)
1 yellow onion, diced
5 garlic cloves, minced
1 bunch scallions,
thinly sliced
1 seasoning pepper,
seeded and
minced (optional;
see page 14)
2 teaspoons fresh
thyme leaves
1 small breadfruit
2 to 3 green bananas
½ pound calabaza or
butternut squash
3 Caribbean
sweet potatoes
(1 to 1½ pounds)
2 large carrots
½ pound okra
1 bunch dasheen
leaves, kale, or
mature spinach
1 Scotch bonnet
pepper
1 teaspoon ground
turmeric, or
1 (1-inch) piece
fresh turmeric,
finely grated
1 (13.5-ounce) can
coconut milk, or
2 cups homemade
Coconut Milk
(page 97)
Dough for 1 recipe
Spinners (page 33)
1 teaspoon kosher salt

SERVES 6 TO 8

Grenada's nickname is the Spice Island. It's one of the world's largest producers of nutmeg and mace and also exports bay leaves, cinnamon, clove, and turmeric, among many other spices. Perhaps because of their spice industry, they've become known for their culinary traditions. Oil down is their national dish, and it's no wonder why. In addition to an impressive list of ingredients and a preparation that demands attention and care, this is a dish associated with community and sharing. It's normally made in a gigantic pot, most traditionally over an open fire, to serve a large number of people. It might be made on the beach as part of a beach lime or in someone's backyard. Wherever it's made, it is a dish for sharing, and though I've scaled this recipe back to be more manageable for your kitchen, it still makes enough to warrant inviting someone over to partake.

The process of "layering the pot" ensures that the ingredients that need to cook longer are closer to the heat, and those that cook faster are farthest from it, which allows you to cook everything all at once rather than in stages. I chose to stick with the pig tails for this recipe because I wanted to honor this culinary representation of the nation, and, well, they make it delicious. You can experiment with different kinds of meat—anything with bones will work, and some people simply use salted cod. You could certainly make this with no meat at all, which would make it a bit like a highly spiced Metemgee (page 64). Much like in Metemgee and Rundown (page 106), the coconut milk cooks down until the oil separates from the liquid. I cannot stress enough that once it's going, you need to leave this pot alone to do its thing. Don't keep removing the lid, as the top layers are steaming, and *do not stir.* Let the layers work the way they're supposed to. You really should have a big pot for this; an 8-quart pot is ideal. Something slightly smaller can work; as long as you're able to cover it tightly, you're fine—there isn't enough liquid to bubble over, and you're not stirring it (*right?*), so you don't need that extra space.

Fresh coconut milk is preferable, and I don't think any self-respecting Grenadian living anywhere in the world would try to make this without it. But if you really can't get your hands on a fresh coconut, you can indeed use canned coconut milk thinned with some water as directed in the recipe. Outside of the coconut milk, the ingredients can be subjective, though breadfruit is almost always involved. If you can't get that, replace it with 2 pounds of other provisions, such as green plantains (or just use more green bananas), yams, malanga, or cassava. Don't forget the turmeric, which gives the dish a lovely pale-yellow color and a hint of earthy fragrance.

RECIPE CONTINUES

Place the pig tails in a medium saucepan and add water to cover. Bring to a boil over medium-high heat. Reduce the heat to low, cover, and simmer for about 1 hour, until they're tender, checking to make sure they are still fully submerged, adding more water if needed. Drain and set aside to cool.

When the pig tails are cool enough to handle, chop them into 2-inch pieces and place them in a medium bowl. Add the chicken, green seasoning, onion, garlic, scallions, seasoning pepper (if using), and thyme. Use your hands to make sure everything is evenly covered with the seasoning. Cover and place in the fridge to marinate for at least 2 hours or up to overnight.

While the meat is marinating, prepare your provisions and other veggies: Cut a small slice off the top of the breadfruit so it sits flat on your cutting board. Quarter the breadfruit, then, using a sharp paring knife, cut off the peel. Next, cut out the core of the breadfruit (the part that looks like rays of light emanating out of the middle). Cut each quarter lengthwise in half so you have 8 wedges in total. Set aside.

Peel the green bananas as you would a green plantain (see page 154). Cut each banana in half lengthwise. Peel the calabaza (see page 45) and cut it into large (3-inch) chunks. Peel the sweet potatoes and cut them in half (or quarters, if they're large). Cut the carrots into 2-inch pieces. Cut the okra pods in half lengthwise. Cut the greens into ribbons; if you're using dasheen leaves, slice the stems as well.

Heat the largest pot you own over medium heat. When it's hot, add the marinated meat and cook until it's releasing its juices, 5 to 10 minutes. Now it's time to begin layering your pot. Put the breadfruit in first, making concentric circles with the wedges. Next add the dasheen stalks, if you have them, then the green bananas. Layer in the carrots, calabaza, sweet potatoes, and okra. Nestle the Scotch bonnet in there somewhere before layering your greens on the very top. Unless you are lucky enough to have a really gigantic pot, this is going to look crazy. Remember, we don't have to stir it while it's cooking.

Stir the turmeric into the coconut milk and pour the milk all over the top of the leaves. If you're using canned coconut milk, fill the empty can with water and pour that into the pot, too. Put the lid on tight and cook over medium-low heat, undisturbed, for 40 minutes.

Meanwhile, make the dough for your spinners. At the 40-minute mark, you can remove the cover. Find a spot where you can access the bubbling liquid and add the salt there. Place the spinners on top of the greens (though if there are any areas where there's open liquid, that's a better spot) and cover. Cook, undisturbed, for 30 minutes more. Do. Not. Stir. I know it's going to be tempting. Don't do it!

When you're serving this, make sure to dig down deep to get all the layers on your plate. As it sits, the provisions will soak up the liquid. The meats should be incredibly tender, and the chicken will not just fall off the bone, but melt. Some of your veggies will get a bit mashed up as you take them out, it's okay. This dish's beauty is not on the outside but radiates from within. It's a celebration of the bounty of Grenada and its people. Oil down can be stored in an airtight container in the refrigerator overnight and reheated, but the provisions will continue to soak up liquid and will start to get a bit mushy, so it's really at its best then and there. All the more reason to share!

CHICKEN COLOMBO

CURRIED CHICKEN ○ MARTINIQUE/GUADELOUPE

COLOMBO CURRY POWDER

1 tablespoon white rice
1 tablespoon cumin seeds
1 tablespoon coriander seeds
2 teaspoons allspice berries
1 teaspoon black mustard seeds
1 teaspoon whole black peppercorns
1 teaspoon fenugreek (optional)
1 tablespoon ground turmeric

CURRY

2 pounds bone-in chicken thighs, skin removed, halved (see page 10)
1 lime, halved
2 teaspoons kosher salt
2 tablespoons extra-virgin olive oil
1 tablespoon unsalted butter
1 yellow onion, diced
4 garlic cloves, minced
3 scallions, thinly sliced
2 tablespoons chopped fresh parsley leaves
1 teaspoon fresh thyme leaves
1 small zucchini or 1 chayote, peeled, pitted, and chopped into 1-inch cubes

When I hit college and realized how little I'd been taught on the subject of half of my lineage, I made it my business to gather up every drop of history I could find. So, even before I began research on this book, I'd considered myself decently well versed in Caribbean history. However, this dish from Martinique and Guadeloupe caught me by surprise. I am certainly no stranger to curry—growing up with a Trinidadian mother made sure of that. But how is it that I had no idea that France, just like England, had brought (read: cajoled or kidnapped) indentured servants from their colonies in India to the Caribbean after slavery was eradicated and they lost their (free) workforce? This dish is a direct result of that moment in history, which has clearly left a legacy on cuisines of these islands. While there aren't nearly as many people of South Indian descent on Guadeloupe and Martinique as there are in places like Trinidad, Guyana, and Jamaica, these descendants of indentured servants still make up about 10 percent of their respective populations.

One of the main things that separates Colombo from other curry powders in the region is the rice—it adds a nutty flavor and helps to thicken the sauce. The addition of eggplant is also unusual in a Caribbean curry and may nod to another French influence.

Make the curry powder: In a small skillet, combine the rice, cumin, coriander, allspice, mustard seeds, peppercorns, and fenugreek (if using) and toast over medium heat for 2 minutes, until fragrant. Remove from the heat and let cool slightly, then transfer the mixture to a spice grinder or pilon and grind into a fine powder. Add the turmeric and blend again. Set aside.

Make the curry: Put the chicken pieces in a large bowl and squeeze the juice of 1 lime half over them. Season with 1 teaspoon of the salt and use your hands to coat the chicken in the lime juice and salt.

In a large Dutch oven or other heavy-bottomed pot, heat the olive oil and butter over medium heat until the butter has melted. Add the chicken, working in batches if need be, and cook for about 3 minutes per side, until browned. Set the chicken aside on a plate.

Add the onion, garlic, scallions, parsley, and thyme to the pot and cook over medium heat for about 8 minutes, until the onion begins to brown.

Add the zucchini, potatoes, eggplant, and curry powder and stir to ensure everything is coated with the spices.

RECIPE CONTINUES

2 russet potatoes, chopped into 2-inch cubes

1 small eggplant, chopped into 1-inch cubes

1 (13.5-ounce) can coconut milk, or 2 cups homemade Coconut Milk (page 97)

1 Scotch bonnet pepper, pricked all over with a fork

"Perfect" White Rice (page 180), for serving

SERVES 6 TO 8

Cook for 3 minutes or so, until the veggies are getting a bit soft, then return the chicken thighs and any juices that have collected on the plate to the pot and stir to coat. Raise the heat to high, pour in the coconut milk, add the Scotch bonnet, and bring to a boil. Add the remaining 1 teaspoon salt, reduce the heat to medium-low, and cover. Simmer, stirring occasionally, for 45 minutes, then remove the lid and cook for 15 minutes more, until the meat is tender and the liquid has reduced. Breaking up some of the potatoes will also help to thicken the curry. Remove from the heat. If you can find the Scotch bonnet, take it out (before someone ends up eating it whole!). Squeeze in the juice from the remaining lime half and serve over rice. Chicken colombo will keep in an airtight container in the fridge for up to 3 days or in the freezer for up to 3 months.

COCONUT BAKE

COCONUT FLATBREAD ○ TRINIDAD AND TOBAGO

2 cups all-purpose
   flour
2 tablespoons sugar
1 tablespoon baking
   powder
1 teaspoon kosher salt
2 tablespoons coconut
   oil, plus more for
   greasing
1½ cups shredded
   fresh coconut
1 cup Coconut
   Milk, homemade
   (page 97) or
   store-bought
1 tablespoon water

SERVES 4 TO 6

For your average Trinidadian, the word *bake* automatically means "fry bake," which is fried dough that sandwiches delicious things such as Buljol (page 206) or fried shark. When I was growing up, however, my mother only made two kinds of bake: what we called "regular bake" (which I learned later in life was actually sada roti) and coconut "pot bake." I liked them both, but my sister and I would silently cheer when we heard she was making the latter. The slighty sweet nuttiness from the coconut always made whatever meal it accompanied feel extra special. It could be breakfast, lunch, dinner, a snack, or a treat, and many a hike with my father was accompanied by fat pieces of coconut bake.

While you can certainly grate the coconut by hand, you'll get perfectly fine results by shredding it in a food processor or using frozen shredded coconut. This is also a great way to use shredded coconut left over from making your own coconut milk. Just don't use desiccated (dried) coconut here, as its texture is all off. Feel free to experiment with your flours, replacing up to 1 cup with any other flour you can think of, gluten-free or not. Breadfruit flour is an unusually delightful option. You can use any kind of oil you like, or even softened unsalted butter. This recipe is very forgiving on every front. It always amazed me how my mother could make this so consistently without measuring a single ingredient while I talked her ear off in the kitchen. No matter what, her coconut bake always came out *exactly* the same. I know she would have been proud of this one.

In a large bowl, mix together the flour, sugar, baking powder, and salt until well combined. Using a fork or your fingers, mix in the oil until grainy pebbles form. Mix in the shredded coconut. Stir in the coconut milk until just combined. Shape the dough into a rough ball with your hands. If you're using homemade milk, the dough will be a bit wet, but don't worry, it will come together. Cover and let the dough rest for about 30 minutes.

Preheat the oven to 350°F. Grease an 8-inch square baking dish or a 9-inch round cake pan with coconut oil.

Transfer the rested dough to the prepared baking dish and spread it out, using your fingers to push it to the edges of the dish. Pierce the dough all over with a fork and let rest for 5 minutes more. Brush the top with the water (this will help it get some color) and bake for 40 to 45 minutes, until a tester inserted into the center comes out clean and the top is lightly browned. The bake will keep in an airtight container at room temperature for up to 3 days or in a zip-top bag in the freezer for up to 3 months.

WILTED DASHEEN LEAVES WITH COCONUT MILK

1 tablespoon extra-virgin olive oil
1 small shallot, sliced
2 garlic cloves, minced
½ Scotch bonnet pepper, seeded and minced
1 (1-inch) piece fresh ginger, peeled and grated
1 bunch dasheen leaves (or other hardy green leaves), stemmed and roughly chopped or sliced into ribbons
Kosher salt
½ cup Coconut Milk, homemade (page 97) or store-bought
2 tablespoons fresh lime juice (from about ½ lime)

SERVES 4 TO 6

This dish evolved out of my always wanting to have greens alongside my Caribbean dishes, but finding a lack of variety when it came to traditional options. My usual go-to greens preparation of garlic, chile flakes, and a squeeze of lemon at the end is fine, but it just doesn't quite gel with Caribbean cuisine. With the knowledge that coconut milk makes everything better, I came up with this variation. If you can find dasheen leaves, also used to make Trinidadian Callaloo (page 135), you owe it to yourself to try them in this dish. If you can't find them, any hardy greens, such as chard, collard greens, or kale, take well to this preparation. The heat level is purely up to you. I like it to have a bit of a kick, but not set off any fire alarms.

In a wide skillet, heat the olive oil over medium heat. Add the shallot and cook until soft, 3 to 5 minutes. Add the garlic, Scotch bonnet, and ginger and sauté for 30 seconds, or until fragrant.

Add the greens and a good pinch of salt and toss with tongs to ensure the greens are coated with the shallot, garlic, and other aromatics. Add the coconut milk and cook for 5 minutes, until the greens have completely collapsed. Remove from heat, then add the lime juice, toss, and taste for salt. These greens are best eaten the same day, but can be kept in an airtight container in the fridge overnight.

RUNDOWN

MACKEREL WITH REDUCED COCONUT MILK ○ JAMAICA

1 (13.5-ounce) can
  coconut milk, or
  2 cups homemade
  Coconut Milk
  (page 97)
1 yellow onion, thinly
  sliced
4 garlic cloves, minced
2 Roma (plum)
  tomatoes, diced
2 scallions, thinly sliced
½ Scotch bonnet
  pepper, minced
  (optional)
1 teaspoon fresh
  thyme leaves
1 teaspoon kosher salt
  (optional)
4 (8-ounce) mackerel
  fillets, or 16 ounces
  salted mackerel
  (see Note)

SERVES 4 TO 6

*Note: If you're using
salted mackerel
fillets, make sure
you desalt them as you
would salted cod (see
page 197) before adding
them to the pan.*

Similar to Oil Down (page 98), the name of this dish refers to the process of cooking down coconut milk until the fat starts to separate and it essentially becomes condensed coconut milk. The result is a slightly sweet, rich dish. Rundown is normally made with salted mackerel, which is delicious, but I have a deep love of fresh mackerel fillets, and they work so perfectly here. You can use any firm, fresh fish fillet. This recipe would also classically be made with fresh coconut milk, but in the interest of time and convenience, canned will certainly do; it can be added as is—no need to thin it. Just make sure the brand you choose has as few ingredients as possible, or it may not cook down and separate properly. This is a surprisingly easy dish to make and really tastes like a lot more than the sum of its parts. Rundown is traditionally eaten with Festivals (page 120), Bammy (page 72), or "Perfect" White Rice (page 180) but is also so good with Coconut Bake (page 103).

In a wide skillet, bring the coconut milk to a boil over medium-high heat. Cook, letting the milk bubble vigorously and stirring frequently, until the fat starts to separate, 15 to 20 minutes. Somewhere around minute 10, you will start to doubt if it will ever happen or wonder if you missed your window. Don't worry—keep going. It will be very obvious when you've hit the sweet spot: The coconut oil (fat) will completely separate, and what's left of the milk will look like cooking caramel.

Reduce the heat to medium and add the onion, garlic, tomatoes, scallions, Scotch bonnet (if using), and thyme. If you're using fresh fish, add the salt. Cook until the onion is soft and the tomatoes are starting to break down, about 10 minutes. Add the fillets skin-side up. Reduce the heat to medium-low, cover, and cook until the fish is cooked through, 10 to 12 minutes. Remove from the heat and serve immediately.

SUGAR CAKE

COCONUT CANDY ○ BARBADOS

2 cups packed
    brown sugar
2 cups grated coconut
    (fresh or frozen)
1 cinnamon stick
1 teaspoon grated
    fresh ginger
2 fresh bay leaves
    (the kind you find
    refrigerated)
½ cup water (or
    coconut water,
    if using a fresh
    coconut)
¼ teaspoon kosher salt

SERVES 8 TO 10

While similar to Kòk Graje (page 109), the Bajan version of coconut candy reminds me more of the Trinidadian ones I would eat growing up. My mother (who was a sweet monster just like Desalin) couldn't take a trip to a Caribbean grocery without coming home with some of these. In Barbados, they add the sugar and coconut together in the beginning and cook it a little faster. The difference is subtle, but the results are slightly grainier, and the sweetness is somewhat more direct compared to the more caramel taste of kòk graje. Though there aren't as many spices here, the result is still fragrant and delicious, and the bay leaf adds a bass note that tempers the extreme sweetness. Use the freshest bay leaf you can get, as the dried ones won't contribute much flavor here.

Line a baking sheet with parchment paper.

In a medium saucepan, combine the brown sugar and coconut. Cook over medium-high heat, stirring frequently, until liquid starts to collect at the bottom of the pot, about 5 minutes.

Add the cinnamon, ginger, bay leaves, water, and salt and cook until the liquid has mostly evaporated, about 15 minutes. Remove from the heat. Remove the bay leaves and cinnamon stick and discard.

Using a tablespoon, drop the coconut mixture onto the prepared baking sheet. You may need to use another spoon to help scoop it out, as it starts to solidify quickly. Let cool completely before serving or storing. These will keep in an airtight container at room temperature for about a week, if you can keep them around that long!

KÒK GRAJE

COCONUT CANDY ○ HAITI

2 cups packed
    brown sugar
2 cinnamon sticks
1 teaspoon grated
    fresh ginger
1 star anise pod
3 strips lime zest
1 teaspoon vanilla
    extract
½ cup water (or
    coconut water,
    if using a fresh
    coconut)
2 cups grated coconut
    (fresh or frozen)
1 teaspoon fresh
    lime juice

SERVES 8 TO 10

Unlike my child and her father, I am not what Desalin calls a "sweet monster." I do enjoy sweets and crave a cookie every now and then, but I don't go crazy for sugary confections. However, kòk graje and all the ways it shows up around the islands is an Achilles' heel for me. There's something about the taste of the coconut mixed with the hard yet chewy sugar that just gets me. I've tried versions of this from just about every island you can think of, and they're all delicious, but I particularly like the highly spiced nature and subtle "tropical" flavor the lime adds in the Haitian version. Using a food processor on the coconut works, and frozen grated coconut is okay, but hand-grated coconut gives a much better texture. This version cooks much longer than the one from Barbados on page 107, resulting in a deeper caramel flavor and candy that's a bit smoother. If you are using a whole brown coconut, be sure to drain the coconut water and use it in place of the regular water, as it adds another layer of coconutty flavor. Kòk graje is something that you'd most often get from a street vendor, but with a little time and elbow grease, it can be made at home. It keeps very well and makes a great host gift.

Line a baking sheet with parchment paper.

In a medium saucepan, combine the brown sugar, cinnamon, ginger, star anise, lime zest, vanilla, and water. Cook over medium-low heat, stirring frequently, until the mixture is thick and syrupy, 12 to 15 minutes.

Stir in the coconut and simmer, stirring frequently, until the mixture looks dry, 35 to 40 minutes. This is a labor of love. You will keep thinking, "Surely it's done *now*," but until this syrupy goo is almost a dry solid, you're not there.

Stir in the lime juice and remove the saucepan from the heat. With a spatula, spread the hot coconut mixture over the prepared baking sheet in a rough square or rectangle, about ¼ inch thick, and remove the cinnamon sticks, star anise, and lime zest. Do this quickly, as the mixture will start to solidify immediately. Let cool completely until the candy is completely hard, then cut it into squares or break it up into irregular shapes. These will keep in an airtight container at room temperature for about a week, if you can keep them around that long!

TEMBLEQUE

COCONUT PUDDING ○ PUERTO RICO

½ cup cornstarch
½ cup sugar
¼ teaspoon kosher salt
1 cinnamon stick
1 star anise pod
2 (13.5-ounce) cans
  coconut milk, or
  4 cups homemade
  Coconut Milk
  (page 97)
Ground cinnamon

SERVES 8 TO 10

Tembleque means "wobbly" in Spanish, which is exactly what this dessert is. The ingredients might not sound like much—some canned coconut milk, cornstarch, and spices—but the result is a coconutty, creamy dream. Many people will swear by using homemade coconut milk here—the tembleque comes out whiter, and the taste is simultaneously more subtle yet more true to a coconut—but to be honest, I don't find the difference great enough to justify the labor. If you're up for it, by all means, try it. I like to top this with just a sprinkle of cinnamon, but you could also try toasted coconut flakes, fruit syrup, or fresh fruit. I make this in my Bundt pan, but the vessel is really up to you, as long as it can fit about 5 cups of liquid. Whatever you use, be sure to rinse it out with very cold water before adding the coconut milk mixture to ensure the tembleque will slide right out once it's set. This is probably one of the easiest desserts you can make, but is sure to impress. It reminds me of those Rice Krispies Treat commercials from the '80s where the moms would throw flour on their faces to make it look like they'd been working hard on a dessert that took mere minutes to make.

In a large Dutch oven or other heavy-bottomed pot, mix the cornstarch, sugar, and salt together. Add the cinnamon stick and star anise. Slowly whisk half the coconut milk into the pot, making sure it's smooth with no lumps, then whisk in the remainder. Cook over medium heat, whisking frequently, until the mixture thickens and falls off the whisk in distinct ribbons, about 10 minutes. Fish out the cinnamon stick and star anise with a fork and discard.

Rinse out your Bundt pan or other vessel with cold water and let any remaining water pool in the bottom, which will help create a seal.

Pour the hot coconut milk mixture into the pan and let cool to room temperature, then cover with plastic wrap and refrigerate for at least 2 hours or up to overnight. To serve, invert the pan over a plate or platter and listen to the tembleque *schhloooop* out. Dust with cinnamon to finish.

PIÑA COLADA ICE CREAM

3 cups cubed
    pineapple (about
    20 ounces, or
    ½ pineapple)
1 (14-ounce) can
    sweetened
    condensed milk
1 tablespoon fresh
    lime juice
¼ teaspoon kosher salt
2 (13.5-ounce) cans
    coconut cream,
    chilled overnight
    in the fridge

SERVES 10 TO 12

This dessert was born on a beach in San Juan. A woman came along offering piraguas (shaved ice) in only two flavors—pineapple or coconut—so clearly, we needed both. As the two flavors started melting together, Desalin and I contemplated the taste. I suggested the coconut chapter of this book might need something with pineapple, and she, between licks, said, "How about coconut pineapple ice cream?" Later on that trip in Piñones, Loíza, Desalin had her first (virgin) piña colada, which she declared to be the best beverage she'd ever had, and the idea was cemented.

Because coconut cream has a higher water content than heavy cream and the pineapple adds even more water, you do have to take steps to prevent this from getting too icy. You can certainly still enjoy the ice cream without extra mixing, but for a creamier, easier-to-scoop texture, follow the instructions in the last step. You can also replace the condensed milk with condensed coconut milk, if you can find it, which will both add to the coconut flavor and make the ice cream vegan. In that case, definitely blend it halfway, as there is more water in the condensed coconut milk. Don't skip the step of chilling the coconut cream in the fridge overnight. You need to separate it from the water in the can, and having it sit in the fridge for just a few hours, or trying to expedite it in the freezer, is not going to cut it.

In a blender, blend the pineapple until completely smooth. You shouldn't need any water to do this, but if it's not blending, add water 1 teaspoon at a time. Water is our enemy in this recipe.

Pour the puree into a medium saucepan and bring to a simmer over medium heat. Cook, stirring frequently, until the liquid has reduced to less than 2 cups, about 20 minutes. I'm not here to make you measure it out and put it back in the pot if it's not enough. Trust your gut. It should have changed from pale yellow to deep golden yellow and be extremely fragrant. Remove from the heat and let cool completely before moving on.

While the puree cools, put a large bowl (preferably metal) and whatever tool you're going to use to whisk the coconut cream in the freezer to chill for at least 30 minutes. (I usually use the whisk attachments on my handheld mixer, but you can also use a stand mixer or [bless you] whisk it by hand. Just remember that chilled coconut cream is much harder than heavy cream.)

In a separate medium bowl, mix together the condensed milk, pineapple puree, lime juice, and salt. This is delicious as it is. This could be the dessert right here. But it's not, so set it aside.

RECIPE CONTINUES

When everything is cooled and chilled, take the cans of coconut cream out of the fridge. Scoop the solidified cream out into the chilled bowl, making sure none of the water in the can comes along for the ride. (Discard the water or save it in the fridge to add a little oomph to your next pot of rice.) Using your mixer or whisk, whip the cream until it's fluffy and smooth-looking, 3 to 5 minutes. Keep in mind that this is very different from whipping heavy cream. Peaks are not the clue, as it will give you a peak right out of the can. You want to make sure it's gotten lighter and has some air in it, and that there aren't any hard chunks of cream remaining.

Gently fold the pineapple mixture into the coconut cream. Scrape everything into a loaf pan and cover it with plastic wrap. Stick it in the freezer. You can stop there if you want, and in about 6 hours, you'll have (very hard) ice cream! However, if you want to get it softer and creamier, you can either stir it every hour for the first 4 hours or so, or freeze it for 4 hours, break it up into chunks, whiz them in the blender for a few minutes, then put it back in the pan to refreeze completely. If you manage not to eat it all at once, it keeps very well in the freezer for up to 1 week.

CORNMEAL

Other names: MAYI MOULEN, HARINA DE MAÍZ

NATIVE TO THE AMERICAS, corn, and therefore cornmeal, was new to both Africans and Europeans alike upon arriving in the Caribbean. It originated as a domesticated plant in Mexico around 8000 BCE and was brought over to the islands by the native peoples who settled them. By the time Columbus arrived, corn was a common ingredient in Indigenous Caribbean cuisine and culture.

As most of the crops brought over from Europe failed to grow in the Caribbean, the Europeans relied on the foods of the Indigenous people, specifically cassava and corn, which grew very prolifically in the region. The Europeans preferred corn to cassava, as it was a bit closer to the grains they had eaten back home. Cornmeal was quickly embraced by slave owners as an inexpensive way to feed the enslaved. In the north of Haiti, the dish mayi moulen, a savory cornmeal porridge whose name literally translates to "ground corn," is sometimes called *tchen tchen*, meaning "here, here," and is what the overseers would say when they handed bowls of porridge to the enslaved. The porridge would be bolstered with small amounts of food that would raise its nutritional value, such as coconut milk (like in pap, see page 126) or salted fish or meat (as in Mayi Moulen ak Aransò, page 118, cornmeal porridge with smoked herring).

While cornmeal was not the food of choice of the enslaved, they adapted to it quickly, taking preparations from home and applying them to this new staple. The dish called Fungee or Funghi (page 138) from Antigua, known as cou cou in other Caribbean countries, is a direct descendant of West African fufu and also fondi, a dish made in Gambia from millet or couscous.

Cornmeal also factors into religious practices. In African-based religions such as Vodoun in Haiti, Orisha in Trinidad, and Santería in Cuba, spirits will often be given offerings of cornmeal porridge. In Haitian Vodoun ceremonies, vèvès, symbols that represent the different spirits and act as their beacon, are often drawn with corn flour, the finest form of ground corn.

While cornmeal still factors largely into the Caribbean kitchen today, there is a certain amount of stigma attached to it, as it is considered a poor man's food. Cornmeal has always been there, economically feeding the masses. It was given to the enslaved to keep them from starvation, and later, in the twentieth century, handed out in rations during troubled economic times. For many years, it was looked down upon and wouldn't show up in fancy restaurants or on the tables of those trying to impress across the region and in the diaspora. However, as many of us return to our roots, cornmeal is starting to have its day. It is so versatile and agreeable to all seasonings and pairings, sweet and savory. I am never without a big jar of cornmeal in my pantry.

NUTRITION: Cornmeal is very high in fiber and is also a good source of magnesium. Stone-ground cornmeal retains more minerals and vitamins than the steel-ground industrial kind, as it keeps more of the shell and germ of the corn kernel, much like rice. However, this also means it has a higher fat content, which means it will spoil faster. I have no problems storing my cornmeal in an airtight jar in my pantry, but I go through it very fast. If you won't use it within 3 months or you don't have a cool place to store it, consider keeping your cornmeal in the fridge or freezer.

HOW TO CHOOSE: As corn is such a ubiquitous vegetable around the Americas, cornmeal is an easy ingredient to find and comes in a variety of textures, from coarse to fine. You can also find corn flour, which has been ground and pounded into a powder. A couple of recipes in this chapter call for corn flour. Some might say it's a different ingredient than cornmeal, but I would argue that it's just the next grade of fine cornmeal. If you can get your hands on organic, small-batch cornmeal that has been stone-ground, do it. You will notice a difference in taste, and personally, I find the coarser, slightly uneven texture of stone-ground cornmeal delightful.

MAYI MOULEN AK ARANSÒ

CORNMEAL WITH SMOKED HERRING ○ HAITI

1 tablespoon extra-virgin olive oil

1 large shallot, minced

2 garlic cloves, minced

½ Scotch bonnet pepper, minced

2 Roma (plum) tomatoes, diced

1 teaspoon fresh thyme leaves

3 smoked herring fillets, diced

1 cup Coconut Milk, homemade (page 97) or store-bought

3 cups water

2 whole cloves

1 cup cornmeal

3 cups baby spinach, roughly chopped

SERVES 4 TO 6

Note: Smoked herring contains bones. Some people spend a lot of time trying to take them out, but they are so fine and flexible, it isn't worth it. Just dice up the bones along with the flesh and you'll be fine. Smoked herring is also usually desalted before it's used, like salted cod. However, unlike in the recipe for Chiktay (page 217), there's only a small amount used here, and leaving it as is provides just enough salt to season the whole dish.

This is exactly the type of dish that would have sustained the enslaved after hours upon hours of labor. Cornmeal was cheap, and the bit of smoked and salted fish would have both provided some extra nutrition, as well as a taste of home. In their native Central and West Africa, they often used pungent dried fish as a flavoring agent, much to the horror of visiting Europeans, who thought the funky smell was grotesque. The first time Atibon made this dish for me, I was initially offended by the smell. "*You're stinking up the whole apartment!*" I yelled as I ran around opening windows dramatically. He ignored me and smirked with satisfaction after I tasted it and rescinded all complaints. The whole place still stank the next morning, but as I ate my leftovers, I didn't care. However you feel about the (*extremely strong*) smell of smoked herring, the smoky, rich, and umami-filled flavor it imparts is worth it. Even in a studio apartment! This has become a favorite dish of mine, and when it's cooking, Desalin takes deep breaths and exclaims, "Yum!" She can even smell it from down the street.

This is a common variation of classic mayi moulen, which is just seasoned cornmeal. To make that version, omit the tomatoes, herring, and baby spinach. The use of coconut milk is mostly found in the southern regions of Haiti. When making plain mayi moulen, people most often use water only.

In a large Dutch oven or other heavy-bottomed pot, heat the olive oil over medium heat. Add the shallot, garlic, Scotch bonnet, tomatoes, and thyme and sauté until the onion softens and the tomatoes begin to break down, 3 to 5 minutes.

Stir in the herring and let it sizzle until the onion and fish are beginning to brown and the liquid begins to thicken, about 5 minutes.

Add the coconut milk, water, and cloves and bring the mixture to a boil. While stirring continuously, add the cornmeal in a steady stream, then cook, still stirring, until it begins to thicken. Reduce the heat to low, cover, and cook, stirring vigorously every 5 minutes or so and adding the spinach with your last stir, for 20 to 25 minutes, until the cornmeal is velvety and the herring is completely incorporated. Remove from the heat and serve immediately.

SORULLITOS DE MAÍZ

CORNMEAL FRITTERS ○ PUERTO RICO

2 cups water
1 teaspoon kosher salt
½ teaspoon sugar
Freshly ground
    black pepper
1½ cups cornmeal
1 cup grated sharp
    cheddar cheese
Neutral oil, for frying
Mayoketchup (recipe
    follows), for serving
    (optional)

SERVES 6 TO 8

These joyous little fritters can be found anywhere you find fried food on the island, which is pretty much everywhere. Sometimes they are sweeter, and sometimes there's no cheese. I prefer the extra bite of sharp cheddar compared to more traditional mild cheeses like Edam. If you want to go the sweet route, try Jamaican Festivals (page 120). Sorullitos are a great snack for a crowd, and this recipe can easily be doubled, or more. Even if you're a mayo hater (I'm a recovering mayo hater myself), you ought to try the mayoketchup, which is served with everything fried in Puerto Rico. It's one of the most addictive condiments I've ever had. You can find it bottled in Puerto Rico and places with large Puerto Rican populations like New York City, but it's also very easy to make.

In a medium heavy-bottomed pot, combine the water, salt, sugar, and a few grinds of pepper and bring to a boil over high heat. While stirring continuously, add the cornmeal in a steady stream, then cook, still stirring until it's thick, stiff, and pulling away from the sides of the pot, 2 to 3 minutes. Remove from the heat, add the cheese, and stir until it has totally melted, about 3 minutes. Let cool. (The cornmeal mixture can be made several hours in advance and kept in the fridge, covered, before frying.)

When it's cool enough to handle, take a heaping tablespoon of the cornmeal mixture and roll it between your hands to create a cigarlike shape that's about 3 inches long. Set it aside on a plate and repeat with the rest of the mixture.

In a wok or deep skillet, heat about 2 inches of oil over medium-high heat until it reaches 350°F. If you don't have a thermometer, you'll know the oil is ready if a wooden spoon dipped into the oil bubbles all around.

Fry sorullitos, in batches if necessary, until golden brown, 6 to 8 minutes, making sure to roll them with a wooden spoon so they cook evenly. Drain on paper towels and serve while hot, preferably with mayoketchup.

MAYOKETCHUP

½ cup mayonnaise
¼ cup ketchup
1 teaspoon garlic
    powder
Hearty squeeze of
    lemon juice

MAKES ¾ CUP

Feel free to experiment with seasonings, like adding a bit of Recaíto (page 22), Sazón (page 23), or a touch of Pepper Sauce (page 215). It's great as a dip or as a spread on burgers or sandwiches.

In a small bowl, mix together all the ingredients. The mayoketchup can be used right away, but the flavors marry better after an hour or so. Store in an airtight container in the fridge for several days.

FESTIVALS

CORNMEAL FRITTERS ○ JAMAICA

1 cup all-purpose flour
1 cup fine cornmeal or
    corn flour
2 tablespoons sugar
2 teaspoons baking
    powder
1 teaspoon kosher salt
½ cup Coconut
    Milk, homemade
    (page 97) or
    store-bought
4 to 6 tablespoons
    water
Neutral oil, for frying

SERVES 6 TO 8

This cornmeal fritter includes more sugar than the Sorullitos (page 119), uses a leavening agent so the fritters puff up, and incorporates coconut milk because, my friends, coconut milk makes everything, *everything* better. My child is unusually obsessed with these and has, on more than one occasion, cried because I would not make "festibals." Though they are a bit sweet, they are most often served as a savory side dish and are amazing with any salted cod dish, such as Ackee and Saltfish (page 203), Buljol (page 206), or Okra and Saltfish (page 137). They're also a traditional companion to escovitch fish (see page 228) and Jerk Chicken (page 222).

In a medium bowl, mix the flour, cornmeal, sugar, baking powder, and salt with a fork. Add the coconut milk and mix until you feel like it's evenly distributed. Add 4 tablespoons of the water and mix that in with the fork. We want the dough to be completely moist, but not *wet*. If it still seems too craggy or dry, add more water 1 tablespoon at a time.

Use your hands to lightly knead the dough until it's somewhat smooth. Don't overwork the dough—you're not looking for perfection. It should just seem completely integrated. Take a heaping tablespoon of the dough and roll it between your hands to create a cigarlike shape, about 3 inches long. Set it aside on a plate and repeat with the rest of the dough.

In a wok or deep skillet, heat about 2 inches of oil over medium-high heat until it reaches 350°F. If you don't have a thermometer, you'll know the oil is ready if a wooden spoon inserted in the oil bubbles all around.

Fry the festivals, in batches if necessary, until they're golden brown, 8 to 9 minutes, making sure to roll them with a wooden spoon so they cook evenly. If they're browning too quickly, reduce the heat to medium and wait a bit for the oil's temperature to drop before adding more. Drain on paper towels and serve immediately.

TAMAL EN CAZUELA

CORNMEAL AND PORK SHOULDER CASSEROLE ○ CUBA

1½ pounds pork shoulder, fat trimmed, cut into 2-inch cubes

6 garlic cloves, minced

¼ cup sour orange juice (see page 14)

1 teaspoon dried oregano

2 teaspoons kosher salt, plus more if needed

1 cup cornmeal

½ cup corn kernels (cut fresh from the cob, canned, or frozen)

2 tablespoons extra-virgin olive oil

1 small yellow onion, diced

½ green bell pepper, finely diced

2 tablespoons dry white wine

½ cup tomato sauce

2 cups water

SERVES 6 TO 8

This dish screams "comfort food" and is something your favorite auntie may have made. Tamal en cazuela may have originated with the people indigenous to Cuba, and the pork would have been an addition inspired by all the wild pigs that ended up roaming all the islands after they were introduced by the Europeans. It's also easy to see how it would have been adopted by enslaved Africans, who may have been the ones to add the cornmeal. For this recipe, I use the Haitian method of simmering the pork first to make it extra tender and infuse it with flavor (it feels right because, historically, Cuba and Haiti had a close relationship). If you want to keep it traditionally Cuban, be sure to marinate the pork with the garlic, sour orange juice, oregano, and salt for at least an hour, then remove the excess marinade and brown the pork for 4 to 5 minutes per side.

In a large Dutch oven or heavy-bottomed pot, add the pork, two-thirds of the garlic, the sour orange juice, oregano, and 1 teaspoon of the salt. Mix the pork with your hands to ensure it's entirely coated. Cover the pot and cook over low heat for 20 minutes, until the pork has released a lot of liquid and appears cooked from the outside.

Meanwhile, in a blender or food processor, combine the cornmeal and corn kernels and blend into a paste. If you need to add a little water to make it work, do so 1 tablespoon at a time.

Transfer the pork to a plate, reserving the liquid from the pot in a bowl or large measuring cup to use later. Wipe out the pot and place it back on the stove over medium heat. Add the olive oil, then brown the pork in batches to prevent crowding the pan; it should only take a minute or two to get some color since it's already cooked and the pot is already hot. As you finish each batch, transfer the pork back to the plate.

When you have finished browning the pork, add the onion, bell pepper, and remaining garlic to the pot and cook until everything is deep brown, 5 to 8 minutes. Add the wine and stir, making sure to scrape up any pork bits from the bottom of the pot, then pour in the tomato sauce and simmer for about 5 minutes, until the tinny taste is gone.

Return the pork and the reserved liquid to the pot, then add the water and the corn mixture. Bring the mixture to a boil, stirring frequently, and add the remaining 1 teaspoon salt (or more, if you like). Reduce the heat to low, cover, and cook, giving it a good stir every 5 minutes or so, for 25 to 30 minutes, until the cornmeal is velvety and the mixture is thick enough that a wooden spoon would stand up in it.

Cornmeal is always best if eaten right away, but this dish can be made a few hours in advance and reheated, as the fresh corn helps keep it a little looser. You can also store it in the fridge overnight in an airtight container and reheat it the next day, though it does firm up quite a bit.

PEN MAYI

SWEET CORNBREAD ○ HAITI

1 cup Coconut
  Milk, homemade
  (page 97) or
  store-bought
1 cup (8 ounces)
  evaporated milk
2 star anise pods
2 cinnamon sticks
½ cup (1 stick)
  unsalted butter,
  plus more for
  greasing
1 cup cornmeal
½ cup all-purpose
  flour
1 teaspoon baking
  powder
¼ teaspoon kosher salt
½ cup packed
  brown sugar
½ cup grated fresh
  coconut
1 ripe banana, mashed
2 teaspoons grated
  fresh ginger
1 teaspoon vanilla
  extract

SERVES 8 TO 10

Clearly a descendant of the arepa on page 125, pen mayi has a bit more going on and uses slightly different cooking methods. The cornmeal isn't cooked first like in the arepa, so the texture of pen mayi is a bit grainier, more like cornbread. The addition of more spices also makes for a more layered experience. Though the ingredient list is long, it's worth every moment of prep.

In a small or medium saucepan, combine the milks, star anise, and cinnamon sticks and bring to a simmer over medium-low heat. Cook for 5 minutes, then turn off the stove. Add the butter, giving it a couple of whirls to help start the melting process, and set the pot aside for 30 minutes to infuse the milks and butter with flavor from the spices.

Preheat the oven to 350°F. Grease an 8-inch square baking pan.

In a small bowl, mix together the cornmeal, flour, baking powder, and salt. In a medium bowl, mix together the brown sugar, coconut, banana, ginger, and vanilla until well incorporated. Strain the infused milk mixture through a sieve into the bowl with the sugar mixture and discard the spices. Stir until well blended, then add the dry ingredients and mix gently until completely incorporated.

Pour the batter into the prepared pan and bake for 1 hour, until the top is golden and a toothpick inserted into the middle comes out clean. Remove from the oven and let cool a bit before slicing. Leftovers can be stored in an airtight container at room temperature for 2 to 3 days.

AREPA

CORNMEAL CAKE ○ DOMINICAN REPUBLIC

3 tablespoons unsalted butter, at room temperature, plus more for greasing
3 cups whole milk
2 cups cornmeal
1 (13.5-ounce) can coconut milk, or 2 cups homemade Coconut Milk (page 97)
1¼ cups packed brown sugar
½ cup raisins (optional)
3 cinnamon sticks, or 1 teaspoon ground cinnamon
2 teaspoons vanilla extract
¼ teaspoon kosher salt

SERVES 10 TO 12

This is not to be confused with the flatbread eaten with fillings that comes from Colombia and Venezuela. In the Dominican Republic, an arepa is an unleavened cake made with cornmeal and a variety of milks, and clearly hails from a simpler time. In certain parts of the island, it would be called torta. Arepa would traditionally be made in a caldero (a big aluminum pot) and cooked over charcoal, which would lend it a beautiful smoky touch. It's a dish that I imagine was originally developed by enslaved Africans, pairing the corn they encountered on the island with their own methods of cooking. I would be willing to bet it hasn't changed much since then, except for all the dairy, which was not common in the islands until more recently. The key here is to work fast when transferring the batter from the pot to the baking pan. The cornmeal will continue to thicken, so be sure to get it straight into the pan. You can substitute additional coconut milk for the whole milk, if you like.

Preheat the oven to 350°F. Grease an 8-inch square baking pan with butter.

In a large Dutch oven or other heavy-bottomed pot, combine the butter, milk, cornmeal, coconut milk, brown sugar, raisins (if using), cinnamon, vanilla, and salt. Cook over medium-high heat, stirring continuously with a sturdy wooden spoon, until the mixture comes to a boil and starts to thicken. Reduce the heat to medium-low and cook, stirring, until it pulls away from the sides of the pot and sticks to your spoon even if you turn the spoon upside down, 10 to 12 minutes.

Fish the cinnamon sticks out and discard. Immediately scrape the mixture into the prepared pan and smooth out the top. Bake for about 40 minutes, until the top is just beginning to turn golden brown. Remove from the oven and let cool before slicing.

This will keep in an airtight container at room temperature for up to 3 days.

CORNMEAL PORRIDGE

JAMAICA

2 cups water
1 (13.5-ounce) can
   coconut milk, or
   2 cups homemade
   Coconut Milk
   (page 97)
1 cup cornmeal
¼ teaspoon kosher salt
1 teaspoon vanilla
   extract
¼ cup (2 ounces)
   sweetened
   condensed milk,
   plus more for
   serving, if desired
A few gratings of
   nutmeg

SERVES 4 TO 6

This hearty Jamaican breakfast is centuries old. Sometimes called cog, pap, or pop—words that come from the various names of West African porridges—this nourishing dish is often the first hard food a baby will eat on the island. It stands out most for my cousin Ashayna when remembering her Jamaican mother's cooking. Auntie Rosie Mae was a beast in the kitchen and could prepare all kinds of complex dishes, from Jamaica and beyond, in the most mouthwatering of ways. But this cornmeal porridge, usually made on weekends, was one of her very best. Ashayna recalls that her mom always made it as simple as possible and didn't even include the condensed milk, though I'm all about the richness it adds.

It is normally made with fine cornmeal, but I love the texture of a coarser grain, even if you may have to cook it a bit longer. When I cook cornmeal, I like to cover the pot and stir it every 5 minutes or so rather than keeping the lid off and stirring it continuously. Either way, the process is a bit laborious, but the rewards are great. If you're using fine cornmeal, mix the cornmeal with ½ cup of the water before adding it to the pot—it's much more prone to lumps. You can sweeten it with whatever you like, but the condensed milk is classic and decadently delicious (if I had to suggest alternatives, I'd go with brown sugar or honey). If you can get your hands on condensed coconut milk, all the better. For a Haitian touch, you can add one star anise pod to the liquid before boiling and remove it just before serving.

In a large Dutch oven or other heavy-bottomed pot, combine the water and coconut milk and bring to a boil over medium-high heat. Stirring continuously, add the cornmeal in a steady stream, then add the salt and cook, stirring, until it begins to thicken, about 3 minutes. Reduce the heat to low, cover, and cook, stirring vigorously every 5 minutes, for 20 to 25 minutes, until the cornmeal is thick and silky, with no grit left.

Turn off the heat and mix in the vanilla, condensed milk, and nutmeg before serving. If you like it sweeter, feel free to drizzle more condensed milk into your bowl. The porridge is best eaten immediately but can be stored in an airtight container in the refrigerator overnight and reheated with a splash more coconut milk the next day.

CONKIES

2 cups fine cornmeal or corn flour
1 cup packed brown sugar
1 cup shredded fresh coconut
1 cup Calabaza Puree (page 54)
1 cup Coconut Milk, homemade (page 97) or store-bought
½ cup all-purpose flour
¼ cup coconut oil, at room temperature
1 egg
1½ teaspoons vanilla extract
½ teaspoon almond extract
½ teaspoon ground cinnamon
½ teaspoon freshly grated nutmeg
¼ teaspoon ground allspice
¼ teaspoon kosher salt
⅓ cup raisins
A pack of banana leaves (optional)

SERVES 10 TO 12

Every island has a version of these dumplings, some made with cornmeal, some with sweet potato, some with plantain. Other names include duckanoo, blue drawers, güanimes, paime, or tie-a-leaf. The earliest recorded mention of them in the islands is from around 1600, and describes cornmeal dough wrapped in banana leaves and cooked in the coals of a fire. Conkey was the sweet version and kankey the savory version. Both words probably come from *kenkey*, which was what the Akan, Ga, and Ewe people of coastal West Africa call a kind of dumpling wrapped in leaves to steam. They were also called dorkunu in West Africa, clearly where the Jamaican name duckanoo came from.

If you can't get your hands on banana leaves, you can wrap the dumplings in a piece of parchment paper using the same method. Instead of tying them together with kitchen twine, you can cover them with aluminum foil to seal. It may not be as cute, and while I find they come out just a bit harder, it's only a slight difference. I like to use a steamer basket to ensure none of the conkies get waterlogged in the pot, but if you don't have one (or anything else that can sit on the bottom of the pot to elevate them), it's fine to just pile them in there with a bit of water. This is a great place to use leftover shredded coconut from making Coconut Milk (page 97).

In a large bowl, mix together the cornmeal, brown sugar, coconut, calabaza, coconut milk, flour, coconut oil, egg, vanilla, almond extract, cinnamon, nutmeg, allspice, and salt until well combined and decently smooth. Fold in the raisins.

If you're using banana leaves, rinse them thoroughly under cold water. If they're still stiff, pass them over the high heat of a stovetop burner a few times, just close enough to warm them up, not to char them. This will make them more pliable.

Next up we're going to wrap the conkies, which is a bit like wrapping a gift. Cut the banana leaves into 8-inch squares. Place a scant ¼ cup of the dough in the center of a square. Fold the bottom of the square up over the dough and the top down over it, then fold in the sides. Use kitchen twine to wrap it all up like a present, securing the folded sides. You can tie it in a bow or a knot. Set your cute little package aside and repeat the process until all the dough is used up.

Fill a large stockpot (or the biggest pot you've got) with a couple inches of water and place a rack or steamer basket inside. Load in the conkies, cover the pot tightly, and steam them over medium heat for about 30 minutes from the moment the heat goes on. You shouldn't run out of water, but listen carefully! If it sounds like it's completely dried out and needs more water, open the pot and add more—otherwise, keep that lid on.

Turn off the heat and let stand for 5 minutes before serving. Conkies are best the same day.

OKRA

ABELMOSCHUS ESCULENTUS

Other names: KALALOU, MOLONDRONES, QUIMBOMBÓ, OCHRO, OKRO

OKRA IS A DIVISIVE VEGETABLE (or fruit, technically) because of its mucilaginous properties—in other words, it's slimy. When I was a kid, you couldn't have paid me to eat okra. But as an adult, I have learned to love the slime and the delicious taste that comes with it.

The history of okra is murky, but it likely originated somewhere around Ethiopia and from there spread throughout North and West Africa, the Middle East, and India. It then probably hitched a ride on slave ships headed to the Caribbean and the Americas. It was first recorded in Brazil in the mid-seventeenth century. The word *okra* comes from the Igbo word *ókùrù*.

A member of the mallow family, this seedpod is related to cacao, cotton, hibiscus, and hollyhock. In parts of Africa, the seeds are roasted, ground, and brewed in place of coffee. In the Caribbean, okra is mostly used in soups and stews but is also sometimes sautéed alone. While there are things that can be done to reduce the slime factor, some slime will always remain. My tip to you is to embrace it! This is one of the ingredients that most connects us to our African roots and is one way enslaved Africans stayed connected to their culture and each other.

NUTRITION: Okra is an incredibly nutritious fruit in a variety of ways. While the leaves and flowers do hold some nutritional and medicinal properties, most of the good stuff is found within the pod. Okra is rich in calcium, dietary fiber, iron, and vitamins B, C, and K. Its mucilage (aka slime) has been shown to lower glucose levels in the blood, which could make it beneficial for those with diabetes. The little pods are full of antioxidants, and studies have shown that the seeds have some anticancerous properties. The pectin (yes, the same stuff you use to make jam) found in okra is known to lower bad cholesterol. And these are just some of okra's benefits!

HOW TO CHOOSE: Choose okra pods that are rich green in color (or red).

HOW TO STORE: Store in the warmest part of your fridge (like the door or the highest shelves). Okra does not keep well, so try to use it within 3 days of purchase.

HOW TO PREPARE: Okra doesn't take much prep. You'll only need to trim the cap where the stem was and trim the tip off before cutting it as directed in the recipe. Just remember to wash the okra *before* you cut it; the second it hits water, the slime will start pumping.

ARROZ CON QUIMBOMBÓ

RICE AND OKRA ○ CUBA

1 tablespoon extra-virgin olive oil
½ pound okra, cut into ¼-inch pieces
1 small yellow onion, diced
½ green bell pepper, diced
3 garlic cloves, minced
2 ounces salted ham or chorizo, cubed (optional)
½ cup tomato sauce
2½ cups water
1 teaspoon kosher salt
1 cup medium-grain rice

SERVES 4 TO 6

In Cuba and Puerto Rico, okra is called quimbombó, a word that probably comes from the Bantu languages of Central Africa, where it is known as tchingombo and ochingombo (also clearly where the word *gumbo* comes from, but that's a story for someone else's book). This list of ingredients is short (by Caribbean standards) but mighty because okra lends its distinctive taste to everything. The addition of pork is traditional, but is optional from a taste perspective, as the dish is still delicious without it. Browning the okra first helps cut down on the slime factor, and the rice soaks up whatever is left. This is a great side dish for any kind of chicken or pork.

In a large Dutch oven or heavy-bottomed pot, heat the olive oil over medium heat. Add the okra and sauté until it begins to brown, about 8 minutes, then add the onion, bell pepper, and garlic. Cook until the onion is soft, 3 to 5 minutes.

Add the ham (if using) and stir to combine. Add the tomato sauce, water, and salt, then raise the heat to high and bring to a boil. Pour in the rice and bring the liquid back to a boil, then reduce the heat to medium-low, cover, and cook, undisturbed, for about 30 minutes, until the liquid has been absorbed. Remove from the heat, fluff, and serve.

CALLALOO

OKRA AND DASHEEN GREENS SOUP ○ TRINIDAD AND TOBAGO

2 tablespoons
    coconut oil
1 yellow onion, diced
4 scallions, thinly sliced
5 garlic cloves, minced
6 tablespoons
    Green Seasoning,
    homemade
    (page 22) or
    store-bought
1 pound dasheen
    leaves (or any hardy
    green or mature
    spinach), stemmed
    and shredded
½ pound okra, roughly
    chopped
2 cups cubed calabaza,
    butternut squash,
    or kabocha squash
    (about 8 ounces),
    peeled
1 tablespoon fresh
    thyme leaves
1 (13.5-ounce) can
    coconut milk, or
    2 cups homemade
    Coconut Milk
    (page 97)
2 cups water
2 teaspoons
    kosher salt
Freshly ground
    black pepper
1 Scotch bonnet
    pepper
"Perfect" White
    Rice (page 180) or
    peeled and boiled
    provisions, for
    serving

SERVES 6 TO 8

A staple in many Caribbean nations, there may be none as proud of callaloo as Trinidad and Tobago, who have claimed it as their national dish. It is easy to see how the enslaved Africans used the ingredients around them in their new environment to create this soupy stew that may have reminded them of their home continent.

Callaloo was something my mother made for special occasions—Easter, a birthday, or when company was coming over. As a child, I could never wrap my head around its appearance—it reminded me too much of the green slime they'd pour on people on *You Can't Do That on Television*. It was almost always served with boiled provisions like sweet plantain, cassava, or Caribbean sweet potato, which I liked, but as a kid, it didn't make up for the green goo. Fortunately, it was also almost always served with fried or stewed kingfish, which I adored. So while I'd always wrinkle my nose and pass on the callaloo, its presence meant a meal I could get excited about, and the smell of it brings me joy to this day. In Trinidad, it is cooked with crab and/or smoked meats just as often as it is cooked vegan, as it is in this recipe. My mother grew up Seventh-day Adventist *and* poor, which made for a largely meat-free life. She never once put any kind of animal product in her callaloo, and this version is as close to hers as I can get. I love the way the earthy green taste comes through and plays with the creamy sweet coconut, something that can get a bit lost with the addition of meat. The dasheen leaves, otherwise known as taro, are traditional and give the callaloo a distinctive taste, but Trinidadians will often substitute spinach. I personally prefer hardier greens like kale or collards, as they are closer to the texture of a dasheen leaf. If you do go with spinach, be sure it's mature, as baby spinach can't stand up to these heavyweight ingredients.

In a large Dutch oven or heavy-bottomed pot, heat the coconut oil over medium heat. Add the onion, scallions, and garlic and sauté until they start to brown, 5 to 8 minutes. Stir in the green seasoning and cook for 3 minutes, until it's very fragrant. Add the greens, okra, calabaza, and thyme. Give a solid stir to coat, then cook for 3 minutes. Raise the heat to high, add the coconut milk and water, and bring everything to a boil. Add the salt and some good grinds of black pepper. Give it one last stir, place the Scotch bonnet in whole, then reduce the heat to low, cover, and cook, undisturbed, for 30 minutes, until the calabaza is very soft.

Remove the Scotch bonnet pepper. This is serious! If you can't find it and you end up blending it up, there will be consequences. Using an immersion blender, blend the stew directly in the pot until smooth (or carefully transfer it to a standing blender, in batches if necessary, and blend until smooth). Serve over plain rice or boiled provisions. Callaloo will keep in an airtight container in the fridge for 3 to 5 days or in the freezer for up to 3 months.

FRIED OKRO

STIR-FRIED OKRA ○ TRINIDAD AND TOBAGO

1 pound okra, cut into
½-inch pieces
2 tablespoons
coconut oil
1 small yellow onion,
diced
2 garlic cloves, minced
1 seasoning pepper,
minced (optional;
see page 14)
Kosher salt

SERVES 4 TO 6

This recipe is perfect for converting slime haters to the okra cause. Traditionally, the okra would be put outside in the sun to dry up, but I had to find alternative measures when living in Brooklyn. I find air-drying them for a few hours is effective, though if you're in a rush, you can certainly cook them straight away and just add a few minutes to the cooking time. They won't be as crispy as they'd be if you had waited, but they will still get a nice golden brown. You might be tempted to try drying them on paper towels to speed up the process—don't do it! The okra will glue itself to the paper and you'll be ruined. My mother used coconut oil whenever possible, and I love the nutty flavor it adds to the okra, but feel free to use another oil suitable for high-heat cooking.

Line a baking sheet with parchment paper. Spread the okra over the parchment and let it sit at room temperature for 2 hours, or refrigerate overnight.

In a wide nonstick skillet, heat the coconut oil over medium-high heat. Add the onion, garlic, and seasoning pepper (if using) and sauté until they start to brown, 5 to 8 minutes.

Add the okra and cook, stirring often, for 8 to 12 minutes, until dry, brown, and slightly crispy. Sprinkle with salt and serve warm.

OKRA AND SALTFISH

GUYANA

1 tablespoon extra-virgin olive oil

1 small yellow onion, thinly sliced

3 garlic cloves, mashed in a pilon or minced

½ pound okra, cut into ½-inch pieces

1 Roma (plum) tomato, diced

2 teaspoons Green Seasoning, homemade (page 22) or store-bought

2 scallions, thinly sliced

½ pound salted cod, desalted (see page 197) and shredded

"Perfect" White Rice (page 180), Coconut Bake (page 103), Fungee (page 138), or plain Mayi Moulen (page 118), for serving

SERVES 4 TO 6

While this dish is most prevalent in Guyana, Jamaica, and Trinidad and Tobago, you can really find it on any island. Most variations differ only by their seasonings. Two Caribbean staples come together to make this delicious and easy dish that could be served for any meal of the day.

In a large skillet, heat the olive oil over medium heat. Add the onion and garlic and sauté until they begin to brown, 5 to 8 minutes. Add the okra and cook until it begins to brown, about 10 minutes.

Add the tomato, green seasoning, and scallions, stirring to mix it all evenly. Cook until the tomato starts to break down, about 5 minutes. Stir in the salted cod and cook for 5 minutes, until the tomato starts to become one with the cod, turning it slightly red. Serve with rice, coconut bake, fungee, or mayi moulen.

FUNGEE

CORNMEAL AND OKRA ○ ANTIGUA

4 cups water
1 teaspoon kosher salt
6 okra pods,
    finely diced
1 cup cornmeal
1 tablespoon unsalted
    butter or olive oil

SERVES 4 TO 6

Sometimes called coo coo, cou cou, funche, fungi, fungie, or funghi, there are variations of this dish all over the Caribbean, and it's almost definitely a descendant of African *fufu*, which means "to pound." In West Africa, it was a dish made with yams, potatoes, or plantains, served either as a porridge or shaped into balls. When they were forcibly taken from their homes, enslaved people adapted a variety of ingredients, such as cassava or, in this case, cornmeal, to suit their purposes, as they were often the only foods they were given. This is one half of Antigua's national dish, the other half being pepperpot—not to be confused with Guyanese Pepperpot (page 73); the Antiguan version is more closely related to Trinidadian Callaloo (page 135).

This simple dish is an excellent vessel for soupy mains, especially fish. It's also a great way to sneak okra past a hater, as my child can testify (or can't, because what she doesn't know won't hurt her). You can substitute olive oil for the butter to make it vegan without losing out. Traditionally, small bowls would be greased with butter and used as a mold for shaping the fungee as in the recipe for Mofongo (page 160); the fat allows it to slide right out. As this is such a weeknight regular for me, I don't bother with the presentation, but if you're making this for guests, give it a try.

In a large heavy-bottomed pot or Dutch oven, combine the water and salt and bring to a boil over high heat. Add the okra and boil for 5 minutes. This will make the water thick and somewhat slimy, but don't be alarmed! The final product will not have this texture.

While stirring, pour in the cornmeal in a steady stream, continuing to stir until it begins to thicken, about 3 minutes. Reduce the heat to low, cover, and cook, giving it a good stir every 5 minutes or so, for 20 to 25 minutes, until the cornmeal is thick and no longer grainy.

Stir in the butter and serve immediately.

GRILLED OKRA

WITH CHARRED SCALLION VINAIGRETTE

Neutral oil for grilling
grates
1 bunch scallions
(about 5), halved
lengthwise
1 pound okra, halved
lengthwise
3 tablespoons plus
1 teaspoon extra-
virgin olive oil
1 small garlic clove,
peeled
¼ teaspoon
kosher salt, plus
more as needed
1 teaspoon fresh
thyme leaves
1 teaspoon Epis
(page 21)
1 tablespoon fresh
lime juice
1 tablespoon apple
cider vinegar
1 teaspoon grated
fresh ginger

SERVES 4 TO 6

*Note: If you don't have a
grill, don't fret! Char the
scallions in a medium
skillet over medium-high
heat with a small splash
of olive oil for 5 minutes.
Broil the okra, spread
out on a baking sheet,
on high for 5 minutes on
each side.*

This recipe is in part inspired by my dear friend Lukas Volger and his love of charred scallions, which he has passed on to me. I first made a vinaigrette of charred scallions when helping test recipes for his cookbook *Start Simple* and have never looked back. The scallions are smoky, but also become a bit sweet and delightfully crispy. Between them and a little bit of Epis (page 21), this dressing is addictive, and leftovers are great on just about any grilled or roasted vegetable, or hardy greens.

Grilling everything makes for the best results, as that smoke taste hits different. Grilling okra directly on the grates without a grill pan is a challenge, a test of focus and Zen. You will lose a few to the flames, but ultimately, you'll win the battle.

If using a charcoal grill, light the charcoal; when the coals are white hot, spread them out evenly. If using a gas grill, set the burners to medium. Make sure your grill grates are nice and oiled.

Place the scallions in a single layer over the grates. Grill them for about 5 minutes per side, until they are quite deeply charred. Set aside to cool.

In a large bowl, toss the okra with about 1 teaspoon of the olive oil. If you have a grill basket, you can put the okra in there, cut-side down; if you don't, very carefully place each piece on the grates (making sure they are placed across the grates so they don't fall in). Cover the grill and cook on the first side for 5 to 7 minutes, until grill marks have formed and the okra begins to soften. Using grill tongs, flip the okra (if you're using a grill basket, you can just stir them around), cover, and cook for 5 to 7 minutes on the second side until they are completely tender.

While the okra is cooking, use a pilon to mash the garlic and ¼ teaspoon salt into a paste. (Alternatively, use the back of a knife to mash them together on a cutting board.) Chop the scallions into small pieces and place them in a small bowl. Add the garlic paste, thyme, epis, lime juice, vinegar, and ginger. Slowly whisk in the remaining 3 tablespoons olive oil.

Toss the okra with the dressing (there may be a surplus of this) and taste for salt. This can be served warm or at room temperature. It's best served the same day but will keep overnight in an airtight container in the fridge.

MOLONDRONES GUISADOS

STEWED OKRA ○ DOMINICAN REPUBLIC

2 tablespoons extra-virgin olive oil
1 pound okra, cut into ½-inch pieces
1 yellow onion, diced
4 garlic cloves, minced
½ red bell pepper, diced
½ green bell pepper, diced
4 Roma (plum) tomatoes, diced
1 cup tomato sauce
2 teaspoons apple cider vinegar
½ teaspoon achiote powder (optional, largely for color)
½ to 1 cup water
Kosher salt and freshly ground black pepper
½ cup fresh cilantro, chopped
"Perfect" White Rice (page 180), for serving

SERVES 4 TO 6

This recipe comes from my dear friend Sarah's abuela Carlita. Carlita came to the United States from the Dominican Republic eight years before Sarah did, and her apartment on 161st Street in Washington Heights was her family's hub. Of all the rooms in the apartment, her grandmother's tiny kitchen—which Sarah swears they converted from a closet, as it was tiny and had no windows—felt like the brightest room in the house. There, her grandmother Carlita would prepare delicious meals without a counter every day for all the people who lived in the apartment (five to eight, at any given time) and regularly for extended family who often came to visit (fifteen to twenty people!). This dish had regular rotation in her kitchen.

One of the many things I love about Carlita's recipe is its simplicity. It doesn't use any of the premade spice or herb blends so many Caribbean recipes rely on now. Whether it was because of her environment or because of how she grew up, Mamá Carlita relied on simple ingredients combined just right.

In a large, deep skillet, heat the olive oil over medium heat. Add the okra and cook, stirring often, until it starts to brown, 8 to 10 minutes. Add the onion and garlic and cook until the onion begins to soften, about 3 minutes. Add the bell peppers and diced tomatoes and stir to combine, then add the tomato sauce, vinegar, and achiote (if using). Bring everything to a simmer, then add ½ cup of the water, salt and freshly ground pepper to taste. Cook for about 20 minutes more, until the veggies are soft and the tomatoes are breaking down. Add up to ½ cup more water if it starts to dry out. You're looking for something like a stew—thick, not soupy.

Remove from the heat and stir in the cilantro. Serve over rice. Leftovers will keep in an airtight container in the fridge for up to 2 days.

TONMTONM AK KALALOU

MASHED BREADFRUIT WITH OKRA ○ HAITI

KALALOU

1 cup djon djon
   mushrooms
   (optional)
1 to 1½ pounds bone-in
   chicken thighs,
   skin removed,
   cut into 3 pieces
   (see page 10)
¼ cup Epis (page 21)
5 garlic cloves, minced
1 yellow onion, diced
2 tablespoons fresh
   thyme leaves
1 teaspoon kosher salt
½ teaspoon
   freshly ground
   black pepper
¼ cup fresh parsley
   leaves, chopped
5 whole cloves
5 or 6 blue crabs,
   cleaned, back shells
   and gills removed
   (see page 182)
1 pound okra, halved
2 cups water

TONMTONM

1 medium breadfruit
1 tablespoon
   kosher salt

SERVES 8 TO 10

I have always assumed that *tonmtonm* was a Haitian Krèyol word that likely derived from one of the Central or West African languages. The preparation of tonmtonm is certainly from the continent, as pounding provisions such as breadfruit until their texture transforms is inherently African. However, if you've ever heard the dish being made, you may start to wonder if the name actually comes from the sound of the big pilon pounding the fruit, *tom tom tom*. In Trinidad, they will mash plantain or green fig banana and call that *tumtum*.

In Haiti, the word *kalalou* refers both to the okra pod itself and to this saucy stew that always accompanies tonmtonm. The dish is native to the westernmost tip of Haiti's southern peninsula, which includes the Grand'Anse and Sud Departments. Traditionally, you are meant to eat this with your fingers, first picking up the breadfruit, then dipping it in the okra, and finally letting it all slide down your throat (I have been reprimanded for chewing it). Different cooks use different kinds of meat in it, often smoked bits or pieces with bone, and most will add crab. Atibon takes this dish very seriously, and spoke to both his *matant* (auntie) Madam Zeno from Les Cayes and his "cousin" Elanie Gervil from Jérémie to get advice on how to make it. He watched me like a hawk the first time I did it. The djon djon mushrooms are optional, but if you can find them, I highly recommend trying them. They are like funkier porcini mushrooms and really add a lot of flair to a dish.

This dish is always made with the pounded breadfruit, but if you cannot find breadfruit, you could use the same method to pound green plantains or green bananas. You could also simply serve the kalalou with boiled provisions. This is one of those dishes for special occasions, often made for a large group to sit and talk around. It takes a fair amount of time and a lot of pots. But it's so, so good.

Make the kalalou: If using djon djon, place them in a small saucepan with 1½ cups water and set aside to soak for 2 hours, then bring to a simmer over low heat for 10 minutes (or skip the soaking step and simmer the djon djon in the water over low heat, undisturbed, for 30 minutes). Let cool slightly, then strain the cooking liquid through a fine-mesh strainer into a bowl, pressing firmly on the mushrooms to get out all the water; discard the mushrooms. You should have a full cup of liquid; if not, add water until you have 1 cup. Set aside.

In a Dutch oven or other heavy-bottomed pot large enough to fit the crabs with room to stir, place the chicken, epis, garlic, onion, thyme, salt, pepper, parsley, and cloves. Cover and cook over medium-low heat for about 30 minutes, until the chicken is mostly cooked through and many juices have collected. Add the crabs, giving them a good stir. Cover once more and let the crabs steam for 10 minutes, until they release some of their juices.

RECIPE CONTINUES

Meanwhile, in a separate medium pot, combine the okra and the water. Bring to a boil over medium-high heat and cook until the okra is soft, about 15 minutes. Let cool slightly, then add 1 cup of water, or the reserved djon djon water, if using. Using an immersion blender, blend the okra with the liquid (or carefully transfer them to a standing blender, in batches if necessary) until the okra is mostly smooth and its fibers have been mostly cut up. Add this to the pot with the chicken and crab, cover, and simmer on low for 30 minutes, until the chicken is falling off the bone.

Meanwhile, make your tonmtonm: Cut a small slice off the top of the breadfruit so it sits flat on your cutting board. Quarter the breadfruit, then, using a sharp paring knife, cut off the peel. Next, cut out the core of the breadfruit (the part that looks like rays of light emanating out of the middle). Put the quarters in a large pot and add

water to cover by 1 inch. Add the salt and cook over medium-high heat until the breadfruit is totally tender, 20 to 25 minutes. Drain.

Place some of the breadfruit in a large pilon and mash it (if your pilon isn't large enough to fit the breadfruit, place it in a large, sturdy bowl and mash it with a pestle). You really need to mash it hard, until the texture starts to take on a gummy sort of look. Keep adding pieces as you go. This could take 10 to 15 minutes.

To serve, spoon a mound of the breadfruit onto each plate and surround it with a lake of kalalou, making sure everyone gets some crab and chicken. If you choose to eat this with a fork, I will not judge you. The tonmtonm is best eaten immediately, but the kalalou will keep in an airtight container in the fridge for up to 3 days.

BREADFRUIT

This import to the Caribbean has possibly one of the most infamous stories of all the ingredients in this book. Originating in New Guinea and the Philippines, breadfruit was a key player in the famous mutiny on the *Bounty*.

In 1787, Captain William Bligh and his crew set off from England on a journey to Tahiti. They were tasked by King George III to find a long spoken-of tree that provided "bread" year-round to bring back to the Caribbean, in response to desiccated crops and a need to feed the enslaved. They were to bring the plants back to propagate in the Caribbean. A variety of factors led to the mutiny, not least of all Bligh's attitude, but whatever the reason, no one was interested in babysitting the plants that Bligh doted on all the way back to England. As a result, in 1789, disaffected crewmen tossed more than one thousand breadfruit plants overboard and set Bligh and his loyalists adrift on open waters. Bligh survived, and despite the rocky first try, his second voyage to Tahiti two years later was successful. In 1793, he brought breadfruit plants to Jamaica, which were then spread throughout the Caribbean.

The fruit gets its name from its texture when cooked, which is like baked bread, and its mild, potato-like taste. In Polynesia, the breadfruit tree is revered for its ability to produce high yields of fruit, which are rich in vitamin C and high in calories, all year long. It is, in fact, one of the highest-yielding food plants on earth, with one tree producing two hundred or more fruits per season, all while requiring little care. It's no wonder some locals in Polynesia call it "the Tree of Life."

Though the plant grew successfully in the Caribbean, the enslaved initially refused to eat this fruit that was so unfamiliar to them. Today it is consumed on every island in the Caribbean and appreciated for its abundance and nutritive value. It is most often simply prepared—boiled, roasted, or fried—and served as a side for any number of meat or vegetable dishes. It may also be pounded out, as it is in the recipe for Tonmtonm ak Kalalou (page 145), or added to soups and stews, such as Grenada's Oil Down (page 98).

CHOP UP

VEGETABLE MASH ○ ANTIGUA

1 tablespoon extra-
  virgin olive oil
1 small yellow onion,
  diced
4 garlic cloves, minced
2 teaspoons Green
  Seasoning,
  homemade
  (page 22) or
  store-bought
  (optional)
1 eggplant (about
  1 pound), peeled
  and cut into
  1-inch cubes
½ teaspoon kosher salt
Freshly ground
  black pepper
1½ cups water
½ pound okra, cut into
  1-inch pieces
1 bunch mature
  spinach, chopped

SERVES 4 TO 6

This dish is exactly what it sounds like: chopped-up vegetables. But what the name doesn't tell you is that those chopped veggies get cooked until they're soft enough to mash. The resulting dish may not be visually appealing—mushy cooked eggplant and okra are not, perhaps, the sexiest of things—but it's a wonderful, simple dish that lets the flavors of the vegetables shine through. Some people don't even season it with anything but a bit of salt and simply boil the vegetables and mash. I can't do anything in my life without a little onion and garlic, and there's certainly room for more experimentation on that front. I've only ever encountered this preparation in Antiguan cuisine, though surely some version of it must exist elsewhere in the Caribbean.

In a large Dutch oven or other heavy-bottomed pot, heat the olive oil over medium heat. Add the onion and garlic and sauté until they begin to brown, 5 to 8 minutes. Stir in the green seasoning (if using) and cook for another minute or so, until it's becoming fragrant.

Add the eggplant, salt, and pepper to taste, give it a good stir to coat, and cook until the eggplant is getting some color, 5 to 8 minutes. Add the water, reduce the heat to low, cover, and simmer for 15 to 20 minutes, until the eggplant begins to soften. Add the okra, cover, and cook for 10 to 15 minutes more, until the okra is soft and the eggplant is breaking down. Mix in the spinach and cook, uncovered, for 5 minutes.

Using a potato masher, a heavy wooden spoon, or a fork if you have to, mash the vegetables until they're mostly blended, but leave some chunks for texture. This will keep overnight in an airtight container in the fridge but does get a little gooier as time goes on.

PLANTAINS

MUSA × PARADISIACA

Other names: BANNANN, PLÁTANOS

PLANTAINS, THE STARCHIER COUSIN of the common banana (known in much of the Caribbean as "fig banana"), are the tenth most important staple food in the world. Thought to have originated in Southeast Asia, the plantain made its way to Africa a few thousand years ago. It is thought that they were brought to the Caribbean from New Guinea by the Portuguese, who were known for traveling the entire world, transporting food everywhere. It would have been immediately embraced by enslaved Africans, who had been eating plantains on their home continent for thousands of years.

Plantains can be eaten in every stage of ripeness. When they're green, they are very starchy and take gloriously to savory preparations like Fried Green Plantains (page 168). They are also the plantain of choice for the Haitian porridge Labouyi Bannann (page 155). As they ripen, they become sweet, which is perfect for Tortilla de Plátano Maduro (page 157), and by the time they're completely black on the outside, they're basically like candy on the inside, which is exactly what you want for something like the Plantain Tarte Tatin on page 170.

For some reason, I grew up only ever eating boiled, usually ripe plantains and felt extremely ambivalent toward them. They'd be served with other provisions and were typically there to soak up the savory juices from another dish, like stewed kingfish or callaloo. I didn't hate on them and would always dutifully eat them, but I just never got *excited* about them. As an adult, I came to New York, and my good friend Geko Jones made me tostones. My world turned upside down. I had no idea this seemingly benign fruit could be so . . . sexy. Then he took me to try mofongo, and I nearly died. That was a long, long time ago, and since then, I have learned to embrace this fruit and its ever-changing persona. There are probably hundreds of traditional plantain recipes across the islands, and there just wasn't room for them all here. Someone could (and should!) write a whole book just about them. Instead, I've chosen to highlight some of my favorites.

Despite the fact that they have little black seeds on the inside (which some cooks go wild trying to remove), plantains are actually propagated via rhizomes. Though we often refer to plantains as growing on trees, the plant is actually a giant herb. A large part of their popularity stems from the ease with which they grow; they're practically weeds. They take very little work to plant relative to other crops and are massively productive. Post-slavery, the upper class felt that the plantain prevented the working classes from working harder to diversify and expand commercial agriculture because the plants were just so easy to grow. I'd venture to suggest that the working classes were just excited to grow something that might keep them from starving.

Though plantains aren't a root vegetable, they are always included in the provisions or viandas category, as they were given to the enslaved to grow on their own plots as a way to feed their families and were one of the foods that sustained life. The many ways they can be prepared is a testament to the women of the Caribbean, who exercised all their creativity in the kitchen to transform this unassuming cousin of the banana into something new and delicious every day.

Plantains have taken on many meanings around the Caribbean. On one hand, there are negative connotations; the concept that they encourage laziness and stupidity in the poor still lurks. On the flip side, they are a chosen symbol of the common people; for instance, they're often used in protests in the Dominican Republic as a sign of resistance and power to the people. Young people there today will hold up plantains to signal they are calling reinforcements to a protest. (The police, apparently, have tried to use it in the same way, possibly to mock the protesters, but were simply laughed at.) The plantain is an intrinsic part of our heritage, and when I see one, I know my people aren't far away.

NUTRITION: Plantains are high in fiber and contain more potassium than bananas. Potassium, which is good for high blood pressure, was the only thing that kept me from having weird leg cramps when I was pregnant. They also contain vitamins A, B6, C, and K and the minerals magnesium, copper, and iron. Plantains are considered a "resistant starch," which is what they call carbs that don't easily or quickly break down in the small intestine. Instead, they move on to the large intestine, where they take their sweet time to break down, fermenting and feeding the good gut bacteria. Because of this, they don't cause a spike in blood sugar the way refined sugars can. While plantains contain resistant starch at all stages of ripeness, green plantains in particular have less sugar and more resistant starch, which is thought to be good for people with diabetes.

HOW TO CHOOSE: If you're buying green plantains, look for ones with smooth, unblemished bright green skin. Some marks are no big deal, but if the plantain has a lot of them, it's been roughed up and has probably seen a lot of things. If I want ripe plantains, I prefer to buy green ones and let them ripen. The green ones are often cheaper, and it brings me a strange satisfaction to watch the ripening process with my own two eyes. If you're looking to use them when they're sweet, you want to wait until they've got at least some brown and black on them. And if you really want to go hard, let those things go black—like, all the way black. They will reward you with candylike sweetness. The taste is similar to a very ripe banana, but with more backbone.

HOW TO STORE: Plantains can be kept on the counter until you're ready to use them. If you need green plantains but can't cook them right away, putting them in the fridge will help slow the ripening process.

HOW TO PREPARE: Trim off both ends. Using a sharp paring knife, make a slit lengthwise down the plantain. If it is ripe, the skin will peel off almost as easily as a banana's. If it is green, make another slit on the other side. Work either the knife or your finger between the peel and the flesh, and pull up. The thick skin will separate, and once you've gotten it started, the rest will come off quite easily. As the fruit oxidizes, the peel might stain your fingers black, but for me it comes off easily with soap and water.

LABOUYI BANNANN

PLANTAIN PORRIDGE ○ HAITI

3 cups water
½ cup evaporated milk
½ cup Coconut
    Milk, homemade
    (page 97) or
    store-bought
2 cinnamon sticks
1 star anise pod
1 (1-inch) piece lime
    zest
1 large green plantain
    (about 10 ounces)
¼ cup packed
    brown sugar, plus
    more as needed
1 teaspoon vanilla
    extract
¼ teaspoon kosher salt

SERVES 2 TO 4

Porridge in the Caribbean is a legacy of both our African ancestors and the lower-income European colonists who brought the dish over. In the Western world, porridge of every kind is often portrayed as a food of the poor, something people would rather not eat. In African society, however, it's seen for what it is: a healthful food that is especially good for small children. I don't want to toot my own horn, but even though Atibon (who is Haitian) and I both make this Haitian dish, Desalin will only get excited if I'm making my version. I think that's because I use some evaporated milk. While pure coconut milk is surely how this dish originated, some dairy really helps round it out and brings the green plantain to the land of the sweet. The old-school way to make this is to peel the plantain with a knife, leaving behind some of the skin's fibers to add to the overall heartiness of the dish. This recipe is easily doubled; if you choose to do so, there's no need to add extra cinnamon or star anise. The quantities here will still do a good job of infusing the milks.

In a medium saucepan, combine 2 cups of the water, both milks, the cinnamon sticks, star anise, and lime zest and bring to a simmer over medium heat. This will take 10 to 12 minutes, which gives the spices a chance to infuse the liquid with flavor.

Meanwhile, peel the plantain and roughly cut into 1-inch slices (see page 154). Transfer the pieces to a blender, add the remaining 1 cup water, and blend until it's a smooth-ish paste. It will be somewhat grainy.

When the liquid reaches a simmer, add the plantain paste, along with the brown sugar, vanilla, and salt. Reduce the heat to medium-low and simmer, uncovered, for about 20 minutes, stirring occasionally to keep anything from sticking to the bottom.

Remove the pot from the heat, fish out the cinnamon, star anise, and lime zest and discard. Taste for sweetness before serving and add more sugar to taste. Leftovers can be stored in an airtight container in the fridge for up to 3 days; reheat with a small amount of coconut milk to loosen it up before serving.

TORTILLA DE PLÁTANO MADURO

SWEET PLANTAIN OMELET ○ CUBA

1 recipe Fried Sweet
  Plantains (page 166),
  using 2 plantains
6 eggs
1 small garlic clove,
  minced
¼ teaspoon kosher salt
Freshly ground
  black pepper

SERVES 4 TO 6

I can imagine that whoever was originally responsible for this dish was likely looking for a way to jazz up their eggs or trying to find another way to use plantains. This may not be one of Cuba's famed recipes, and I've seen it on a menu in a restaurant exactly once (at Rincon Criollo in Queens, and they killed it!), but you'll find an endless number of videos about it on YouTube, which is, let's face it, where all the best Caribbean cooking videos are. This dish is so delicious, but so easy to make. Aside from flipping the eggs, there isn't much here anyone can't do. I prefer to use less ripe plantains (the ones that are yellow with a few brown spots), but you can try it with whatever stage of yellow plantain you like or have on hand. Use a nonstick skillet if you have one, or bump up the amount of oil if you don't, leaving a bit more oil than a tablespoon when pouring out the oil after cooking the fried sweet plantains. Lastly, garlic is not a traditional ingredient in this dish but makes a nice counter to the sweet plantains and adds another dimension to the flavor.

Prepare the plantains as directed on page 166. While they cook, beat the eggs, garlic, salt, and pepper to taste in a medium bowl and set aside.

Pour out most of the oil from making the plantains, leaving a glossy film in the pan, about 1 tablespoon. Set the pan over medium heat. Arrange the maduros in the pan in whatever pattern you like, then pour the eggs over them, ensuring they're evenly spread over and around the plantains. With a spatula, lift the edge of the eggs, which will begin to solidify immediately, and tilt the pan to allow raw egg to run underneath, continuing all around the pan until the top of the eggs starts to firm up. Cover the pan, reduce the heat to low, and cook for about 5 minutes, until the eggs are set.

Here's where your nonstick pan and some sturdy oven mitts will really help you out. Slide the tortilla onto a large plate, preferably larger than your pan (nudge it with the spatula if it gives you trouble), then place the pan over the plate. Holding the plate in place firmly with one hand and the bottom of the pan with the other (protected with the oven mitt!), flip over the whole operation so the tortilla is now upside down in the pan. This is like removing a Band-Aid—the quicker you do it, the better your success. If for some reason the tortilla tries to escape, remain calm. You can probably slide it back into the pan safely.

Cook on the second side, uncovered, for about 2 minutes, until it's firm and just getting a bit of brown. Slide it out onto a cutting board or plate and cut it into wedges for serving.

MANGÚ

MASHED GREEN PLANTAINS WITH QUICK-PICKLED ONIONS
○ DOMINICAN REPUBLIC

Kosher salt
3 green plantains,
    peeled and cut
    into 4 pieces each
    (see page 154)
3 tablespoons extra-
    virgin olive oil
½ red onion, thinly
    sliced
1 tablespoon sherry
    vinegar
3 tablespoons unsalted
    butter at room
    temperature
1 to 3 tablespoons
    cold water

SERVES 4 TO 6

Mangú dates back to the 1500s, when plantains first showed up on the islands. The African roots of this dish are clear. It's another example of West African fufu showing up in the Caribbean, as the key to this dish is mashing or pounding the plantain until it changes texture. The subject of African origins can be a touchy one in Dominican culture and has, throughout the history of the island, given rise to some truly brutal xenophobic and racist acts. Haitians living in the Dominican Republic are often the targets of these acts, along with anyone else who presents what are thought of as African features. Some examples include dictator Rafael Trujillo's Parsley Massacre in 1937, and the more recent legal and administrative actions of President Luis Abinader and his government that aim to expel people of Haitian descent from the country, regardless of their residency status, and specifically target the Black population, even if they have no Haitian background.

While this recipe looks simple, there is a real skill to getting the plantain to a smooth texture. If you find it's still looking dry, you can keep adding more water, butter, or olive oil as you mash, but one of the vital tricks is using a bit of cold water at the end. Traditionally served with salami frito, queso frito, and huevos fritos—Los Tres Golpes—Mangú is delicious with anything saucy, but I particularly love it with the Sòs Ti-Malice with Shrimp (page 225), pairing dishes from each side of the island as a symbol of unity. If you ever want to impress a person from the Dominican Republic, tell them you made mangú.

Bring a large pot of water to a boil over high heat. Add 2 tablespoons salt and the plantain pieces, and cook for 25 to 35 minutes, until the plantains are very tender, very yellow, and starting to fall apart when you try to stab one with a fork.

Meanwhile, in a small skillet, heat the olive oil over medium heat. Add the onion and sauté until it's just beginning to soften but still retains some crunch, about 3 minutes. Turn off the heat and carefully stir in the vinegar to avoid splatters from the hot oil. Set aside.

Using tongs or a slotted spoon, transfer the plantains to a large, sturdy bowl, reserving the cooking water. Start mashing them immediately with a fork or potato masher. Add 1 teaspoon salt, half the butter, and ¼ cup of the reserved cooking water and mash until they are incorporated. Mash in the rest of the butter, then add up to another ¼ cup of cooking water, until it's looking relatively smooth. Add the cold water 1 tablespoon at a time, and continue to mash until the plantains are positively creamy.

Scrape the onions and every bit of oil and vinegar you can from the pan on top of the plantains and serve immediately. The mangú will harden quickly, so it's best to eat it as soon as possible.

MOFONGO

FRIED MASHED PLANTAINS
WITH CHICHARRÓNES ○ PUERTO RICO

Neutral oil, for frying
3 green plantains,
    peeled and cut
    into 2-inch pieces
    (see page 154)
4 garlic cloves, peeled
    (see Note)
1 teaspoon kosher salt
1 cup chicharrónes
    (optional)
3 to 4 tablespoons
    extra-virgin olive oil
3 to 4 tablespoons
    chicken stock or
    water

SERVES 4 TO 6

*Note: If you are omitting
the chicharrónes, add
one more clove of garlic.*

Mofongo is another ode to Africa, sort of like Mangú 2.0. The word may be from the Angolan term *mfwenge-mfwenge*, which means a great amount of anything at all, or the word *mfwongo*, which means plate or flat surface, possibly referring to the act of mashing it. My first ever mofongo was eaten with the same person who made me my first tostones, Geko Jones, in Bushwick, circa 2003. He told me it would change my life and I said he was being a ridiculous Aries. But he was right. The *best* mofongo I ever had was out in Rincón, on the west coast of Puerto Rico. It was stuffed with freshly fried chicharrónes and doused in a garlic sauce. People will stuff or top mofongo with all kinds of things, and all of them are delicious. It's also pretty great on its own, but it does do well with something saucy or soupy to hydrate it a bit. I love it served with shrimp, like the Sòs Ti-Malice with Shrimp on page 225.

Mofongo can be a bit tricky to get in the perfect place between too dry and too wet. One key is to make sure you're not overcooking the plantains. They shouldn't be deeply golden and crispy like Fried Green Plantains (page 168), but just have a slight coloring. Overcooking them will result in a dry mofongo no matter what else you do. Nuyorican chef and food historian César Pérez says one way to avoid this is to not cut the plantains too small. Adding enough liquid helps, too. In Illyanna Maisonet's *Diasporican*, she suggests adding one ripe plantain in place of a green one, as the ripe fruits have a higher water content to minimize the amount of water you'll need while mashing. The next secret is the mashing itself. A fork is not going to cut it. Traditionally it would be done in a large pilon, the kind that stands on the floor. This is one of Desalin's favorite activities. However, I'm aware not everyone has one of these in their home. If you have a decent sized one, you can mash them a few at a time, which can get tedious, but the kind of pressure you get in the pilon is really the best. If your mortar is too small, you can try using just the pestle and a large bowl. If you don't have any of these, try a heavy-bottomed cup, or another heavy object you don't mind getting plantain all over. Keep in mind that if it's wide rather than narrow like a pestle, you will have to use a bit more force. My last note is that this dish is *all* about garlic. You will repel vampires for several hours after eating this.

In a wok or deep skillet, heat 2 inches of neutral oil over medium-high heat until it reaches 350°F. If you don't have a thermometer, you'll know the oil is ready if a piece of plantain touches the oil and bubbles all around.

Add the plantain pieces to the hot oil and fry until they are *just* beginning to brown, 4 to 5 minutes on each side.

Meanwhile, use a pilon to mash the garlic and salt into a paste. (Alternatively, use the back of a knife

to mash them together on a cutting board.) Set aside.

Using tongs, transfer the fried plantains to paper towel–lined plates. When you have finished frying all the plantains, start mashing them in your pilon or bowl, working with 5 or 6 rounds at a time, until they're mostly, but not completely, smooth. As you go, alternate adding the chicharrónes (if using), garlic, the olive oil, and stock, 1 tablespoon at a time, making sure it's all well incorporated before adding more. If they keep falling apart, add more olive oil and stock. You want them to stick together on their own, but not be wet. This process is going to take a while, so be patient. You may be mashing for 10 to 15 minutes.

When it's all smashed, grease a few small bowls (or one bigger bowl) with a little bit of olive oil, then mold the plantains into them, using your hands to really pat it down. Flip the bowl(s) over on whatever plate you're using for serving and let the plantains slide out. Mofongo is best eaten immediately.

PASTELÓN

PLANTAIN "CASSEROLE" ○ DOMINICAN REPUBLIC

CARNE MOLIDA

1 pound ground beef
1 small onion, diced
6 garlic cloves, minced
1 teaspoon dried
   oregano
2 teaspoons
   kosher salt
1 tablespoon extra-
   virgin olive oil
½ Scotch bonnet
   pepper, minced
   (optional)
¼ cup Dominican
   Sazón (page 23)
   or store-bought
   tomato sofrito
3 tablespoons tomato
   paste
¼ cup water, plus
   more if needed

4 tablespoons (½ stick)
   unsalted butter at
   room temperature,
   plus more for
   greasing the pan
4 ripe plantains,
   peeled and cut in
   half (see page 154)
2 cups shredded
   cheddar cheese

SERVES 4 TO 6

I should start this off with a disclaimer: The terms *pastelón* and *piñon*, what they mean, and who (Dominican Republic or Puerto Rico) created the recipe are highly debated. There are some who say pastelón is actually the piñon recipe on page 165, and vice versa. There are some who say "This belongs to one country, and the other to another." What I can tell you is that both versions, more or less, are found in both countries, and whatever you call it, plantains (or plátanos as they are called in Cuba, the Dominican Republic, and Puerto Rico) are the star.

This pastelón recipe originates from my friend Sarah's Dominican grandmother and was cooked up for special occasions in huge batches in her tiny kitchen in Washington Heights. On paper, it may not make sense. Sweet plantains, savory minced meat, and cheese? But trust me, it works. Seasoned beef—called carne molida in the Dominican Republic or picadillo in Cuba and Puerto Rico, and also eaten with rice or put into empanadas—is layered between mashed sweet plantain and cheese. Traditional recipes call for olives, but as Sarah is cooking for two young olive haters, she sometimes omits them, which I do as well. She also replaces the tomato sauce with tomato paste in favor of its color, and I think it adds a deeper flavor. Sarah, like many others from the Dominican Republic, prefers to remove the little black seeds from the plantains to make it even smoother, but I am not that dedicated. I couldn't help but add a little Scotch bonnet pepper because, for me, meat is just not the same without it. This dish is a group activity; I've made and eaten this with Sarah's family, and everyone is always involved in some step of the process. I encourage you to share this experience with loved ones as well.

Make the carne molida: In a large bowl, season the ground beef with half the onion, half the garlic, the oregano, and 1 teaspoon of the salt, mixing it all together with a fork. Set aside.

In a wide pan, heat the olive oil over medium heat. Add the remaining onion, remaining garlic, and the Scotch bonnet (if using) and sauté until the onion is translucent, 3 to 5 minutes. Stir in the sazón and cook for another minute. Raise the heat to medium-high and add the beef. Cook, continuously breaking up the meat with a wooden spoon, until well browned and completely

crumbled, 10 to 15 minutes. Add the tomato paste, water, and remaining 1 teaspoon salt. Stir to combine. Reduce the heat to low, cover, and cook for 10 minutes more, until the beef is infused with flavor and saucy. If it starts to look too dry, add a bit more water.

Preheat the oven to 350°F. Grease a 9 by 13-inch baking dish with butter.

Bring a large pot of water to a boil over high heat. Add the plantains and cook until they are very soft, 20 to 25 minutes. Using a slotted spoon or tongs, transfer the plantains to a medium

RECIPE CONTINUES

bowl. Reserve the plantain cooking water. In a separate large bowl, mash 2 plantains at a time with 2 tablespoons of the butter and 2 tablespoons of the reserved plantain water. Use whatever utensil you have for this; I find a fork works fine. Your plantains should be quite smooth, but there's no need to remove every last lump. If they look too crumbly, add more water 1 tablespoon at a time until they are smooth. In the same bowl, repeat with the remaining 2 plantains, 2 tablespoons butter, and 2 tablespoons of the plantain water.

Evenly spread half the mashed plantains over the bottom of the prepared baking dish. Spread all the carne molida over the plantains, cover with half the cheese, then add the remaining plantains, smoothing them out with a spatula. Cover with the remaining cheese.

Bake until the cheese starts to brown, about 40 minutes. Remove from the oven and let rest for at least 10 minutes before serving.

PIÑON

PLANTAIN "CASSEROLE" ○ PUERTO RICO

3 ripe plantains,
    peeled (see
    page 154)

PICADILLO

1 tablespoon extra-
    virgin olive oil, plus
    more for greasing
1 onion, diced
6 garlic cloves, minced
¼ cup Recaíto
    (page 22)
½ green bell pepper,
    diced
1 pound ground beef
½ cup tomato sauce
¼ cup olives, pitted
    and roughly
    chopped
¼ cup raisins (optional)
Kosher salt

½ pound green beans,
    blanched
2 cups shredded
    cheddar cheese
2 eggs, beaten

SERVES 4 TO 6

As mentioned in the pastelón recipe on page 163, pastelón and piñon are a highly debated topic in Puerto Rico and the Dominican Republic. Some say the names are interchangeable, some say otherwise. If I had to try to break it down in simple terms, I would say in the Dominican Republic, pastelón usually appears as the recipe on page 163, and in Puerto Rico what is called piñon most often refers to this recipe (but that is also up for debate!). Traditionally, the plantains, or plátanos, would be fried, and listen, it's damn delicious that way. However, between the meat and cheese and the egg, it's just too much for me and my heart, and not frying really doesn't make the texture of the final dish suffer. Should you want to try it the traditional way, fry each plantain slice until light golden brown and drain on paper towels before layering them in the dish. The biggest difference between the picadillo and Dominican carne molida is the raisins. They probably sound completely bizarre here, but they add a pop of sweetness that's both subtle and unexpected and marries so beautifully with the whole scene. The other thing that makes this different from pastelón are the green beans, which some say are optional and others fiercely counter that they are *not*. I think if you're going for this recipe, you should go all in. This is a maximalist, decadent dish that's great for a special occasion, but it also freezes very well, perhaps better than pastelón, as the plantains aren't mashed.

Cut the plantains in half crosswise, then slice them lengthwise into pieces about ½ inch thick. In a large pot, pour a couple inches of water and place a rack or steamer basket inside. Add the plantains, cover, and steam over medium-high heat until they are tender but not falling apart, 10 to 15 minutes. Set aside.

Make the picadillo: In a large skillet, heat the olive oil over medium heat. Add the onion and garlic and cook until they begin to brown, 5 to 8 minutes. Add the recaíto and cook for 2 to 3 minutes, until it is very fragrant, then add the bell pepper, cooking for a few more minutes until it begins to soften. Add the ground beef and cook, using a wooden spoon to break up the meat, until all the meat is browned,

about 10 minutes. Add the tomato sauce, olives, raisins (if using), and salt to taste, then reduce the heat to low. Simmer until all the flavors have blended, 15 to 20 minutes.

Preheat the oven to 350°F. Grease a 9 by 13-inch baking dish with olive oil.

Spread half the picadillo evenly over the bottom of the dish. Layer on half the green beans, a third of the cheese, and half of the plantain slices. Repeat, ending with a layer of cheese on top. Pour the eggs carefully over everything, getting them into any cracks or crevices. Bake until the cheese starts to brown, about 40 minutes. Remove from the oven and let rest for at least 10 minutes before slicing and serving.

FRIED SWEET PLANTAINS

ACROSS THE CARIBBEAN

Neutral oil, for frying
2 to 4 ripe plantains,
    peeled and cut into
    ½-inch-thick slices
    on the diagonal
    (see page 154)
Kosher salt (optional)

SERVES 4 TO 6

Fried sweet plantains, called maduros in Cuba, the Dominican Republic, and Puerto Rico, are little jewels of wonder: deeply colored and crisp on the outside, sweet and soft on the inside. The most coveted maduros are made from the ripest, blackest plantains, which are of course the sweetest. However, as a green plantain lover, I do prefer the ones that are just solidly ripe—yellow skins with blotches of black—which retain a bit of their savory personality. Because the plantains are ripe and not as starchy, maduros can be pan-fried rather than deep-fried to make them a less fussy affair. They can be eaten as is, with a sprinkling of salt, or used in other recipes such as the Tortilla de Plátano Maduro (page 157). They can even be sprinkled with sugar for a sweet snack. There isn't a nation in the Caribbean or, likely, in all the tropics that doesn't fry plantains in every state of ripeness.

In a wide skillet, heat about ⅛ inch of oil over medium-high heat until it shimmers. Carefully add the plantain slices, being sure not to crowd the pan (cook them in batches, if necessary). Fry each plantain until golden brown, about 3 minutes per side. If they're browning too fast, reduce the heat to medium and wait a moment before adding more. Using a slotted spoon or tongs, transfer the fried plantains to a paper towel–lined plate to drain. Sprinkle with salt, if desired. Don't expect them to last long.

FRIED GREEN PLANTAINS

ACROSS THE CARIBBEAN

2 cups water
1 garlic clove, smashed
   and peeled
Kosher salt
Neutral oil, for frying
2 to 4 green plantains,
   trimmed, peeled,
   and cut into
   1-inch rounds
   (see page 154)

SERVES 4 TO 6

I could probably wax poetic about twice-fried plantains—called bannann peze in Haiti, pressed plantains in Jamaica, or tostones in Cuba, the Dominican Republic, and Puerto Rico—for pages in this book. I grew up only eating boiled ripe plantain, usually served with something saucy, like stewed king fish or callaloo (I mention my feelings on that on page 152), or sometimes buljol. And as I've said, that was fine but nothing special. I spent all my younger years with very neutral feelings toward plantains, until I moved to New York, and one of my very first friends, Geko Jones, half Puerto Rican, half Colombian, made me tostones for the very first time. I watched with interest while he went through the whole involved process. (I was particularly intrigued by the container of water with a clove of garlic in it. What was *that* for!?) I had my first one and was transported. If you told me I could only ever have one fried food ever again, this would be it. The crispy crunch, the starchy flavor, the way it's the perfect vehicle for dipping or topping . . . I love tostones for this and so much more. And then I came to find out that *everyone* who eats plantains fries them like this. In every Caribbean nation and territory, people have been frying their green plantains. Why was my family holding out on me? What did I do to deserve this? But no matter—over twenty years ago this wrong was righted, and I am forever indebted to Geko for bringing me into the light. There is very little, if any, variation on how this is done from island to island. If you plan to fry plantains often—and you should be—it's worth investing in a tostonera, a simple device with two flat surfaces, usually wood, connected by a hinge, that allows you to easily smash each piece of plantain. However, in a pinch, using a heavy-bottomed glass or cup on a sturdy flat surface like your cutting board will do just as well.

These pieces of fried gold are an operation. They aren't *hard* per se, but it's a long process that's almost entirely active. The end result is worth it. I am a french fry lover, but I'd throw french fries in a river forever for fried plantain. You're likely to have these with Mayoketchup (page 119) in Puerto Rico, topped with Pikliz (page 214) in Haiti, or dipped in Mojo Sauce (page 76) in Cuba. They're also great as a side to Buljol (page 206), Snapper Escovitch-ish (page 228), or Jerk Chicken (page 222). The recipe is easy to scale up if you're serving a crowd (or down, if you're craving a snack) by simply using more or less plantains.

Fill a small bowl or other small container with the water and add the smashed garlic. Salt the water until it tastes like the ocean. Set aside.

In a wok or deep skillet, heat 2 inches of oil over medium to medium-high heat until it reaches 350°F. If you don't have a thermometer, you'll know it's hot enough if you drop in a piece of plantain and the oil bubbles all around it.

Working in batches, fry the plantain rounds until they only just begin to brown, 3 to 4 minutes per side. When they're ready, they should sound sort of hollow if you tap on them. If they're browning too fast, reduce the heat a bit and wait a few minutes before adding more. Using tongs or a slotted spoon, transfer the plantains to a plate or tray. Smash each round using a tostonera or by placing them on a flat surface (like a cutting board) and pressing down on them with the bottom of a heavy cup. The thickness is up to you. The thinner they are, the crispier they will be.

Dip each smashed plantain into the salted water and immediately return it to the skillet, adding as many as will fit in the pan at a time. Be careful—they will sputter! A wok is especially useful here as you can slide them down the side, rather than splash in from above. Fry the smashed plantains for 3 to 4 minutes on each side, until deep golden. Using tongs or a slotted spoon, transfer the plantains to a paper towel–lined tray to drain. Season with salt. Repeat the whole process until all the plantains are cooked. The fried plantains stay enjoyable a little longer than most other fried things, but are still best eaten right away.

PLANTAIN TARTE TATIN

CRUST

1 cup all-purpose
 flour, plus more
 for dusting
1 tablespoon sugar
½ teaspoon kosher salt
6 tablespoons (¾ stick)
 cold unsalted
 butter, cut into
 cubes
3 to 5 tablespoons
 ice water

TOPPINGS

2 ripe plantains
6 tablespoons sugar
½ teaspoon ground
 cinnamon
¼ teaspoon freshly
 grated nutmeg
¼ teaspoon ground
 allspice
2 tablespoons unsalted
 butter
1 teaspoon vanilla
 extract
Coconut Whipped
 Cream (recipe
 follows), for serving
 (optional)

SERVES 6 TO 8

This is possibly the most tested recipe in this book, as I took forever to get it just right. My family was more than happy for my follies. One thing I learned is that the plantains must be par-cooked, or the end result will be a hard surface that's nearly impossible to cut and difficult to chew. Another thing is to let it cool only slightly before flipping, otherwise your plantains will most definitely get stuck to the bottom of your skillet. This dish came about because I saw someone from Martinique make a banana tarte tatin, and my brain immediately went to ripe plantains. They don't get enough love as a dessert in their fully ripe state, when they become almost like candy. If cutting the whole plantain down its length seems daunting, don't fret. Cut them in half crosswise before doing the long cut; they will still look cute, and they'll be a lot easier to work with. This crust recipe is courtesy of my longtime friend Lukas Volger and comes from his book *Start Simple*. I have struggled with pie and tart dough for the better part of a decade, but this one comes out just right every single time.

Make the crust: In a medium bowl, mix the flour, sugar, and salt. Add the butter cubes and work them into the flour with your fingers, squeezing and squishing the cubes until you have a pebbly mixture with pieces of butter that range in size from a lentil to a peanut. With a fork, mix in the ice water 1 tablespoon at a time, until the mixture is moistened just enough to come together with some shaggy flour bits left behind. Gather the dough into a rough ball and place it on a piece of plastic wrap. Using the plastic wrap, shape it into a disc about ½ inch thick, wrap it tightly, and refrigerate for at least 30 minutes or up to overnight. (The dough can also be frozen for up to 4 months; just thaw in the refrigerator overnight before using.)

Preheat the oven to 350°F.

Make the toppings: Peel the plantains. In a large pot, pour a couple inches of water and place a rack or steamer basket inside. Add the plantains, cover, and steam over medium-high heat until they are tender but not falling apart, about 10 to 15 minutes. Remove the plantains with tongs and set them aside until they're cool enough to handle. Cut each plantain lengthwise into ¼-inch-thick slices and set aside.

Remove the dough from the fridge and let it warm up just a bit so you're able to manipulate it, then flour a piece of parchment paper on a flat surface. Using a floured rolling pin, roll out the dough into a round that is only slightly bigger in circumference than a 9-inch skillet. Start from the middle and roll outward, rotating the dough as you go. Transfer the dough on the parchment paper back into the fridge while you finish the toppings.

In a small bowl, mix the sugar, cinnamon, nutmeg, and allspice until they're evenly distributed. Heat an ovenproof 9-inch skillet (like a cast-iron pan) over medium-high heat. Melt the butter with the spiced sugar until everything is a beautiful bronze color, bubbles all over, and starts to look smooth and cohesive, 5 to 8 minutes. Immediately remove from the heat, as the caramel will continue to darken, especially in a cast-iron skillet. Carefully arrange the plantain slices on top of the caramel as tightly as possible without overlapping them. Drizzle the vanilla over the plantains, then carefully but quickly arrange the dough over the top, tucking the edges between the skillet and the plantains. Cut four 1-inch slashes in the middle and bake for 35 to 40 minutes, until the crust begins to turn golden and the caramel is bubbling.

Remove from the oven and let cool for just about 5 minutes, then don your oven mitts. Place a large plate or serving platter on top of the skillet and, holding the plate in place, flip the whole thing over. The tarte tatin should come out cleanly and immediately, but if it doesn't, don't panic! If the entire thing is stuck, firmly shake the skillet and it should release. If a few rogue pieces of plantain get stuck, just slide them out with a spatula and get them back into place. Let cool before slicing. Serve alone or with coconut whipped cream. Leftovers keep well overnight in an airtight container at room temperature.

COCONUT WHIPPED CREAM

2 (13.5-ounce) cans coconut cream, chilled overnight in the fridge
½ cup powdered sugar

MAKES ABOUT 2 CUPS

It should first be stated that coconut whipped cream is never going to be the same as whipped cream made from heavy cream. Coconut whipped cream is heavier and, of course, tastes strongly of coconut. I love both these qualities, but they do mean coconut whipped cream won't always work in lieu of dairy. I have seen recipes that call for coconut milk, but I have never had success with anything but coconut cream.

Chill a large bowl, preferably metal, and the beaters from your hand mixer in the freezer for about 30 minutes. When they are cold, open the cans of coconut cream and scoop out only the solid white cream on top into a large bowl. Save the coconut water for another use, like replacing some of the water in your next pot of rice.

Add the powdered sugar and beat for 3 to 4 minutes. When the cream is smooth and seems airy, it's ready. It will hold up in the fridge, covered, for several hours, and is still pretty good the next day.

RICE

Other names: ARROZ, DIRI

RICE IS ARGUABLY ONE OF the most prevalent ingredients in Caribbean cooking, which is no surprise as it's the most common food staple in the world. You'd be hard-pressed to find a Caribbean household that doesn't center its meals around rice most days of the week, and in fact there are many nations where a meal is not considered complete without this well-loved grain. "But where is the rice?" is a question asked from the Bahamas down to Trinidad and everywhere in between. How did this little grain come to play such an important role in the food culture of these Caribbean nations? Asia is probably most famous for its rice production, but some may be surprised to know that it is believed the first rice cultivars came to the islands via the African people.

It is generally agreed that rice was first domesticated in China 13,500 to 8,200 years ago and that the most common type worldwide today is *Oryza sativa*, or Asian rice. However, another strain, *Oryza glaberrima*, was domesticated in Africa more than two thousand years before rice appeared in the Americas, and it now seems very likely that the *glaberrima* strain was introduced to the Caribbean via West Africa before any other variety showed up. Though there were many scholars in the West that argued this fact for years, it wasn't until the 1970s—over 400 years after the beginning of the Atlantic slave trade—that the rest of the Western world finally accepted it as truth. Due to inherent racial biases, Westerners originally refused to acknowledge that Africans were directly responsible for introducing many of the plants that now grow in the Caribbean today. The knowledge of rice cultivation at home in Africa allowed the grain to flourish at the hands of the enslaved in the Caribbean. The *glaberrima* strain was likely later replaced by Asian rice, which is what dominates the Caribbean today, with the introduction of indentured servants from South Asia in the nineteenth century. One exception to this seems to be Puerto Rico, where rice was brought by the Spanish before the slave trade began. However, with the communication Spain already had with the African continent, the rice they brought over is still likely to have been African rice.

Rice grows very easily and is a particularly appealing crop because you can get more than one harvest per plant. It also keeps very well; the bran layer protects the grain's kernel from the elements, keeping out fungus and preventing the breakdown of its enzymes. The caveat to all this is that rice needs a moist area to grow. The lowlands on a variety of islands were perfect for this, and for a long while, rice cultivation flourished. In many islands, two factors brought the demise of the crop: a steep increase in population and the expansion of other crops, specifically sugarcane, for export. The sugarcane took well to the lowlands where rice was grown, and the rice didn't grow well in higher elevations. The colonists could only see dollar signs, and therefore prioritized the more valuable sugarcane.

By the time rice production stopped in most Caribbean nations around the 1960s, rice had long been a staple in every household. As such, rice needed to be imported from other countries who grew it en masse and pretty much ended any remaining rice production in the Caribbean. One exception to this was Haiti, where they continued to produce rice for consumption up until the '90s. At that time, then-president Bill Clinton forced Haiti to drop tariffs on importing rice to the country so he could export rice grown by farmers in Arkansas. This effectively killed the last surviving rice industry in the Caribbean and brought ruin to many farmers. Rice in Haiti is now also imported and sold at high prices many people cannot afford.

NUTRITION*:* The average white rice we eat is, on the whole, less nutritious. Modern milling techniques remove and break down the bran, where all the good stuff is. Brown rice has the bran and germ intact and has a slew of nutritional benefits. White rice is a good source of carbohydrates, which has become a dirty word in modern, wealthy Western society, but they provide essential calories in many parts of the world. It also is a good source of folate. Because its excess fiber has been removed, white rice is easy to digest and is great for people with stomach issues. If you do experiment with brown rice (which I encourage you to do!), remember that it has a much longer cooking time. Should you ever want to try cooking brown rice in the Haitian style (such as in Diri ak Pwa, page 28, or Diri ak Djon Djon, page 185), add up to an extra cup of water to buffer the longer cooking time it needs, even while boiling with the lid off. I once brought diri ak pwa made with brown rice to the beach and my Haitian friend thought I bought it from a Haitian restaurant!

HOW TO CHOOSE: There are far too many types of rice to list here. I will stick to the types used most in the Caribbean, but I encourage you to experiment and use the cultivars you like best. At home I most often cook with brown basmati rice, as that's what my mother preferred, but you do you! Basmati rice is most often used in places with a South Indian population. It is long-grained and fragrant, and is great when you're looking for a rice whose grains remain separate and mostly intact after cooking. I use it for most of my rice cooking unless I need something specifically short. Jasmine rice is another long-grain variety, and you will often find it used in Haitian cooking. It's not quite as long as basmati but has the same effect. In Puerto Rico, the rice of choice is usually medium- or short-grain. If a recipe calls for medium, you can get away with long, but if it calls for short, you have to comply, as those varieties are much starchier, usually an important element of the dish. I like to use sushi rice when recipes call for short-grain.

HOW TO PREPARE: I may get myself into trouble saying this, but I don't rinse my rice. This was not something I ever saw my mother do, so it wasn't a practice I took on, and at this late stage of my life I just can't seem to remember to do it. The main reason people rinse their rice is to remove debris that might have traveled with it. It's possible my eyesight isn't great, but I've rarely found my rice to be filled with debris. It is also said that removing excess starch from the grain helps it cook up fluffier, and not rinsing can result in gummy rice. I have not, to be honest, noticed that much of a difference between cooked rice that has been rinsed versus not, especially because I use longer-grained varieties, but there are *many* people who would fiercely debate me on that. If you want to do it, simply put the rice in a fine-mesh strainer and rinse with cold water.

"PERFECT" WHITE RICE

4 cups water
2 cups white rice
1 tablespoon extra-
virgin olive oil
1 teaspoon kosher salt

SERVES 6 TO 8

I am well aware that, for some, making rice can be daunting. I remember being much younger and watching my mother make rice—she mostly just eyeballed it, occasionally measuring the rice-to-water ratio with her finger. She never timed how long it cooked, and she never really paid it much mind, but it came out perfectly every time. *Every. Time.* I don't claim to have the magic secret that will make you a rice guru, too, but as the daughter of one, I can tell you this method has never let me down. I don't always add oil to my rice (or not this much, anyway), but if you're looking for rice that will wow, here it is. Halve this recipe, or double it, or sauté some onions and garlic first before adding the water if you're feeling extra fancy. Knowing exactly when it's time to lower the flame does take some practice, but know that even if you overcook it a little, you'll end up with the golden, crunchy goodness at the bottom that's coveted by so many cultures around the globe. They call it bubun in places like Jamaica and Trinidad and Tobago, concon in the Dominican Republic, graten in Haiti, pegao in Puerto Rico, and raspa in Cuba. Don't you dare soak your pot with that still inside—the ancestors will be angry!

In a heavy-bottomed pot or Dutch oven, bring the water to a boil over medium-high heat. Add the rice, olive oil, and salt, and boil, uncovered, until the water has visibly evaporated, 10 to 15 minutes. There will be little pockets of air on the top, and you may still hear some bubbling from below. Reduce the heat to low, cover, and cook for 15 minutes more. Remove from the heat and fluff the rice before serving.

CRAB AND RICE

TURKS AND CAICOS

1 tablespoon
  coconut oil
1 small yellow onion,
  diced
4 garlic cloves, peeled
½ green bell pepper,
  diced
1 seasoning pepper
  (optional; see
  page 14)
2 teaspoons Green
  Seasoning,
  homemade
  (page 22) or
  store-bought
1 teaspoon fresh
  thyme leaves
2 tablespoons tomato
  paste
1 cup water
4 or 5 small blue crabs,
  cleaned, back shells
  and gills removed
  (see page 182)
1 cup Coconut
  Milk, homemade
  (page 97) or
  store-bought
  (see Note)
1 teaspoon kosher salt
1 cup long-grain rice

SERVES 4 TO 6

*Note: Coconut milk is
not traditional, but,
as you may know by
now, my mantra is that
coconut milk makes
everything better.
There's not enough
to make it coconutty;
instead, it counters some
of the sharper tastes in
the dish. If you prefer,
you can use all water
instead, or even stock.*

Turks and Caicos is actually made up of many little islands, with a total population of less than 50,000. The nation imports much of its produce and is in large part known for its tourism. However, local culture is still very much alive and well, as can be seen by this dish. Crabs are not in short order on these islands! The land crabs used for this dish in the Caribbean are significantly larger than the small blue crabs they sell at my local seafood shop. Traditionally, you would remove the crab "fat" inside the head and use it to sauté your vegetables. That yellow stuff is not really fat but rather the crab's hepatopancreas, an organ similar to a liver! It's consumed by many around the world as a delicacy, and is fine in moderation, but can be toxic in large amounts. The little guys in this recipe don't have enough crab fat to make it worth trying to remove it, or enough that you need to worry about accidentally poisoning yourself, so I just add them in whole. If you're lucky enough to have something big like a Dungeness crab, you can scoop the crab fat into a bowl and add it after you've cooked the tomato paste and before you've added the crabs themselves. Cook it until it becomes liquid. The crab both lends its flavor to the rice and gives you something fun to do while you're eating.

In a large Dutch oven or other heavy-bottomed pot, heat the coconut oil over medium heat. Add the onion and garlic and sauté until they begin to brown, 5 to 8 minutes. Add the bell pepper, seasoning pepper (if using), green seasoning, and thyme and cook for 3 to 5 minutes, until the bell pepper is a bit softened and the green seasoning is fragrant. Add the tomato paste, stirring aggressively to get it worked into the veggies, and cook until it begins to darken, 2 to 3 minutes.

Add ¼ cup of the water, give it a stir, then add your crabs. Stir them all around until they're completely coated, then reduce the heat to low,

cover, and cook for 5 minutes, until the crabs have begun to release some juices. Raise the heat to medium-high, add the remaining ¾ cup water and the coconut milk, and bring to a boil. Add the salt. Reduce the heat to medium-low, cover, and cook for 10 minutes more to really get those crab juices going.

Add the rice, cover, and cook for 30 minutes, until the liquid has been absorbed and the rice can be fluffed with a fork. If you find the rice isn't quite dry, cook on low with the lid off until the water has evaporated. This dish is best served immediately.

CRABS

If you're like me and have a hard time dealing with live animals in your sink, you may want to ask your fishmonger if they have frozen whole crabs, or to clean them for you. Science has finally proven what we all ought to know: Crabs do indeed feel pain. This doesn't mean we can't eat them, but please kill your crab before you start removing its body parts! To kill a crab humanely, you need to "spike" it, or cut the front and rear nerve centers with a very sharp knife. It's worth a look on YouTube to see how to do it. Once you've done this, pry the pointy back shell off and remove the dark gills. The neon-orange stuff is the crab's eggs, which are edible. The yellow part, sometimes called crab fat or crab butter, is actually the crab's hepatopancreas, an organ that functions like a liver. Because these crabs are so small, you can keep them whole, but if you want to try this with something larger, you'll want to remove the legs before putting the crabs in your pot.

DIRI AK DJON DJON

RICE WITH MUSHROOMS ○ HAITI

1 cup well-packed djon
  djon mushrooms
2 cups water
2 tablespoons extra-
  virgin olive oil
1 small yellow onion,
  diced
1 small shallot, minced
2 garlic cloves, minced
½ cup lima beans or
  green peas (fresh
  or frozen)
2 whole cloves
2 thyme sprigs
1 Scotch bonnet
  pepper
1 cup jasmine rice
1 teaspoon kosher salt

SERVES 4 TO 6

Many years ago, this rice dish was part of my first-ever Haitian meal. Of all the things I ate, it intrigued me the most. There was an unusual taste I wanted to know more about. The key to the dish is djon djon, a mushroom that appears to only grow in the north of Haiti and is considered a delicacy. Its smell is not for the faint of heart, but the taste is delicious. It reminds me of porcini mushrooms but funkier (in all senses of that word), and I've often substituted djon djon for porcinis. The stem of the mushroom is inedible, and rather than eating the fungus itself, it is soaked in water, then discarded. The soaking water is then used to cook the rice, imparting a beautiful purplish-black hue. I have tried a variety of ways to extract the flavor—both soaking for hours before boiling or just boiling for a longer period of time, but the difference is small. If you have the time (and foresight) to soak the mushrooms, definitely do, but if not, you can make up for it with a slightly longer simmering time.

If you live in a city with a large Haitian diaspora like I do, djon djon is easily found at Caribbean markets. There are plenty of online sellers (like Kalustyan's), but watch out for sources that don't clean the debris collected with the mushrooms, or you'll end up paying partly for sticks and leaves. Djon djon is on the pricey side, so it's not a surprise this dish is often reserved for special occasions such as weddings or birthdays. Some people do use a djon djon–flavored Maggi cube instead, which is more economical but certainly not as tasty. This recipe is easily doubled.

Place the djon djon in a small sauce-pan with the water and set aside to soak for 2 hours, then bring to a sim-mer over low heat for 10 minutes (or skip the soaking step and simmer the djon djon in the water over low heat, undisturbed, for 30 minutes). Let cool slightly, then strain the cooking liquid through a fine-mesh strainer into a bowl, pressing firmly on the mush-rooms to get out all the water; discard the mushrooms. You should have a scant 2 cups of liquid; if not, add water to make up the difference. Set aside.

In a heavy-bottomed pot, heat 1 table-spoon of the olive oil over medium heat. Add the onion, shallot, and garlic and sauté until soft, 3 to 5 minutes.

Add the reserved mushroom water, the lima beans, cloves, thyme, and Scotch bonnet and bring to a boil over medium-high heat. Add the rice and salt and boil until the water has been almost completely absorbed, 15 to 20 minutes. It should look very dry, and you should feel concerned it will burn (it won't—it's just the Haitian way!).

Drizzle the remaining 1 tablespoon oil on top. Reduce the heat to low, cover, and cook for 15 to 20 minutes, until the remaining liquid has completely evaporated. Remove the cloves, thyme sprigs, and Scotch bonnet, which will all have floated to the top. When fluffed, the rice should be separate and grainy.

PEAS AND RICE

BAHAMAS

1 cup dried pigeon
  peas, soaked
  overnight and
  drained
6 cups water
2 tablespoons
  coconut oil
3 tablespoons sugar
1 small yellow onion,
  diced
½ green bell pepper,
  diced
3 garlic cloves, minced
1 Roma (plum) tomato,
  diced
¼ cup tomato sauce
1 teaspoon fresh
  thyme leaves
1 cup Coconut
  Milk, homemade
  (page 97) or
  store-bought
2 cups basmati rice
1 tablespoon
  kosher salt

SERVES 6 TO 8

The secret to this dish is burnt sugar, which makes the base of many dishes from the English-speaking Caribbean, but can feel intimidating for a first timer. Many recipes will instruct you *not* to burn the sugar, but that's not quite right. A more accurate way to phrase it would be to *just* burn the sugar. Let it *just* pass the point of comfort, where it crosses the line from caramel to something else. Let it smoke and get dark, but just for the blink of an eye. Anything less, and the dish will be sweet, which is not what you're looking for; anything more, and it will be a black, smoky mess. Properly burnt sugar adds a depth and is something that toes the line between sweet and mysterious umami. Pigeon peas are a direct link to our African heritage and are combined with rice in every Caribbean nation.

In a large, heavy-bottomed pot, combine the peas and water and bring to a boil over medium-high heat. Reduce the heat to low, cover, and cook for 1 to 1½ hours, until tender. Drain the peas, reserving the cooking water, and set both aside.

Wipe out the pot and place it back on the stove over medium-high heat. Add the coconut oil and heat until it shimmers, then add the sugar. Cook, watching it constantly and stirring it occasionally with a wooden spoon to make sure it cooks evenly, for 5 to 8 minutes, until the sugar bubbles all over, turns dark brown, and *just* starts to smoke. (This will vary from stove to stove; if it hasn't happened by minute 8, just hang in there; the moment will happen quickly after.) Immediately add the onion, bell pepper, and garlic. You will hear a very satisfying singing, sizzling noise that encapsulates my youth. Cook the vegetables until soft, 3 to 5 minutes.

Add the diced tomato, tomato sauce, and thyme, and cook for 3 to 5 minutes, until the tomatoes begin to break down. Add the peas, give them a stir to coat, then add the coconut milk and 3 cups of the reserved pea cooking water. Bring to a boil over high heat, then add the rice and salt, and let it boil rapidly for 5 minutes. Reduce the heat to low, cover, and cook for 30 minutes, until all the water has been absorbed. Fluff before serving.

Leftovers will keep in an airtight container in the fridge for several days or in the freezer for up to 3 months.

ARROZ CON POLLO

CHICKEN AND RICE ○ PUERTO RICO

ADOBO

3 garlic cloves, mashed
   in a pilon or minced
2 teaspoons
   kosher salt
2 teaspoons fresh
   lime juice
2 teaspoons extra-
   virgin olive oil
1 teaspoon dried
   oregano
Freshly ground
   black pepper

2 pounds bone-in
   chicken thighs, skin
   removed, halved
   (see page 10)
1 tablespoon extra-
   virgin olive oil
1 onion, diced
2 garlic cloves, minced
½ cup Recaíto
   (page 22)
1 teaspoon Puerto
   Rican Sazón,
   homemade
   (page 23) or
   store-bought
¼ cup tomato sauce
¼ cup pimento-
   stuffed olives,
   roughly chopped
   (optional)
3 cups water
2 cups long- or
   medium-grain rice
1 to 1½ teaspoons
   kosher salt, plus
   more as needed

SERVES 4 TO 6

To me, this is one of the most iconic Puerto Rican dishes. It's the first thing I ever tried from the cuisine when I first started coming to NYC many decades ago. Nuyorican chef and food historian César Pérez remembers his mother making huge amounts of arroz con pollo in her caldero and taking it along for a beach day. He says when he's back on the island, he and his friends do the same, and all the older people on the beach love that they're keeping tradition alive. It isn't difficult to make, but it does take some practice to not burn the bottom of the rice and make sure it isn't soggy. One trick is to make sure the water you're adding to the rice is hot. I have an aversion to using more pots than necessary, so I prefer bringing the water in the pot to a boil first before adding the rice. Everything hangs out in there anyway and the flavor doesn't suffer a bit. César also says he'll usually make this with long-grain rice, which also helps prevent the rice from getting soggy. Other versions of this dish show up around the Caribbean (cook up rice and pelau are common names) and in Latin America. Our African ancestors were making rice dishes like this long before their forced arrival on the islands. I'm 100% going to start bringing a pot of this to beach days in the Rockaways.

Make the adobo: In a bowl large enough to fit your chicken, mix together the garlic, salt, lime juice, olive oil, oregano, and black pepper.

Add the chicken and use your hands to mix it with the adobo, making sure the seasoning is evenly distributed. Cover and marinate in the fridge for at least 2 hours or up to overnight.

About 30 minutes before cooking, remove the chicken from the fridge to bring it to room temperature.

In a large Dutch oven, caldero, or other heavy-bottomed pot, heat the olive oil over medium heat. Add the chicken pieces and cook until browned on each side, about 4 minutes per side. The chicken pieces need space to get good color, so do this in batches if necessary. Transfer the chicken to a plate and set aside.

Add the onion and garlic to the pot and sauté in the fat left over from the chicken until they begin to brown, 5 to 8 minutes. Add the recaíto and cook for 3 minutes, until it's very fragrant, then add the sazón, tomato sauce, and olives (if using). Give everything a good stir, then return the chicken to the pot, along with any juices that have collected on the plate. Pour in the water, raise the heat to high, and bring to a boil. Add the rice and 1 to 1½ teaspoons of salt. Cook until the water is close to being evaporated, 10 to 15 minutes. Give it another hearty stir to bring all the things at the bottom to the top so it doesn't burn and taste for salt. Reduce the heat to low, cover, and cook for 20 minutes more. Serve while hot.

PELAU

CHICKEN AND RICE ○ DOMINICA

3 pounds bone-in
    chicken thighs, skin
    removed, cut into
    bite-size pieces
    (see page 10)
¼ cup plus
    2 tablespoons
    Green Seasoning,
    homemade
    (page 22) or
    store-bought
6 garlic cloves, minced
2 teaspoons
    kosher salt
1 teaspoon paprika
½ teaspoon
    freshly ground
    black pepper
2 tablespoons
    coconut oil or
    other neutral oil
2 tablespoons
    brown sugar
1 yellow onion, diced
2 scallions, thinly sliced
1 large carrot, diced
2 teaspoons fresh
    thyme leaves
1 (15-ounce) can
    kidney beans,
    drained
¼ cup ketchup
3 cups water
2 cups basmati or
    jasmine rice

SERVES 6 TO 8

While Arroz con Pollo (page 188) may be the most famous version of chicken and rice outside of the Caribbean, pelau is the one I know best. My mother never made it, but it always showed up at family functions at my aunt's house around the corner. This rendition from Dominica is very similar to what I knew growing up. The main difference is the use of kidney beans, which show up a lot in Dominican cuisine, instead of pigeon peas, and the omission of coconut milk. As a person who, prior to having a small child, *never* had ketchup in my house, I have to admit it is really the secret sauce. You could substitute tomato paste if you must, and I have, but the magic will be missing. I've eaten a lot of pelaus in my life, but this one from Dominica might be my favorite.

In a medium bowl, mix the chicken with ¼ cup of the green seasoning, two-thirds of the garlic, the salt, paprika, and pepper, using your hands to make sure the seasoning is evenly distributed. Place in the fridge to marinate for at least 2 hours or up to overnight.

About 30 minutes before cooking the chicken, remove it from the fridge to come to room temperature.

In a large Dutch oven or other heavy-bottomed pot, heat the coconut oil over medium-high heat until it shimmers, then add the brown sugar. Cook, watching it constantly and stirring it occasionally with a wooden spoon to make sure it cooks evenly, for 5 to 8 minutes, until the sugar bubbles all over, turns dark brown, and *just* starts to smoke. (This will vary from stove to stove; if it hasn't happened by minute 8, just hang in there; the moment will happen quickly after.) Immediately add the chicken and listen to it sing and sizzle. Cook the chicken, uncovered, for 5 minutes, until it's releasing its juices, then add the onion, remaining 2 table-spoons green seasoning, remaining garlic, the scallions, carrot, and thyme. Reduce the heat to low, cover, and cook for 10 minutes, until the vegetables are soft.

Add the beans and ketchup and cook until the ketchup has darkened, 3 to 5 minutes. Add the water, raise the heat to high, and bring it all to a boil. Add the rice, reduce the heat to medium, and cook, uncovered, until the water has mostly evaporated, about 15 minutes. Give everything a hearty stir to make sure nothing sticks to the bottom of the pot. Reduce the heat to low, cover, and cook for 15 to 20 minutes more, until the liquid has completely evaporated. Pelau is great immediately and heats up well for several days after; store it in an airtight container in the fridge.

ASOPAO DE POLLO

CHICKEN AND RICE STEW ○ PUERTO RICO

ADOBO

- 3 garlic cloves, mashed in a pilon or minced
- 2 teaspoons kosher salt
- 2 teaspoons fresh lime juice
- 2 teaspoons extra-virgin olive oil
- 1 teaspoon dried oregano
- Freshly ground black pepper

- 2 pounds bone-in chicken thighs, skin removed, halved (see page 10)
- 1 tablespoon extra-virgin olive oil
- 1 medium yellow onion, diced
- 1 large carrot, diced
- ½ green bell pepper, diced
- 2 garlic cloves, minced
- ½ cup Recaíto (page 22)
- 1 cup tomato sauce
- 1 teaspoon Puerto Rican Sazón, homemade (page 23) or store-bought
- 4 cups chicken stock
- 1 bay leaf
- 1 teaspoon kosher salt
- 1 cup short-grain rice
- ½ cup green peas (fresh or frozen)

SERVES 6 TO 8

At first glance, this might look similar to Arroz con Pollo (page 188), but it's soupy and has a more complex flavor, probably due to the massive amount of seasoning within it. Really, don't hold back on the seasoning in this one; it's an all-hands-on-deck situation. A staple dish on many restaurant menus in Puerto Rico and in home kitchens alike, this is a rainy-day, home-from-school dish. It was also traditionally made on Christmas Eve to feed rotating visitors, because it's an easy, economical thing to have simmering on your back burner. Short-grain rice here is key, as it adds its starch to the liquid and makes it a bit thick and creamy. Longer-grained varieties just don't have the same effect. This dish is a deeply comforting, satisfying one-pot meal.

Make the adobo: In a bowl large enough to fit your chicken, mix together the garlic, salt, lime juice, olive oil, oregano, and black pepper. Add the chicken and use your hands to mix it with the adobo, making sure the seasoning is evenly distributed. Place in the fridge to marinate for at least 2 hours or up to overnight.

About 30 minutes before cooking the chicken, remove it from the fridge to come to room temperature.

In a large Dutch oven or other heavy-bottomed pot, heat the olive oil over medium heat. Add the chicken pieces, in batches if necessary, and cook until browned, 4 to 5 minutes on each side. Transfer the chicken to a plate and set aside.

Add the onion, carrot, bell pepper, and garlic to the pot and cook until the onion begins to brown, 5 to 8 minutes, scraping up the golden chicken bits from the bottom of the pot as you go.

Add the recaíto and cook for 5 minutes, until it is deeply fragrant. Add the tomato sauce and sazón and simmer for 5 minutes. Return the chicken to the pot, along with any juices that have collected on the plate. Add the stock and bay leaf and bring it all to a boil. Add the salt, then reduce the heat to medium-low, cover, and simmer for 20 minutes, until the chicken is cooked through. Add the rice and cook, covered, for 15 minutes, until the rice is cooked and has soaked up all the flavor. Add the peas, cover the pot, and let them heat through, 5 minutes or so. Remove the bay leaf before serving.

Asopao de pollo is at its very best within 30 minutes or so of making it, but it does reheat well enough the next day. Store it in an airtight container in the refrigerator. Just keep in mind that the rice will continue to absorb liquid, so the longer it sits, the less soupy it will be.

ARROZ CON DULCE

RICE PUDDING ○ PUERTO RICO

1 cup short- or
    medium-grain rice
2 (13.5-ounce) cans
    coconut milk, or
    4 cups homemade
    Coconut Milk
    (page 97)
1 cup water
2 cinnamon sticks
6 whole cloves
1 star anise pod
1 (1-inch) piece fresh
    ginger, sliced
½ cup packed
    brown sugar
½ cup raisins

SERVES 4 TO 6

Rice is so ubiquitous in Caribbean cuisine that of course other islands, aside from Puerto Rico, make sweet rice pudding. In Trinidad, it's called sweet rice; in Haiti, it's called diri labouyi (which is more of a breakfast than a dessert). But as it happens, Puerto Rico has the claim to fame on this one. Traditionally, there is a lot more coconut milk (if you can believe that!), and it's added gradually over time, with more stirring. This helps to release the starches in the rice and make it thick, like a risotto. However, out of the necessity that arises from being a working mother to a four-year-old who doesn't have much patience for you constantly stirring rice, I developed this recipe using less coconut milk and less active time. The result is still creamy and delicious. Do be sure to soak the grains, however, as this helps them become plump with moisture rather than mushy. Also make sure to use short-grain (top choice) or medium-grain (runner-up) rice, as long-grain rice just won't get creamy. I like to keep the spices in even after adding the rice for more flavor, then fish them out (usually imperfectly) in the end, but the more practical thing to do is to take them out with a slotted spoon right before adding the rice. This rice pudding is traditionally eaten chilled, but I also love it warm, straight from the pot.

Place the rice in a medium bowl with water to cover and set aside to soak for about 2 hours. Drain the rice in a fine-mesh sieve.

In a large Dutch oven or other heavy-bottomed pot, combine the coconut milk, water, cinnamon sticks, cloves, star anise, and ginger and bring to a simmer over medium-low heat. Cook for 15 minutes. Add the rice, brown sugar, and raisins, give it all several healthy stirs, and bring to a boil. Stir again, reduce the heat to low, cover, and cook for 25 minutes. Stir it heartily after the 25-minute mark. Really put your back into it! If it's still very liquidy, cover again and cook, checking every 5 minutes and giving it a stir, until the mixture has a wet pudding consistency, like a loose risotto. It will thicken up as it cools. Remove the spices.

If serving the rice pudding chilled, spread it evenly in a pan or in serving dishes. Let cool, then cover and refrigerate for up to 3 hours before serving.

SALTED COD

Other names: BACALAO, MORI, MORUE, SALTFISH

THOUGH WE USE OTHER salted fish as well, such as herring and mackerel, none is as ubiquitous as salted cod, which can be found prepared a million ways throughout the Caribbean. This food's popularity in the region has everything to do with the Atlantic slave trade and capitalism: In order to sustain ships' crews and enslaved Africans on the long journeys to and from Africa, the colonists needed to give them a source of protein that could withstand the long journey, humidity, and wetness of the boat and the tropics. Once on the island, salted cod continued to be a popular dish made to feed the enslaved. Preserving fish in salt was a tried-and-true technique used across the world and was a staple in the cuisines of Central and West Africa. Hot-smoked, dried, fermented, and salted fish were all used as flavoring agents in the stewy dishes so common to the region.

Atlantic cod is not by any means native to the Caribbean, but rather comes from the icy-cold waters of the northern regions of the world. Originally, the fish was imported to Europe from settlements in what would later become Greenland and Newfoundland. Cod became popular in part because it was so prolific. It also lends itself to salting because of its lower fat content. Though the Caribbean seas were abundant with fish, their high fat content made them difficult to preserve.

The codfish trade was vital to the Atlantic slave trade and became a currency in itself. Salted codfish made all those sea voyages sending sugar, cotton, rum, and human labor back and forth across the Atlantic possible. It became an ingrained part of the cuisine, and today can be found on every island in dishes that range from stews to salads and even gratins.

In a post-slavery world, salted cod has continued to be a popular source of protein for lower classes, with some caveats. Once cheap to purchase in the Caribbean, the overfished species is now becoming an expensive commodity. It's becoming more common to see salted pollack or hake, which work easily as substitutions.

NUTRITION: Salted cod is very high in protein, which is one of the main reasons it was so desirable as food for the enslaved. Despite only having 18 percent protein when fresh, salted cod flesh becomes about 80 percent protein. Salted cod retains a lot of sodium even after you desalt the fish, so it should only be consumed in moderation.

HOW TO CHOOSE: If you live somewhere with Caribbean grocery stores, you may find salted cod in a variety of forms. Sometimes it's boneless and skinless (my preference); sometimes it's bone-in, skin-on; and sometimes you'll find whole fish. You may also find salted pollack or hake that's been prepackaged. These also work well, though keep in mind that they do have some water in them so they are a little heavier, which means you're getting less fish in a pound than you would if it was dried. I recommend buying salted cod without the bones, if possible, to save yourself the trouble of picking them all out. They are many and they are sharp! Even if you buy boneless cod, you should double-check, as there are often still some lurking about. The pollack and hake fillets are reliably bone-free. I keep my salted cod in the fridge (where the fruit flies can't get to it!), even though in theory it can be left out.

HOW TO PREPARE: A key step to preparing saltfish is desalting it. It takes a bit of work to get all that salt out of the cod. Many believe the best way to do so is to soak it overnight, changing the water every few hours. I, however, have never been one to have that much active foresight. Therefore, I do exactly what my mother did, and don't find the difference to be that great:

1. Rinse the fillets under cold water until the visible salt has been removed.
2. Place the fish in a medium saucepan and cover it with cold water.
3. Bring it to a boil over medium or medium-high heat. You can do this covered or uncovered. (Note that if you do this with the lid on, it will happen faster, but you'll also get boiling salty water all over your stovetop, which will dry into a big mess. Not that this happens to me . . . all the time.) Boil for 10 minutes, then drain the fish, rinse, and repeat. At this point, you can taste a bit to see how salty it is. If you aren't sure if it's desalted enough, it doesn't hurt to boil and rinse it again. You can always add salt back in when you're cooking, but you can't take it out!
4. Drain the fish a last time and let it cool before breaking it up into smaller flakes with your hands. Your saltfish is now ready for whatever preparation you like.

If you want to try the soaking method, follow steps 1 and 2. Soak the fish 4 to 6 hours. Then drain it, rinse it, and submerge it in fresh water for 4 to 6 hours more. After this process, you may find it still is a bit too salty. If so, you can boil it for just about 5 minutes in fresh water, then drain. Let it cool before breaking it up into smaller flakes. Soaked saltfish can be a little tougher to shred.

ACCRAS DE MORUE

SALT COD FRITTERS ○ MARTINIQUE

½ pound salted cod, desalted (see page 197) and shredded

3 garlic cloves, minced

2 scallions, minced

¼ cup fresh parsley leaves, minced

1 teaspoon fresh thyme leaves

½ to 1 Scotch bonnet pepper, minced (optional)

2 large eggs

1 cup whole milk

1½ cups all-purpose flour

½ teaspoon baking soda

Freshly ground black pepper

Neutral oil, for frying

SERVES 6 TO 8

Language is a funny thing. In West Africa, an akara is a fritter made of black-eyed peas, and the connection is obvious to the Caribbean, where the same thing is called akkra or accra in Jamaica. In Aruba, those are called Cala (page 29). In Haiti, akra or accra is a fritter made from malanga (otherwise known as taro, but not actually a taro—confused yet?). In Martinique and Guadeloupe, accras refer to these salted cod fritters, and I believe that the word *accra* has come to be a generic term for "fritter," though it didn't originate as such. As confusing as that path was, there's one thing I know: Every single nation or territory makes a version of a codfish fritter, and I am here for all of them. There is little more satisfying than eating some of these on the beach with a cold beer. I love every version of salt cod fritters I've ever met (some I had on a beach in Rio once are a top contender), but I do still have my favorites! I have to say, the combination of spices in these, and the somewhat unusual addition of milk—which is perhaps a French influence—give these a special place in the fried food section of my heart.

In a medium bowl, mix the cod, garlic, scallions, parsley, thyme, and Scotch bonnet (if using) until evenly distributed.

In a large bowl, beat the eggs, then whisk in the milk. With a fork, mix in the flour and baking soda until well incorporated. Add the fish mixture and some good grinds of black pepper. The batter should be thick, like cookie or muffin dough.

In a wok or deep skillet, heat about 2 inches of oil over medium-high heat until it reaches 350°F. If you don't have a thermometer, you'll know the oil is ready if a bit of dough makes it bubble intensely when dropped in.

Using a heaping tablespoon, carefully place balls of dough into the oil. Try to make the fritters as round as possible; you may need to use another spoon to help shape the balls. Fry until golden on all sides, 8 to 10 minutes total. If they're browning too fast, reduce the heat to medium and wait a bit before adding more. Remove the fritters from the oil and drain on paper towels. Serve immediately.

BACALAITOS

SALT COD FRITTERS ○ PUERTO RICO

½ pound salted cod,
    desalted (see
    page 197), water
    from the last soak
    (about 2 cups)
    reserved, and
    shredded
½ small yellow onion,
    minced
2 garlic cloves, minced
2 tablespoons minced
    fresh cilantro leaves
2 tablespoons minced
    fresh parsley leaves
1 tablespoon Recaíto
    (page 22)
1 cup all-purpose flour
1 teaspoon baking
    soda
1 teaspoon fresh lime
    juice
Neutral oil, for frying

SERVES 4 TO 6

As mentioned in the recipe for Accras de Morue (page 198), everyone in the Caribbean makes some version of a codfish fritter. What makes bacalaitos unique, other than the specific seasonings true to Puerto Rican food, is their shape: They are large and flat, unlike everyone else's fritters, which are round. It can take a bit of practice to get the shape down, but they'll be delicious no matter what they look like.

While at the famous Kiosko El Boricua right by the beach in Piñones, Loíza, Atibon, Desalin, and I conquered the biggest bacalaito I've ever seen, bigger than Desalin's head. If you find yourself in Puerto Rico, do yourself a favor and make the trip. Loíza is known for its African roots; people from the Yoruba tribe were brought to the islands as slaves in the sixteenth century. This tie to their culture has made Loíza a hot spot for delicious food. There are so many of these food stalls selling frituras on the sides of the road on the way to and through Loíza from San Juan, but this one is famous for good reason. You'll likely encounter a line and you'll definitely wait forever for your name to be called to get your food, but just relax. Get a drink. Soak it in. Dance to some salsa. I haven't had any bacalaitos as good on the island or off, but I strive to match them every time.

In a medium bowl, mix the cod, onion, garlic, cilantro, parsley, and recaíto together with a fork or, even better, your hands until evenly distributed.

Mix in the flour and baking soda. Add about 2 cups of the reserved cod soaking water and the lime juice, and use a fork to mix until all the flour is incorporated. The mixture should be fairly liquidy and much looser than your average fritter. Thinner than pancake batter, more like crepe batter. Let sit for 10 minutes. (You can also cover and refrigerate the batter overnight, then fry the fritters the next day.)

In a wok or deep skillet, heat 2 inches of oil over medium-high heat until it reaches 350°F. If you don't have a thermometer, you'll know it's ready if a bit of batter makes it bubble intensely when dropped in.

Using about ¼ cup at a time, pour the batter into the hot oil in a line that's about 3 inches long. The batter will spread itself flat when it comes into contact with the oil, rather than forming a rounded shape. Fry until golden, about 4 minutes on each side. If they're browning too fast, reduce the heat to medium and wait a bit before adding more. Drain on a paper towel–lined tray and eat ASAP.

APORREADO DE BACALAO

SCRAMBLED EGGS WITH SALTED COD ○ CUBA

1 tablespoon extra-virgin olive oil
1 small yellow onion, diced
½ green bell pepper, diced
3 garlic cloves, minced
½ cup tomato sauce
½ pound salted cod, desalted (see page 197) and shredded
2 tablespoons apple cider vinegar
2 tablespoons dry white wine
2 tablespoons water
1 bay leaf
Freshly ground black pepper
4 eggs, beaten

SERVES 4 TO 6

It's easy to see the connection here to Ackee and Saltfish (page 203), a Jamaican dish featuring the ackee fruit that has been compared to scrambled eggs. One almost wonders if the ackee was in place of the eggs, or vice versa. The other difference here is, of course, in the seasonings, which are quite different than in the Jamaican dish. Otherwise, the two are made similarly, with the ackee or egg being added at the end. You'll see wine used in cooking in Cuba more than in other Spanish-speaking islands, which could be a nod to the Spanish colonial power's influence on the food.

In a wide skillet, heat the olive oil over medium heat. Add the onion, bell pepper, and garlic and sauté until the onion begins to brown, 5 to 8 minutes. Add the tomato sauce and let it cook down until it thickens, 3 to 5 minutes. Add the fish and stir to coat, then add the vinegar, wine, water, bay leaf, and several grinds of black pepper. Reduce the heat to low, cover, and simmer for 15 minutes.

Remove the lid and add the eggs. Cook, stirring continuously, until they firm up, 3 to 5 minutes. Remove the bay leaf before serving. This dish is at its best served immediately, but can be stored in an airtight container in the fridge overnight and reheated the next day.

ACKEE AND SALTFISH

JAMAICA

1 tablespoon extra-
  virgin olive oil
1 small yellow onion,
  diced
3 garlic cloves, minced
½ green bell pepper,
  diced
½ Scotch bonnet
  pepper, minced
2 teaspoons fresh
  thyme leaves
2 Roma (plum)
  tomatoes, diced
½ pound salted cod,
  desalted (see
  page 197) and
  shredded
1 (19-ounce) can
  ackee, drained
2 scallions, thinly sliced
½ teaspoon
  freshly ground
  black pepper

SERVES 4 TO 6

Ackee is a fruit that originated in Africa and came to the islands with the enslaved. If it's picked unripe or the wrong part of the fruit is used, it can be deadly. It was, in fact, one of the silent weapons the enslaved used against their masters; the enslavers lived in constant fear of death by poison, which maybe should have been a sign to their conscience. Ackee can cause what was called Jamaican vomiting sickness, or barfing to death, which was probably as awful as it sounds. While ackee trees exist all over the world (and in West Africa the seeds are used to make soap), it seems to be eaten only in the Caribbean, and specifically in Jamaica at that. I've been trying to get an answer to that for years. I'm sure the whole death-by-vomit plays into things, but why is it only in Jamaica they've put fear aside and got ackee harvesting and eating down to a science? It's even their national dish! Whatever the reason, there's no need to worry about using ackee in this dish. Unless you're planning on going out alone, with no knowledge, to pick a fresh ackee fruit—don't do that—you won't be in any danger. The fruit that is sold in Caribbean markets, or more likely in a can stateside, is ripe and safe.

I have not myself ever eaten ackee beyond this dish, but I think it's worth some experiments. Do be gentle when stirring it, as the pieces of fruit break apart very easily. It doesn't really matter taste wise, but it does make a more striking visual if you can keep the ackee flesh intact. I'm waiting for ackee to have its day, but until then, Jamaica will keep it going. In the summer on our many trips out to Rockaway Beach, if I don't have it in me to pack a picnic, we'll pick up Jamaican food on Nostrand Avenue on our way. This dish is always top on Desalin's requests. Serve with Bammy (page 72), Festivals (page 120), or "Perfect" White Rice (page 180).

In a wide skillet, heat the olive oil over medium heat. Add the onion, garlic, bell pepper, Scotch bonnet, and thyme and cook until the onion starts to brown, 5 to 8 minutes. Add the tomatoes and cod and cook for 5 minutes, until the tomatoes just start to break down.

Add the ackee, scallions, and black pepper. Fold the ackee in carefully, trying to keep it mostly intact. Cook for 5 minutes, until the ackee has picked up all the flavor and is heated through, then serve immediately.

BOULÈT LAM VERITAB AK LANMORI

FRIED BREADFRUIT AND SALT COD BALLS ○ HAITI

1 pound salted cod, desalted (see page 197) and shredded

5 garlic cloves, mashed in a pilon or minced

1 shallot, minced

¼ cup fresh parsley leaves, minced

1 tablespoon Epis (page 21)

½ Scotch bonnet pepper, minced (optional)

2 cups breadfruit flour

2 to 2½ cups water

Neutral oil, for frying

¼ cup all-purpose flour, for coating

SERVES 8 TO 10

My take on this recipe is inspired by the fact that even here in Brooklyn, home to the biggest Caribbean diaspora in the entire world, it can be impossible to find breadfruit. It's a bit of a mystery, really, considering how prolific breadfruit is and how the trees yield fruits all year long. However, New York City will see long stretches with nary a breadfruit in sight. Fortunately, the internet makes breadfruit flour available at your fingertips. It doesn't work as a flour substitute for most recipes, but it lends itself to these fried fritter balls perfectly. Though a lot of fritters are something you might find at a roadside stall, these are more likely found as part of a home-cooked meal. They are fantastic with Pikliz (page 214). Leftover breadfruit flour also makes a great substitute for half the flour in Coconut Bake (page 103).

In a medium bowl, mix the cod, garlic, shallot, parsley, epis, and Scotch bonnet (if using) evenly. Your hands make the best work of this, but make sure to wash them afterward because of the Scotch bonnet! Stir in the breadfruit flour until well incorporated, then mix in 2 cups of the water. The dough should be thick, like cookie dough. Add up to ½ cup more water, 1 tablespoon at a time, if necessary. (The dough can be covered and refrigerated overnight and fried the next day.)

In a wok or deep skillet, heat 2 inches of oil over medium-high heat until it reaches 350°F. If you don't have a thermometer, you'll know the oil is ready if a bit of batter makes it bubble intensely when dropped in.

Put the all-purpose flour in a small bowl or plate. Roll 1 tablespoon of the dough into a ball, then roll the ball in the flour to coat.

Working in batches, add the balls to the hot oil and fry until firm and golden on all sides, 8 to 10 minutes, making sure to move them around and roll them over as they cook. If they're browning too fast, reduce the heat to medium and wait a bit before adding more. Transfer to a paper towel–lined tray to drain, then eat ASAP.

BREADFRUIT PIE

3 tablespoons unsalted butter, plus more for greasing
1 small breadfruit (about 2 pounds)
1 tablespoon extra-virgin olive oil
1 small yellow onion, diced
4 garlic cloves, minced
½ Scotch bonnet pepper, seeded and minced (optional)
1 Roma (plum) tomato, diced
1 teaspoon Green Seasoning, homemade (page 22) or store-bought
1 pound salted cod, desalted (see page 197) and shredded
3 tablespoons all-purpose flour
1 cup Coconut Milk, homemade (page 97) or store-bought
1 teaspoon mustard
1 teaspoon fresh thyme leaves
½ teaspoon kosher salt
Freshly ground black pepper
1 cup shredded cheddar cheese

SERVES 4 TO 6

This recipe isn't claimed by one particular island, and is something someone from a place like Barbados, Jamaica, Saint Lucia, or Trinidad might make. It's not a traditional recipe, but there are versions of it floating around the internet. It takes a bit of work but is well worth the result: a comforting, somewhat decadent pie with layers of flavor. The breadfruit is really the star of the show, but the saltfish and spices complement it so well. The secret superhero might be what I guess could be called a coconut béchamel. There is no world in which I would have believed that salted cod and cheese belonged together, but here I am, in that world, telling you they are destined to be.

Preheat the oven to 350°F. Grease a 2-quart casserole dish with butter.

Cut a small slice off the top of the breadfruit so it sits flat on your cutting board. Quarter the breadfruit, then, using a sharp paring knife, cut off the peel. Next, cut out the core of the breadfruit (the part that looks like rays of light emanating out of the middle). Place the wedges in a medium saucepan with enough water to just barely submerge them and cover the pot. Bring the water to a simmer over medium heat and cook until soft, about 20 minutes. Drain the breadfruit and transfer to a plate. Set aside.

Wipe out the pot and put it back over medium heat. Add the olive oil. Add the onion, garlic, and Scotch bonnet (if using) and sauté until the onion begins to brown, 5 to 8 minutes. Add the tomato and green seasoning and cook for 5 minutes, until the green seasoning is very fragrant. Add the shredded fish and cook until the tomato begins to break down, 3 to 5 minutes. Remove the pot from the heat.

In a small saucepan, melt the butter over medium heat. Sprinkle the flour evenly over the melted butter and cook, stirring frequently, until the butter begins to brown and smell fragrant and nutty, 3 to 4 minutes. Add the coconut milk, mustard, thyme, salt, and black pepper to taste and stir until thick and well combined. Add half the cheese and stir again until it's melted and remove from the heat.

Cut your cooled breadfruit wedges into ½-inch-thick slices (you can make them thinner if you like, but try to keep them intact). In the prepared casserole dish, layer one-third of the breadfruit, half the salt cod, then one-third of the sauce, spreading out each layer evenly with a spatula. Repeat the layers once, then add a final layer of breadfruit and top it with sauce. There should be three layers of breadfruit and two layers of salt cod. Sprinkle the remaining cheese over the top.

Bake for 35 to 40 minutes, until the pie is bubbling and the top is golden brown. Remove from the oven and let the pie stand for at least 10 minutes to firm up before cutting and serving. Though breadfruit is often best eaten immediately, this keeps very well overnight in an airtight container in the fridge.

BULJOL

STEWED SALTED COD ○ TRINIDAD AND TOBAGO

1 tablespoon extra-
  virgin olive oil
1 small yellow onion,
  sliced
4 garlic cloves, minced
4 thin scallions (or
  2 fat ones), thinly
  sliced
1 seasoning pepper,
  minced (optional;
  see page 14)
½ to 1 Scotch bonnet
  pepper, minced
  (optional)
3 culantro leaves, or
  ¼ cup fresh cilantro,
  chopped
1 pound salted
  cod, desalted
  (see page 197)
  and flaked
2 Roma (plum)
  tomatoes, diced
Kosher salt

SERVES 4 TO 6

Since salted cod is so connected to the slave trade (see page 196) and cured fish is such an integral part of West and Central African cuisine, every Caribbean nation has some version of this dish. Trinidadians make buljol fresh as a salad or stewed like this, but I grew up eating only the latter. Though my father remembers Mom calling it buljol, I only remember her referring to it as simply "saltfish." Most often eaten for breakfast in Trinidad, it was a staple weeknight dinner in my house growing up. It was one of those things Mom cooked so often that when your daily what's-for-dinner question was answered with "Saltfish!," you'd roll your eyes and sigh, "*Again*?" Nevertheless, once I was sitting in front of it, I would always eat it enthusiastically. In Trinidad, it is most often served with fry bake (a fried flatbread my mother never made at home, much to my dismay), but we usually ate it with sada roti, Coconut Bake (page 103), or over rice.

This dish is simple to prepare with a short list of ingredients; just make sure to factor desalting the fish into your cooking time. Mom never added culantro (called chadon beni in Trinidad), but it's a pretty standard ingredient for others. This preparation is identical to how it's made in other English-speaking islands such as Barbados, Jamaica, Saint Vincent, and many more. Whenever I make this, I can see my mother in the kitchen, whipping it up.

In a large saucepan, heat the olive oil over medium heat. Add the onion and garlic and sauté until translucent, 3 to 5 minutes. Add the scallions, seasoning pepper (if using), Scotch bonnet (if using), and culantro and cook for 3 minutes, until fragrant and the onions are starting to brown.

Stir in the fish, then the tomatoes. Bring the mixture to a simmer, then reduce the heat to low, cover, and cook until the tomatoes begin to break down, about 20 minutes. Taste for salt.

Serve warm. Leftovers will keep in an airtight container in the fridge for up to 3 days.

SÒS MORI

STEWED SALTED COD ○ HAITI

2 tablespoons extra-
  virgin olive oil
1 yellow onion, sliced
½ green bell pepper,
  sliced
4 garlic cloves, minced
2 tablespoons
  chopped fresh
  parsley
1 teaspoon fresh
  thyme leaves
3 tablespoons tomato
  paste
1 pound salted
  cod, desalted
  (see page 197)
  and shredded
½ cup water
3 whole cloves
Freshly ground
  black pepper

SERVES 4 TO 6

I should start off by saying that every single version of stewed saltfish I've ever tried has been a beautiful experience. It doesn't matter that they don't taste like my mother's version—salty cod with seasonings just equals goodness. I've had bacalao guisado from Puerto Rico that made me want to cry tears of joy. In Saint Lucia, I tried a version with turmeric that blew my mind. But at the end of the day, the different types of stewed saltfish are all *very* similar. Here, I chose to highlight the Haitian version as a variation because of three things: One, it's delicious. Two, it's different from many others because it's slightly saucier; the tomato paste gives it a deeper flavor than the acidic zip you'd get from fresh tomatoes. And three, the cloves, a standard seasoning in Haitian food, marry with the saltfish in the most unusual way, giving a hint of warm spice to a dish that generally doesn't have it.

In a medium saucepan, heat the olive oil over medium heat. Add the onion, bell pepper, garlic, parsley, and thyme and cook until the onion and bell pepper are soft, 3 to 5 minutes.

Add the tomato paste, stir to completely combine, and cook for about 2 minutes, until it's dark and fragrant. Add the cod and stir to coat it completely. Pour in the water and give it a good stir before adding the cloves and black pepper to taste.

Bring everything to a simmer, then reduce the heat to low, cover, and simmer for 20 minutes, until all the flavors have melded together. Fish out the cloves if you can find them (if not, just warn everyone that they're hanging around) and serve.

SERENATA DE BACALAO

SALTED COD SALAD ○ PUERTO RICO

1 green plantain, peeled and cut in half (see page 154)

2 or 3 small potatoes (about 10 ounces total)

1 pound salted cod, desalted (see page 197) and shredded

3 hard-boiled eggs, peeled and cut into wedges

1 cup diced tomatoes or halved cherry tomatoes

1 small red onion, thinly sliced

½ green bell pepper, sliced

½ yellow bell pepper, sliced

1 garlic clove, minced

1 tablespoon capers, rinsed and roughly chopped

¼ cup extra-virgin olive oil

3 tablespoons sherry vinegar or white wine vinegar

Freshly ground black pepper

SERVES 4 TO 6

This salad is a great hot-summer-day meal or bring-to-the-cookout go-to. It can be as simple or complicated as you want to make it. I like mine somewhere in between. The eggs might seem like overkill, but they add some substance to the dish that helps take it to full-meal status. It does take a bit of prep work and time, but once everything is boiled and chopped, it comes together quickly. I suppose you could consider it a cousin to the fresh version of Buljol (page 206), but the flavor profile and ingredients are so different, I think they're more like second cousins once removed. Other possible additions are olives, any firm, boiled provisions you like, or red bell peppers. Many people make this with red wine vinegar, but I particularly like the hint of sweetness you get from sherry vinegar. It's another great example of the many ways the people of the region can find to dress up some salted cod.

Bring a medium saucepan of water to a boil over high heat. Add the plantain to the pot and cook for 15 minutes, until it's getting soft. Add the potatoes and cook everything until the potatoes and plantain are tender and the plantain flesh is bright yellow, about 10 minutes more. Drain the potatoes and plantain and set aside until cool enough to handle, then peel the potatoes and cut the plantain and potatoes into ½-inch-thick rounds.

Transfer the plantain and potatoes to a large bowl and add the fish, eggs, tomatoes, onion, bell peppers, garlic, and capers. Mix with your hands to thoroughly combine. Pour the olive oil and vinegar on top, give it a few grinds of black pepper, and use a large spoon to mix it all again. If you have the time, this salad tastes best if given about an hour to sit before serving, but is still good straight away. It will keep overnight in an airtight container in the fridge.

SCOTCH BONNET PEPPERS

CAPSICUM CHINENSE

Other name: PIMAN

I HAVE TO START THIS CHAPTER with a disclaimer: While Scotch bonnet peppers may be the taste I most associate with Caribbean food, they are not, in fact, used across the entire region. The Spanish-speaking countries—Cuba, the Dominican Republic, and Puerto Rico—don't use them, and in fact hardly use any kind of hot pepper at all (though their ají dulce peppers look deceivingly similar to Scotch bonnets). On other islands, the go-to hot pepper differs—for instance, in Guyana, it's the wiri wiri pepper—but most Caribbean countries where English and French are spoken either prefer the distinctive Scotch bonnet or fall back on it as a close-second option. I cannot imagine cooking without them, and they find their way into nearly all my dishes, from pasta sauces to burgers. They are possibly the only food that is directly native to the Caribbean and were first seen growing in Cuba by Europeans. They are named for their resemblance to a tam-o'-shanter hat from Scotland. Belonging to the species *Capsicum chinense*, which includes habanero peppers, the group known as Scotch bonnets are one of the hottest chile peppers around, with a heat rating of 100,000 to 350,000 Scoville heat units (SHU). To put that into context, most jalapeños have a rating of 2,500 to 8,000 SHU.

Scotch bonnet peppers are loved not just for their heat, which is largely located in their seeds, but also for their flavor. I think they're the most flavorful chile peppers and have what I describe as a smoky taste. On our first date, Atibon made me turkey burgers and had me guess what the "secret" ingredient was. It took me about a second to figure out it was Scotch bonnet. The taste is very singular, so please note that if you're substituting another chile, like the related habanero, you are changing the flavor profile of the dish.

In addition to being used in food, the Scotch bonnet has had many other uses throughout the history of the islands. Chile smoke was used as a type of chemical weapon by Indigenous people in attacks on Columbus's fort in Santo Domingo (one of the names for the island shared by Haiti and the Dominican Republic). Chiles also play a role in spiritual ceremonies. For instance, in Haitian Vodoun, the Gede—the family of *lwa* (spirits) associated with the life cycle of fertility and death—love spice and are particularly fond of a drink called piman—white rum infused with (many) Scotch bonnet peppers for a year. Those that are inhabited by these spirits during a Vodoun ceremony might rub this spicy libation on their body, or eat a pepper whole, with seemingly no ill effects. Don't try that at home!

HOW TO CHOOSE: Look for fruits with smooth, unwrinkled skin and no dark blemishes. The color of the pepper doesn't matter; a ripe pepper will be very hot whether it's green, yellow, or red.

HOW TO STORE: For short-term storage, Scotch bonnets keep well in a zip-top bag in the fridge for 2 to 4 weeks. You can also store them in a zip-top bag in the freezer for 6 months or so, though they do seem to lose some heat the longer they are in there.

HOW TO PREPARE: When working with these peppers, it's important to be very careful. Some people recommend using plastic gloves while you prep them; I personally do not wear them, but I make sure not to touch the inside of the peppers or the seeds, where the heat is, when I'm handling them. In some dishes, the pepper is used whole and can be pricked with a fork to let some of the heat escape. To cut them, first halve the pepper lengthwise (through the stem end), then, if you'd like to cut down on some heat, scrape out the seeds with a small spoon. Place the chile halves face down on the cutting board, slice and mince them carefully, and thoroughly wash your hands afterward if you weren't using gloves. Be mindful that your cutting board now has very spicy oils on it, and anything you cut on it will be spicy, too! And be *very* careful about touching any part of your body immediately after cutting them, even after you've washed your hands. The amounts of peppers listed in these recipes are more of a guideline. Most of us like our food *spicy.* But you have to be able to eat it! In recent years, I've dialed down the amount of pepper I use for the sake of my daughter, but I won't leave it out. She's developing a nice heat tolerance. A real Caribbean gyal!

PIKLIZ

2 cups shredded
green cabbage
(about ½ small)
1 cup shredded carrot
(about 1 large)
½ cup thinly sliced
yellow onion
(about 1 small)
4 to 5 Scotch bonnet
peppers, thickly
sliced
2 garlic cloves, peeled
and halved
4 whole cloves
1 teaspoon kosher salt
½ teaspoon
freshly ground
black pepper
¼ cup fresh lime juice
(from about 1 juicy
lime)
1½ to 2 cups distilled
white vinegar

MAKES 3 CUPS

Pikliz is a magical Haitian condiment that I understood in theory but didn't truly *get* until the first time I tried it. Atibon would explain it to me, and (as usual) I would roll my eyes at his Haitian superiority and say, "Okay, so it's hot sauce?" No. He'd try to explain again. "Okay, so it's spicy coleslaw?" Then it was his turn to roll his eyes. Trying to define pikliz is an impossible feat, but I suppose you could say it falls somewhere between those two things. The acid from the pickling liquid creates a refreshing bite that combines perfectly with the intense heat from the peppers. The cloves add a mysterious allure, and all together I can't think of anything better to top fried food, or grilled meat, or . . . well, just about anything. Every family makes their pikliz differently, but I promise you every Haitian kitchen has a jar going. The vinegar from your pikliz is also a treasured cooking ingredient. Try substituting it anywhere vinegar is called for, if you like things spicy. If you like, you can shred the cabbage, carrot, and onion in a food processor using the S-blade.

Combine the cabbage, carrot, and onion in a large bowl, using your hands to make sure everything is evenly distributed. In a 1-quart jar, layer the cabbage mixture with the Scotch bonnet slices, garlic, and cloves, making sure there are some ingredients at every level. Sprinkle in the salt and black pepper, then add the lime juice and enough vinegar to cover the ingredients completely. Close the jar tightly and turn it upside down a few times. You can certainly use it right away, but the flavors develop best if you let it sit for a week in the refrigerator before using it. It will keep in the fridge almost indefinitely, but I guarantee it won't last long before being eaten up.

PEPPER SAUCE

HOT SAUCE ○ TRINIDAD AND TOBAGO

15 Scotch bonnet peppers, halved

3 seasoning peppers, halved (optional; see page 14)

1 head garlic, cloves smashed and peeled

6 culantro leaves, or ½ cup fresh cilantro, roughly chopped

½ cup apple cider vinegar

Juice of 1 to 1½ limes (3 to 4 tablespoons)

1 heaping tablespoon whole-grain mustard

1½ teaspoons kosher salt

1 teaspoon grated fresh ginger

MAKES JUST OVER 1 CUP

This recipe is inspired by my uncle Richard, a man of few words whose pepper sauce was one of our family's most sought-after export items from the island. I will always remember coming back to the house in Princes Town after a day out in San Fernando and finding him on the couch, calmly watching his Westerns with his hands up in the air covered in Vaseline. When asked what happened, he shrugged nonchalantly and said he'd made a batch of pepper sauce. This pepper sauce appeared to have given him at least first-degree burns, and if that's not a cautionary tale, I don't know what is! His sacrifices did not go in vain; that stuff was liquid gold in our households, and the moment the last little speck was done, my mom would be on the phone asking who was going to the island next to bring more back home. I wish I could have gotten his secret recipe before he passed, but I feel strongly that if he were still here, he'd taste the pepper sauce I've developed over many, many years of trying to replicate his, and just smile.

Use any kind of mustard you have on hand. If you can't find seasoning peppers, it's okay to omit them. They simply amplify the smoky taste of the Scotch bonnets, which is what makes this sauce so distinctive. As always, be careful when handling the peppers, and take extra care when washing up after. (I've heard of someone passing out from the fumes when hot water hit the blender where the peppers had been!) This sauce can go on just about anything, but it makes a great addition to rice dishes, such as Arroz con Pollo (page 188) or Pelau (page 189). Remember, a little goes a long way.

Place all the ingredients in a food processor or blender and process for a few minutes until completely blended and almost smooth. Transfer the sauce to a glass jar and store in the fridge until infinity.

FÉROCE D'AVOCAT

SPICY SALTED COD AND AVOCADO PÂTÉ ○ MARTINIQUE

1 or 2 avocados (about
  25 ounces total)
¼ cup fresh lime juice
8 ounces salted cod,
  desalted (see
  page 197) and
  roughly shredded
1 cup cassava flour
1 small shallot,
  chopped
1 garlic clove, smashed
  and peeled
1 to 2 Scotch bonnet
  peppers, chopped
¼ cup fresh parsley
  leaves
3 tablespoons extra-
  virgin olive oil
Freshly ground
  black pepper

SERVES 8 TO 10

The name of this dish translates to "ferocious avocado." That does not mean there's an evil avocado plotting your downfall—rather, the ferocity comes from the hot pepper, which should be *very* prominent. This dish is highly addictive. In Martinique, it's often rolled up into little balls and eaten on its own, but it's also great on crackers, toasted baguette, corn chips, or Casabe (page 69). This is traditionally made with large "Caribbean" or "tropical" avocados—these are often more than twice the size of a Hass avocado and have relatively smooth, bright-green skin—but any variety will do. Just know that if you're looking to serve it in the shell, you'll need something on the larger side. Cassava flour is gaining popularity these days and you might even find it at your local grocery store. If not, health food stores are a great place to look, and of course the internet will always help you out. Féroce d'avocat is a great party snack and will have your guests making a lot of full-mouthed exclamations of joy.

Cut up the avocado and put it in a food processor. Sprinkle it with the lime juice to prevent it from browning. If you have a large avocado, keep the shell for serving, if you like.

Add the fish, cassava flour, shallot, garlic, Scotch bonnet, parsley, olive oil, and black pepper to taste to the food processor and process until smooth. Serve in the reserved avocado shell or in a bowl. Leftovers will keep in an airtight container in the fridge overnight.

CHIKTAY

SPICY SMOKED HERRING SALAD ○ HAITI

6 smoked herring
  fillets
5 tablespoons extra-
  virgin olive oil
1 shallot, minced
¼ cup finely diced
  green bell pepper
¼ cup finely diced
  red bell pepper
3 garlic cloves, minced
1 or 2 Scotch bonnet
  peppers, minced
¼ cup fresh parsley
  leaves, chopped
1 teaspoon fresh
  thyme leaves,
  chopped
2 tablespoons fresh
  lime juice
Freshly ground
  black pepper

SERVES 6 TO 8

Chiktay always makes me think of parties, as that's where I always seem to have it. If smoked herring were a person, they would have a *strong* personality, so chiktay doesn't need a lot of bells and whistles to dress it up. The oil factor, however, can be tricky, as it's hard to find a sweet spot between too dry (as desalting it removes much of its oil) and too oily, but I've got you covered. While I would say chiktay should always be *hot*, I wouldn't say it's something that should make your mouth feel like it's going to fall out. You want a heat level that will be a slow, sort of pleasant and tingly burn. I describe my first experience with smoked herring on page 118, and I'll say again that cooking smoked herring is fragrant. If you feel differently about the taste, that may not be the adjective you'd use. But it's worth it. You can serve chitkay warm or at room temperature on top of Fried Green Plantains (page 168), Casabe (page 69), crackers, or chips.

First, desalt the herring: Place the fillets in a small saucepan, add water to cover, and bring to a boil over medium-high heat. Cook for about 10 minutes, then drain the herring. You'll only need to do this once. Let the herring cool a bit, then shred it in a food processor. Don't worry about the bones. They are very fine, and the blades will make short work of them.

In a medium skillet, heat the olive oil over medium heat until shimmering. Add the shallot, bell peppers, garlic, Scotch bonnet (use 1 for less heat, 2 for more!), parsley, and thyme and sauté until the shallot and peppers begin to soften, 3 to 5 minutes.

Add the herring to the pan and stir in the lime juice, along with several good grinds of black pepper. Mix everything together well before removing from the heat and transferring to a serving bowl. Chiktay will keep in an airtight container in the fridge for about a week; just bring it to room temperature before serving.

MANGO CHOW

SPICY MANGO SALAD ○ TRINIDAD AND TOBAGO

2 half-ripe large
    mangoes, peeled,
    pitted, and sliced
    lengthwise into
    thick strips
Juice of 2 limes
1 teaspoon kosher salt
5 garlic cloves, minced
½ Scotch bonnet
    pepper, seeded and
    minced
¼ cup fresh cilantro,
    roughly chopped

SERVES 4 TO 6

Trinidadian writer, recipe developer, and food expert Brigid Washington contributed this recipe for mango chow, one of my favorite dishes in the world. She remembers how, on her way home from school, she would buy chow from Ms. Dolly, a crotchety woman who had no love of children but made the best chow Brigid had ever had. Though she'd never say it, you knew Ms. Dolly liked you when she gave you the mango seed to suck on.

As Brigid got older, this daily ritual began to take on meaning, as she began to understand that she had control over what she chose to do with her money. In a world when many choices were made for her, she could choose what she wanted to do with this money, and she chose chow. For her, chow became a symbol of her own agency. What makes this dish so good? How does it have the power to change lives? It's in part its simplicity. As Brigid says, it's so accessible at every point—to eat it and to make it. All parts of it are so rewarding.

I have made all kinds of chow, with pineapple (even grilled pineapple), cucumber, or tomatoes. But the classic chow, ideally made with what Trinidadians call "force ripe" mangoes, sort of a half-ripe fruit, is both my and Brigid's favorite. The heat level is up to you. I like mine *very* fiery, but Brigid prefers hers a bit more mellow. No matter what, there should always be a kick.

Place the mangoes in a medium bowl. Add the lime juice, salt, garlic, Scotch bonnet, and cilantro. Toss to combine using a fork. Serve immediately.

MAROONS

Though perhaps most famous in Jamaica because of their ties to jerk seasoning, Maroons, or Mawons in Haitian Kreyòl, existed anywhere the Atlantic slave trade did, all across the Caribbean islands and up and down the Atlantic Coast from North America to South America. The first recorded slave rebellion, which created the first group of Maroons, took place in the sixteenth century, on the island of Ayiti (the original Taíno name for the island shared by Haiti and the Dominican Republic today, meaning "mountainous island"), on the side that would later become the Dominican Republic.

When escaping the terrifying conditions of the plantations where they were enslaved, the most common thing for enslaved Africans to do was to flee up into the mountains. In those days, the densely forested mountains would have been nearly impossible to navigate (there are many places in the Caribbean that still are), and the enslavers would have had a hard time chasing them. While some Maroons left by boat, and some, especially skilled laborers, fled to cities where they could blend in with the population, most headed upward and settled in the mountains with the help of the Indigenous people already living there. Not much is recorded about the interactions between the enslaved Africans and the native peoples of the Caribbean, but we know they mixed, had children together, lived together, and traded culinary traditions.

In this wilderness, communities of Maroons were established, and from it they raided the plantations at night. They were a scourge on the plantation owners, both because their escape was a loss of labor, and because these raids, during which they took food, weapons, tools, and, when possible, their own family members, cost a lot. Anyone who attempted to escape the plantation and was captured (especially folks who made the journey more than once) suffered some of the cruelest punishments that resulted in horrific deaths. I suppose this was to make an example out of them and deter anyone else from trying to escape.

But the colonizers underestimated both the enslaved Africans' ability, and their will, to escape the sheer horror of their conditions. It was worth trying to escape and suffer a terrible fate, because the way they lived day in and out was intolerable. They were successful in part because of their ability to live off the land, with the help of the Indigenous people, and because they became well versed in guerilla warfare, which baffled European soldiers who were only familiar with war on the battlefields of Europe.

Perhaps one of the most famous Maroons was an escaped slave named Dutty Boukmann in Haiti. His backstory is murky: We know he was originally from a region in West Africa historically known as Senegambia. The story says he came to Haiti from Jamaica, but more recent research suggests he may have been in Haiti all along. Boukmann was a huge man with a charismatic persona who preached freedom everywhere he went. It is said he taught himself how to read and helped others learn as well. He was, one might say, the original Malcom X. On August 14, 1791, Boukmann presided over the famous Bwa Kayiman ceremony, alongside a Vodoun priestess named Cécile Fatiman. Vodoun ceremonies had long been a chance for the enslaved to meet and plan. Legend has it that the drums were heard all through the mountains that night as the group called on the many manifestations of Ogoun, the *loa* of war, such as Ogoun Feray and Ogoun Balendjo, to help them with their uprising. This led to the great slave revolt of 1791, which some look at as the beginning of the Haitian Revolution. Many of the Taíno people living up in the mountains with the Maroons joined in this fight. Boukmann was eventually caught a few months later, and his head was put on a spike by the French to try to scare others into submission. This had the opposite effect, however, instead making the man a legend, inspiring those for centuries to come to stand up and fight against those who tried to hold them down.

JERK CHICKEN

JAMAICA

JERK SEASONING

1 yellow onion,
  chopped
1 large head garlic,
  cloves smashed and
  peeled
1 bunch scallions,
  roughly chopped
3 tablespoons
  brown sugar
2 tablespoons allspice
  berries, toasted and
  crushed in a pilon
2 tablespoons fresh
  thyme leaves
1 tablespoon
  kosher salt
1 (2-inch) piece fresh
  ginger, peeled and
  roughly chopped
2 to 3 Scotch bonnet
  peppers, halved
1 teaspoon
  freshly ground
  black pepper
½ teaspoon freshly
  grated nutmeg

3 pounds bone-in,
  skin-on chicken
  thighs
Neutral oil, for the
  grill grates

SERVES 4 TO 6

Jerk chicken is probably the most iconic dish from Jamaica, if not the entire Caribbean. Though so many around the world claim to love it, few really know what it is. The jerk sauces you see at your local grocery store are *not* it. To get to the bottom of it, you have to first start with the Maroons (see page 220), enslaved Africans who escaped from plantations into the mountains, and the food they needed to sustain them on their journey. The term *jerk* comes from a word the Maroons used for the Taíno method of "jirking" meat, which involved cutting it up, salting it, seasoning it, and curing it in the sun before cooking it in the fire. Legend says the Taíno taught the Maroons this art and also taught them how to create underground firepits so the smoke would not be detected. These methods were perfect for a group of people on the move who needed food that could keep for long stretches and ways of cooking that wouldn't attract attention. At the time, jerk pork was most common, as wild pigs abounded on the island.

Though there were Maroons all throughout the Caribbean, jerk didn't seem to catch hold anywhere the way it did in Jamaica. When slavery was abolished there in 1838, the Maroons were free to come down from the mountains and sell their particular preparation of meat. It turns out, while jerk chicken served a crucial purpose for survival, its combination of spices, the hot pepper, and the smoking method resulted in some of the most delectable meat you'd ever eat. While it's rare to find people cooking this in a pit now, the tradition of using the wood of the allspice tree to build the fire has continued today on the island, which gives the meat a particular flavor. This recipe cannot possibly claim to be *true* jerk, as there are a lot of factors that come together to claim that word. But I'll tell you, I stand by this version of jerk seasoning, and a charcoal grill will get you close to the real deal. If you have to use gas, go for it, and if you don't have a grill, you can certainly roast the thighs in the oven and still have a delicious meal. But do know that the low-and-slow method, as well as the smoke, are really integral parts of this dish. Jerk chicken is great with Diri ak Pwa (page 28), Bammies (page 72), or Festivals (page 120).

Note: Please do remember the marinated thighs have hot pepper on them! While I normally recommend using your hands to cover meat with marinade, I don't do so here. Either wear plastic gloves or use the method described in the second step because you must get that marinade in every nook and cranny.

RECIPE CONTINUES

To make the jerk seasoning: Put the onion, garlic, scallions, brown sugar, allspice berries, thyme, salt, ginger, Scotch bonnet, black pepper, and nutmeg in a blender or food processor and blend until smooth.

Using a sharp paring knife, make some slashes in the chicken thighs to help ensure the flavor (and the heat!) gets everywhere. Put the thighs in a large zip-top bag, then pour in the jerk seasoning (see Note on page 223). Massage the seasoning around to make sure it's evenly distributed and gets in all the slashes, then seal the bag and refrigerate for 24 hours.

About 30 minutes before cooking the chicken thighs, take them out of the fridge to bring them to room temperature.

Prepare a grill: If using a charcoal grill, stack the coals on one side and get a fire going. When the coals are all blazing and the grates are well heated up and oiled, shake the excess seasoning off the chicken. (You can do this wearing plastic gloves, or use tongs. Or, if you're like me, live wild and use your bare hands.) Reserve the marinade. Place the thighs skin-side down on the side of the grill opposite the coals, so they get indirect heat. Cover the grill, open the vent all the way, and position it directly over the chicken. (If using a gas grill, light the burners on one side and heat the grill to about 250°F. Place the chicken skin-side down on the side with no flame and cover the grill.)

Cook, flipping the chicken every 20 minutes and basting it with about a third of the remaining seasoning each time, for about 80 minutes, until the thighs are a deep mahogany brown with some charring in parts, and perfectly tender. If you find that the skin needs more crisping, give it 5 minutes over the flames with the lid off.

Allow the thighs to rest 15 minutes or so before serving.

SÒS TI-MALICE WITH SHRIMP

SHRIMP WITH HOT SAUCE ○ HAITI

SÒS TI-MALICE

1 tablespoon extra-
virgin olive oil
½ small yellow onion,
diced
2 small shallots
4 garlic cloves, minced
½ cup diced green
bell pepper
¼ cup diced red
bell pepper
1 to 2 Scotch bonnet
peppers, minced
2 tablespoons tomato
paste
1 teaspoon fresh
thyme leaves
2 tablespoons Pikliz
vinegar (page 214)
or apple cider
vinegar
2 tablespoons fresh
lime juice (from
about ½ lime)
1 cup water
½ teaspoon kosher salt
Freshly ground
black pepper

1 pound shelled shrimp
2 tablespoons fresh
lime juice
Kosher salt and
freshly ground
black pepper
1 tablespoon extra-
virgin olive oil
1 tablespoon salted
butter

SERVES 4 TO 6

This sauce gets its name from Ti-Malice, a character in Haitian folklore. Ti-Malice is very sharp and is always getting one over on his friend (or frenemy) Tonton Bouki. Bouki is very greedy and is always stopping by uninvited at mealtimes to eat all of Ti-Malice's food. In an effort to stop this, Ti-Malice tries making a sauce that is so hot, it will scare off Bouki forever. However, his plan backfires when his friend falls in love with the sauce, then sets off to tell everyone how good "Ti-Malice's sauce" is.

Sòs Ti-Malice is often used as a condiment, but I prefer to cook with it. For that reason, I don't put as many peppers in as you could (though it still packs a major punch!), but adjust the number of peppers to your heat tolerance. In addition to shrimp, as it's served here, the sauce is also wonderful to cook fish in, or to add to any type of soup or stew. This particular dish is great over "Perfect" White Rice (page 180), but also works well with Mangú (page 158) or Fungee (page 138).

Make the sòs Ti-Malice: In a medium saucepan, heat the olive oil over medium heat. Add the onion, shallots, and garlic and sauté until they begin to soften, 3 to 4 minutes. Add the bell peppers, Scotch bonnet, tomato paste, and thyme, and cook for 3 minutes, until the tomato paste is dark and fragrant. Add the vinegar, lime juice, water, salt, and black pepper to taste. Reduce the heat to low and simmer for 15 minutes, until the mixture is thick and the flavors have blended together. Remove from the heat.

Sprinkle the shrimp with the lime juice and lightly season them with salt and pepper. Set aside.

In a large skillet, heat the olive oil and butter over medium heat until the butter has melted. Add the shrimp and cook until mostly pink, about 2 minutes per side. Add ¾ to 1 cup of the sòs Ti-Malice and stir to coat. Cook until the shrimp is cooked through, about 5 minutes, and serve immediately.

PEPPER SHRIMP

SPICY WHOLE SHRIMP ○ JAMAICA

1 pound head-on,
  shell-on large
  shrimp
½ small yellow onion,
  minced
2 Scotch bonnet
  peppers, minced
3 garlic cloves, minced
1 tablespoon crushed
  allspice berries
2 teaspoons fresh
  thyme leaves,
  minced
2 scallions, thinly sliced
2 teaspoons annatto
  powder (optional)
2 teaspoons
  kosher salt
Freshly ground
  black pepper
1 tablespoon
  coconut oil
¼ cup water
2 tablespoons distilled
  white vinegar

SERVES 4

Pepper shrimp is most often found as a roadside snack, particularly in the area of St. Anne, Jamaica. Shrimp in the shell is key, as it has so much more flavor, and peeling them is half the fun. Today, some people use red food coloring to give the dish its signature color, but traditionally it was tinted with annatto seeds. It's also perfectly acceptable for the shrimp to not be red. What's *not* acceptable is for them to be anything less than burning hot, hence the name. My sweet spot is two Scotch bonnet peppers, seeds and all, but adjust to your heat tolerance.

In a medium bowl, mix the shrimp with the onion, Scotch bonnet, garlic, allspice, thyme, scallions, annatto powder (if using), salt, and black pepper to taste. Set aside in the fridge for an hour.

In a wide skillet with a lid, heat the coconut oil over medium heat. Add the shrimp in one layer, with all the marinade, and add the water and the vinegar. Cover and cook until the shrimp are pink on the bottom, about 4 minutes. Flip each shrimp, cover the skillet, and cook for 4 minutes on the second side. Transfer the shrimp to a serving bowl, discarding any liquid in the pan. The shrimp can be served warm or at room temperature. Be sure to warn anyone eating them that these shrimp will make your fingers burn a little and your mouth a lot.

SNAPPER ESCOVITCH-ISH

GRILLED SNAPPER WITH SPICY SHALLOT VINAIGRETTE
○ JAMAICA

3 garlic cloves, minced

2 teaspoons fresh thyme leaves, chopped

1 tablespoon extra-virgin olive oil, plus more as needed

4 pounds whole red snapper or other white-fleshed fish, cleaned

Kosher salt and freshly ground black pepper

Thyme sprigs

1 lime, sliced

ESCOVITCH

2 tablespoons extra-virgin olive oil

2 shallots, thinly sliced

¼ red bell pepper, thinly sliced

¼ yellow bell pepper, thinly sliced

1 to 2 Scotch bonnet peppers, thinly sliced

1 large carrot, julienned

2 garlic cloves, sliced

5 allspice berries

3 tablespoons apple cider vinegar

1 tablespoon fresh lime juice

½ teaspoon kosher salt

SERVES 4

Escovitch fish is a dish that was all around me growing up. I love all the parts of this dish individually, but I have come to realize that (and stay with me here, for any Jamaicans reading this) it's just a bit too vinegary for me, so I've made some adjustments. Yellow onions are more traditional than shallots, but I like how the shallots mellow out faster. And while I also love fried fish, frying a whole fish at home is just not a thing I do very often. I prefer to grill the whole fish, even if the process can be a bit daunting. Because the fish gets completely covered with this highly spiced and fragrant mixture of, essentially, quick pickled veggies, I don't think you're missing out that much by grilling it instead of frying it. If you don't have a grill, broil the fish for about 15 minutes, until browned and charred and cooked through to the bone.

This dish may have been an import from the Portuguese, who are known for dousing cooked fish with something acidic and who have quietly influenced food across the Caribbean in some surprisingly profound ways. Jamaica has 100% made it their own, and though my take is slightly different, I'd say it still keeps to its roots. This recipe works well with other white-fleshed fish, and I've had particular luck with sea bass.

In a small bowl, combine the garlic, thyme leaves, and olive oil. With a sharp paring knife, make two or three slashes on each side of the fish. Generously rub the fish all over with salt and black pepper, paying special attention to the slits and cavities. With your fingers, stuff the slits with the garlic mixture, rubbing any you have left over inside the cavity. Lightly rub the whole fish with olive oil and stuff the fish with the thyme sprigs and lime slices. Let the fish sit while you heat the grill.

Prepare a grill: If using a charcoal grill, stack the coals on one side and light them, or set half the burners on a gas grill to high. Make sure the grill grates are very well oiled.

Place the fish on the side of the grill opposite the coals (or the lit burners) and cook, uncovered, for 8 to 12 minutes on each side (it could be less if they're small), or until the skin is nice and charred.

While the fish is grilling, make the escovitch: In a wide saucepan, heat the olive oil over medium heat. Add the shallots, bell peppers, Scotch bonnet, carrot, garlic, and allspice berries and cook until the veggies are *just* beginning to soften, about 3 minutes. You want them to retain some crunch. Carefully pour in the vinegar and lime juice, being mindful of splatters. Stir in the salt, remove from the heat, and set aside.

When the fish is done cooking, place it on a large serving platter and cover it with the veggie mixture. Allow the fish to sit at room temperature for at least 1 hour to let the flavors deepen and settle, or preferably in the fridge for 2 hours or more. Bring to room temperature before serving.

ACKNOWLEDGMENTS

First and foremost, I must thank my dear longtime friend and food guru of my life, Lukas Volger. This book wouldn't have even been an idea without your tireless guidance and belief. Thank you for being my mentor, cheerleader, editor, reality check, and, of course, friend.

Secondly, I have to thank Atibon Nazaire for believing in this book from its inception and inspiring it with your embrace of all our cultures. Thank you for looking at everyone from the African diaspora (and the continent itself) as your brother and sister. Thank you for being a daily sounding board, allowing me to talk in circles until I got it right. Thank you for digging deep in your connections and knowledge to make this book as great as it could be, for sitting through meal after meal after meal of (sometimes not winning) tests, for being an honest critic and a steadfast advocate. Thank you for constantly peering over my shoulder with questions, suggestions, and critiques while I was cooking. Even though it usually annoyed me, I know the book is better for it. And thank you for being a caretaker of your culture—it is inspiring.

Thank you to my daughter, Desalin, for your spirit, your love of helping me in the kitchen, your willingness to try new foods, and your early embrace of your culture. Thank you for being one of the only three- (and then four-!) year-olds I know who would actually eat all the food I tested.

Thank you to my agent, Kari Stuart, for believing in this project from the outset, for putting up with all my novice questions with such grace, for being a badass on my behalf, and being genuinely concerned with honest representation for all cultures on the bookshelves. Thank you to Allison Renzulli for being all in for this from day one and for answering so many late night text questions! Thank you to Dervla Kelly for really understanding what I was trying to do and advocating for this book. And thank you to my editor, Claire Yee, who came on to the project with so much enthusiasm. Your mindful edits and thoughtful (and plentiful!) questions made this book infinitely better. Thank you to Ivy McFadden for your ability to turn what was sometimes word vomit into wine! Thank you Lizzie Allen for really listening and changing things again (and again) to make this gorgeous book.

Thank you to the rest of the Ten Speed team: Natalie Blachere, Abby Oladipo, Gabby Ureña Matos, Mari Gill, and Jane Chinn.

I have so much appreciation and love for the team that made these stunning photos a reality. Thank you Marc Baptiste and Paul Storey for the beautiful photos. Nicole Taylor told me Gerri Williams and her props were the secret sauce to her book, and I believe it! Thank you, Gerri, for being so committed to this project, for your artistic vision, and for being so ride-or-die! Thank you, Luciana Lamboy, for killing it on the food, for understanding where it's all coming from, and for truly doing whatever it takes. Thank you, Sadie Frost, Rosanna Añil, and Skye Baptiste for all your creativity, hard work, and laughter. Thank you all for making magic happen and keeping a sense of humor while doing it. Thank you, Leslie Siegel, for the beautiful surfaces from your rental shop, Surface Workshop (surfaceworkshop .nyc)! They truly made the images shine. Thank you Roodolph, Jessica, Saul, and Kaia Senecal for letting us completely take over your lovely home (and fridge!) for this photo shoot. Thank you Deanna Wallach for those sexy beans.

Thank you to my sister, Kelly Enston, for being so hype about this book on my behalf, for testing recipes, for sharing memories of Mom and the food we ate growing up. Thank you, Sarah Arias; her mami, Caridad Santana; and the whole Arias-Peralta family, for the knowledge, the meals, the recipes, the answers to my late-night text questions, and the love. Thank you to my cousin Ashayna for answering all my random Jamaican food questions. Thank you to César Pérez for one of the most enjoyable phone calls I've had since I was a teenager, and all the amazing knowledge and anecdotes about Puerto Rican cuisine. Thank you Malcolm Livingston for helping to answer a Bajan mystery. Thank you to our neighbor Miss Bibi for always sharing food with us, and for sharing her recipes for this book.

Thank you to all my chosen family, who have supported me through this process, who listened to all the saga of writing a cookbook while working and mothering, who both tested recipes for me, and who sat at my table as my guinea pigs time and time again: Gabriel Cyr, Geko Jones, Abena Koomson-Davis, Blair Smith (also for regularly contributing your copy skills), and Jane Son. Thank you, Amisi and Fidel Nazaire Hicks, for testing recipes and sitting through and eating them! Thank you, Kasey Hearns, Joe Dyson, and Sage Dyson, for sitting for so, *so* many test dinners and eating so many fried things in the name of science. And a special thank-you, Kasey, for testing so many recipes in your small but mighty kitchen—your feedback was invaluable. Thanks to Richard Renzulli for being the discerning tester I knew you would be! Thank you Liz Mulholland and Chris Nelson (and Bess!) for eating my experiments and being so supportive of this process. Thank you to Susan Morgan, Cheickh Aidara, Alioune Aidara, and Assane Aidara for coming through and letting me burn your mouths with all this hot peppa! Thank you to my team at GMHC for being so supportive of this book and all my "I won't be online todays." Thank you Chris Spinelli for your eye and helping me speak design.

Thank you to those who came before me and set the stage for me to be able to do this at all.

ABOUT THE AUTHOR

For **LESLEY ENSTON**, cooking has always been a way to connect to her Caribbean roots. After growing up in Toronto, moving to Brooklyn, and spending a few years in London, she ultimately settled in Bedford-Stuyvesant, Brooklyn. Along the way she's consistently found herself over a stovetop, preparing the dishes her Trini mother first introduced her to, along with all her favorite foods from around the islands—and putting Scotch bonnet in just about everything. Lesley is a seasoned home cook and takes great pleasure in spreading the joy (and heat) of these flavors to her friends and loved ones by way of her famed backyard dinner parties. Better yet, Lesley's young daughter, Desalin, now plays the role of sous-chef, enjoying the flavors her mother and grandmother cherish so deeply. You can find Lesley's recipes in *Bon Appétit*, Food52, and the *New York Times*.

FURTHER READING

These books were invaluable resources for researching this book, and if the subject matter interests you, I encourage you to check them out.

Judith A. Carney, *Black Rice: The African Origins of Rice Cultivation in the Americas* (Cambridge, MA: Harvard University Press, 2001).

Alfred W. Crosby, *The Columbian Exchange: Biological and Cultural Consequences of 1492* (Westport, CT: Praeger Publishers, 2003).

Richard S. Dunn, *Sugar and Slaves: The Rise of the Planter Class in the English West Indies, 1624–1713* (Chapel Hill, NC: University of North Carolina Press, 1972).

Hannah Garth and contributors, *Food and Identity in the Caribbean* (New York: Bloomsbury, 2013).

Candice Goucher, *Congotay! Congotay! A Global History of Caribbean Food* (New York: M.E. Sharpe, 2014).

Lynn Marie Houston, *Food Culture in the Caribbean* (Westport, CT: Greenwood Press, 2005).

Christine Mackie, *Life and Food in the Caribbean* (New York: New Amsterdam Books, 1991).

Sidney W. Mintz, *Sweetness and Power: The Place of Sugar in Modern History* (New York: Penguin Books, 1985).

Cruz Miguel Ortíz Cuadra, *Eating Puerto Rico: A History of Food, Culture and Identity* (Chapel Hill, NC: University of North Carolina Press, 2013).

H. D. Tindall, *Vegetables in the Tropics* (London, UK: Macmillan, 1983).

FURTHER COOKING

To dive deeper into the cuisines of the islands, I highly recommend these books, both new and old. The dates on many of these should highlight that we need new cookbooks!

Cuba María Josefa Lluriá de O'Higgins, *A Taste of Old Cuba* (New York: HarperCollins Publishers, 1994).

Mary Urrutia Randelman and Joan Schwartz, *Memories of a Cuban Kitchen* (New York: Wiley Publishing, 1992).

Dominica Mayma Raphael, *Dominica Gourmet: A Unique Spin on Traditional Dominican Cuisine* (Palo Alto, CA: Mom Publishing, 2022).

Haiti Nadege Fleurimond, *Haïti Uncovered: A Regional Adventure into the Art of Haitian Cuisine* (Gaithersburg, MD: Signature Book Printing, 2014).

Mirta Yurney-Thomas, *A Taste of Haiti* (New York: Hippocrene Books, 2004).

Jamaica Enid Donaldson, *The Real Taste of Jamaica* (Kingston, Jamaica: Ian Randle Publishers, 2000).

Melissa Thompson, *Motherland: A Jamaican Cookbook* (Northampton, MA: Interlink Books, 2022).

Puerto Rico Carmen Aboy Valldejuli, *Puerto Rican Cookery* (Gretna, LA: Pelican Publishing Company, 1975).

Illyana Maisonet, *Diasporican: A Puerto Rican Cookbook* (New York: Ten Speed Press, 2022).

Yvonne Ortiz, *A Taste of Puerto Rico* (New York: Penguin Books, Ltd., 1994).

Trinidad and Tobago Ramin Ganeshram Ramin, *Sweet Hands: Island Cooking from Trinidad and Tobago* (New York: Hippocrene Books, 2010).

Pan-Caribbean Jessica B. Harris, *Beyond Gumbo: Creole Fusion Food from the Atlantic Rim* (New York: Simon & Schuster, 2003).

Jessica B. Harris, *Sky Juice and Flying Fish: Traditional Caribbean Cooking* (New York: Simon & Schuster, 1991).

Elisabeth Lambert Ortiz, *The Complete Book of Caribbean Cooking* (New York: M. Evans and Company, 1973).

INDEX

Note: Page references in *italics* indicate photographs.

A

Ackee and Saltfish, 203
Allspice, 10
Avocado and Salted Cod Pâté, Spicy, 216

B

Bananas
    Sweet Cornbread, 123
    Vegetables Stewed in Coconut Milk, 98–100, *99*
Bean(s), *25,* 26–27
    Black, Stewed, 36, *37*
    Black-Eyed Pea Fritters, 29
    Chicken and Rice (Dominica), 189, *190–91*
    Curried Chickpeas and Potatoes, 30, *31*
    Peas and Rice, 186, *187*
    Pigeon Pea Mash, 34
    Red, Stewed, 41
    Rice and, 28
    Rice with Mushrooms, *184,* 185
    Split Pea Fritters, *38, 39*
    Stew Peas, *32,* 33
    White, Sauce, 35
Beef
    Chayotes Stuffed with Picadillo, 83
    Freedom Soup, 47–49, *48*
    Meat Stew, 73–75, *74*
    Plantain "Casserole" (Dominican Republic), *162,* 163–64
    Plantain "Casserole" (Puerto Rico), 165
    Stuffed Cho Cho, *85,* 86
Bell peppers, 10
    Epis, 21
    Green Sofrito, 22
    Sazón (Dominican Republic), 23
    Trini Chow Mein, *88,* 89
Black-Eyed Pea Fritters, 29
Blender, 18
Breadfruit
    about, 147
    Fried, and Salt Cod Balls, 204
    Mashed, with Okra, *144,* 145–46
    Pie, 205
    Vegetables Stewed in Coconut Milk, 98–100, *99*

Breads
    Cassava, Soaked in Coconut Milk, 72
    Cassava Flatbread, *68,* 69–70
    Coconut Flatbread, 103
    Sweet Cornbread, 123

C

Cabbage
    Chayote Slaw, 90, *91*
    Spicy Pickled, 214
Cake, Cornmeal, *124,* 125
Calabaza, *43,* 44–45
    Freedom Soup, 47–49, *48*
    Okra and Dasheen Greens Soup, *134,* 135
    Pancakes, *56,* 57
    Pie, 58, *59*
    Pumpkin Fritters, 55
    Pumpkin Rice, 52
    Pumpkin Soup, 51
    Puree, 54
    Steamed, with Garlic, 50, *50*
    Steamed Sweet Cornmeal Dumplings, 127, *128–29*
    Stewed, and Salted Cod, 53
    Stewed Red Beans, 41
    Vegetables Stewed in Coconut Milk, 98–100, *99*
Candy, Coconut
    from Barbados, 107
    from Haiti, *108,* 109
Cassareep
    about, 75
    Meat Stew, 73–75, *74*
Cassava, *61,* 62–63
    Boiled, with Mojo Sauce, 76, *77*
    Bread Soaked in Coconut Milk, 72
    cassareep made from, 75
    and Coconut Pudding, 71
    Flatbread, *68,* 69–70
    Fritters, 66
    Hash, 67
    Meat Stew, 73–75, *74*
    Provision Stew, 64–65
Chayote(s), *79,* 80–81
    Cheese-Stuffed, 84
    Slaw, 90, *91*
    Soup, Cream of, 87

Chayote(s), continued
  Stuffed Cho Cho, *85,* 86
  Stuffed with Picadillo, 83
  Trini Chow Mein, *88,* 89
  Vegetable Stew, 82
  and Watercress Salad with Sour Orange
    Vinaigrette, 81
Cheese
  Breadfruit Pie, 205
  Cornmeal Fritters (Puerto Rico), 119
  Plantain "Casserole" (Dominican Republic),
    162, 163–64
  Plantain "Casserole" (Puerto Rico), 165
  -Stuffed Chayotes, 84
  Stuffed Cho Cho, *85,* 86
Chicharrónes, Fried Mashed Plantains with,
    160–61
Chicken, 10
  Curried, 101
  cutting into pieces, 10
  Jerk, 222–24, *223*
  Mashed Breadfruit with Okra, *144,* 145–46
  and Rice (Dominica), 189, *190–91*
  and Rice (Puerto Rico), 188
  and Rice Stew, 192
  Vegetables Stewed in Coconut Milk, 98–100, *99*
Chow Mein, Trini, *88,* 89
Chutney, Mango, 40
Cilantro
  Green Seasoning, 22
  Sazón (Dominican Republic), 23
  substituting, for culantro, 11
Cinnamon, 10–11
Cloves, 11
Coconut, *93,* 94–96. *See also* Coconut cream;
    Coconut Milk
  Candy (Barbados), 107
  Candy (Haiti), *108,* 109
  and Cassava Pudding, 71
  Flatbread, 103
  Steamed Sweet Cornmeal Dumplings,
    127, *128–29*
  Sweet Cornbread, 123
Coconut cream
  Coconut Whipped Cream, 171
  Piña Colada Ice Cream, 111–13, *112*
Coconut Milk
  canned, note on, 96
  Cassava Bread Soaked in, 72
  Coconut Flatbread, 103
  Coconut Pudding, 110

Curried Chicken, 101
  recipe for, 97
  Reduced, Mackerel with, 106
  Vegetables Stewed in, 98–100, *99*
  Wilted Dasheen Leaves with, 104, *105*
Coriander
  Sazón (Puerto Rico), 23
Cornbread, Sweet, 123
Corn flour, about, 117
Cornmeal, *115,* 116–17
  Cake, *124,* 125
  Dumplings, Steamed Sweet, 127, *128–29*
  Fritters (Jamaica), 120, *121*
  Fritters (Puerto Rico), 119
  and Okra, 138, *139*
  and Pork Shoulder Casserole, 122
  Porridge, 126
  with Smoked Herring, 118
  Sweet Cornbread, 123
Crab
  killing humanely, 182
  Mashed Breadfruit with Okra, *144,* 145–46
  and Rice, 181
Culantro, 11
  Green Seasoning, 22
  Green Sofrito, 22
  Sazón (Dominican Republic), 23
Cumin
  Sazón (Puerto Rico), 23
Curried Chicken, 101
Curried Chickpeas and Potatoes, 30, *31*

D
Dasheen Leaves
  Okra and Dasheen Greens Soup, *134,* 135
  Vegetables Stewed in Coconut Milk, 98–100, *99*
  Wilted, with Coconut Milk, 104, *105*
Desserts
  Calabaza Pie, 58, *59*
  Cassava and Coconut Pudding, 71
  Coconut Candy (Barbados), 107
  Coconut Candy (Haiti), *108,* 109
  Coconut Pudding, 110
  Cornmeal Cake, *124,* 125
  Piña Colada Ice Cream, 111–13, *112*
  Plantain Tarte Tatin, 170–71, *173*
  Rice Pudding, 193
  Steamed Sweet Cornmeal Dumplings, 127,
    128–29
Duff, 64–65

Dumplings
    Duff, 64–65
    Spinners, *32,* 33
    Steamed Sweet Cornmeal, 127, *128–29*

E
Eggplant
    Curried Chicken, 101
    Vegetable Mash, 148
    Vegetable Stew, 82
Eggs
    Salted Cod Salad, 209
    Scrambled, with Salted Cod, 201, *202*
    Sweet Plantain Omelet, *156,* 157
Epis, 21
Equipment, 18–19
Evaporated milk, 11

F
Food processor, 18
Freedom Soup, 47–49, *48*
Fritters
    Black-Eyed Pea, 29
    Cassava, 66
    Cornmeal (Jamaica), 120, *121*
    Cornmeal (Puerto Rico), 119
    Fried Breadfruit and Salt Cod Balls, 204
    Pumpkin, 55
    Salt Cod (Martinique), 198, *199*
    Salt Cod (Puerto Rico), 200
    Split Pea, *38,* 39

G
Garlic, 11–12
    Epis, 21
    Green Seasoning, 22
    Green Sofrito, 22
    Hot Sauce, 215
    Steamed Calabaza with, 50, *50*
Ginger, 12

H
Haitian Revolution, 46
Hash, Cassava, 67
Herbs. *See specific herbs*
Hot Sauce, 215

I
Ice Cream, Piña Colada, 111–13, *112*

J
Jerk Chicken, 222–24, *223*

K
Ketchup
    Chicken and Rice (Dominica), 189, *190–91*
    Mayoketchup, 119
Knives, 18–19

L
Limes, 12–13

M
Mackerel with Reduced Coconut Milk, 106
Mango
    Chayote Slaw, 90, *91*
    Chutney, 40
    Salad, Spicy, *218,* 219
Maroons, history of, 220–21
Mayoketchup, 119
Meat. *See also* Beef; Pork
    Stew, 73–75, *74*
Milk, evaporated, 11
Mushrooms
    Mashed Breadfruit with Okra, *144,* 145–46
    Rice with, *184,* 185
    Trini Chow Mein, *88,* 89

N
Noodles. *See* Chow Mein
Nutmeg, 13

O
Oils, 13
Okra, *131,* 132
    and Cornmeal, 138, *139*
    and Dasheen Greens Soup, *134,* 135
    Grilled, with Charred Scallion Vinaigrette, *140,* 141
    Mashed Breadfruit with, *144,* 145–46
    and Rice, 133
    and Saltfish, 137
    Stewed, 142, *143*
    Stir-Fried, 136
    Vegetable Mash, 148
    Vegetables Stewed in Coconut Milk, 98–100, *99*
Omelet, Sweet Plantain, *156,* 157
Onions, Quick-Pickled, Mashed Green Plantains with, 158, *159*

Oxtail
    Freedom Soup, 47–49, *48*
    Meat Stew, 73–75, *74*

P

Pancakes, Calabaza, *56,* 57
Parsley
    Epis, 21
    Green Seasoning, 22
Pâté, Spicy Salted Cod and Avocado, 216
Pea(s)
    Black-Eyed, Fritters, 29
    Pigeon, Mash, 34
    and Rice, 186, *187*
    Rice with Mushrooms, *184,* 185
    Split, Fritters, *38,* 39
Peppers. *See also* Bell peppers; Scotch bonnet
      peppers
    dried seasoning, 14
    Green Sofrito, 22
Picadillo, Chayotes Stuffed with, 83
Pies
    Breadfruit, 205
    Calabaza, 58, *59*
Pigeon Pea(s)
    Mash, 34
    Peas and Rice, 186, *187*
Pilon (mortar and pestle), 18
Piña Colada Ice Cream, 111–13, *112*
Pineapple
    Piña Colada Ice Cream, 111–13, *112*
Plantain(s), *151,* 152–54
    "Casserole" (Dominican Republic), *162,* 163–64
    "Casserole" (Puerto Rico), 165
    Fried Green, 168–69
    Fried Mashed, with Chicharrónes, 160–61
    Fried Sweet, 166, *167*
    Mashed Green, with Quick-Pickled Onions,
      158, *159*
    Porridge, 155
    Provision Stew, 64–65
    Salted Cod Salad, 209
    Sweet, Omelet, *156,* 157
    Tarte Tatin, 170–71, *173*
Pork
    Shoulder and Cornmeal Casserole, 122
    Vegetables Stewed in Coconut Milk, 98–100, *99*
Porridge
    Cornmeal, 126
    Plantain, 155

Potatoes. *See also* Sweet potatoes
    and Chickpeas, Curried, 30, *31*
    Curried Chicken, 101
    Salted Cod Salad, 209
Pots, 18
Provisions, about, 13
Provision Stew, 64–65
Pudding
    Cassava and Coconut, 71
    Coconut, 110
    Rice, 193

R

Rice, *175,* 176–78
    and Beans, 28
    and Chicken (Dominica), 189, *190–91*
    and Chicken (Puerto Rico), 188
    and Chicken Stew, 192
    and Crab, 181
    with Mushrooms, *184,* 185
    and Okra, 133
    and Peas, 186, *187*
    "Perfect" White, 180
    Pudding, 193
    Pumpkin, 52

S

Salads
    Chayote and Watercress, with Sour Orange
      Vinaigrette, 81
    Chayote Slaw, 90, *91*
    Salted Cod, 209
    Spicy Mango, *218,* 219
    Spicy Smoked Herring, 217
Salted Cod, *195,* 196–97
    Ackee and Saltfish, 203
    and Avocado Pâté, Spicy, 216
    Breadfruit Pie, 205
    Fried Breadfruit and Salt Cod Balls, 204
    Okra and Saltfish, 137
    Salad, 209
    Salt Cod Fritters (Martinique), 198, *199*
    Salt Cod Fritters (Puerto Rico), 200
    Scrambled Eggs with, 201, *202*
    Stewed (Haiti), 208
    Stewed (Trinidad and Tobago), 206, *207*
    and Stewed Calabaza, 53
Sauces
    Hot, 215
    Mayoketchup, 119

Tamarind, 40
White Bean, 35
Sazón (Dominican Republic), 23
Sazón (Puerto Rico), 23
Scallion, Charred, Vinaigrette, Grilled Okra with, *140,* 141
Scallions, about, 13
Scotch bonnet peppers, *211,* 212–13
Grilled Snapper with Spicy Shallot Vinaigrette, 228, *229*
Hot Sauce, 215
Jerk Chicken, 222–24, *223*
Shrimp with Hot Sauce, 225, *226*
Spicy Mango Salad, *218,* 219
Spicy Pickled Cabbage, 214
Spicy Salted Cod and Avocado Pâté, 216
Spicy Smoked Herring Salad, 217
Spicy Whole Shrimp, 228
Seafood. *See also* Salted Cod
Cornmeal with Smoked Herring, 118
Crab and Rice, 181
Grilled Snapper with Spicy Shallot Vinaigrette, 228, *229*
killing crabs humanely, 182
Mackerel with Reduced Coconut Milk, 106
Mashed Breadfruit with Okra, *144,* 145–46
Shrimp with Hot Sauce, 225, *226*
Spicy Smoked Herring Salad, 217
Spicy Whole Shrimp, 228
Trini Chow Mein, *88,* 89
Seasoning peppers, 14
Seasonings
Epis, 21
Green, 22
Green Sofrito, 22
Sazón (Dominican Republic), 23
Sazón (Puerto Rico), 23
Shallot Vinaigrette, Spicy, Grilled Snapper with, 228, *229*
Shrimp
with Hot Sauce, 225, *226*
Spicy Whole, 228
Trini Chow Mein, *88,* 89
Slaw, Chayote, 90, *91*
Smoked Herring
Cornmeal with, 118
Salad, Spicy, 217
Snapper, Grilled, with Spicy Shallot Vinaigrette, 228, *229*
Sofrito, Green, 22

Soups
Cream of Chayote, 87
Freedom, 47–49, *48*
Okra and Dasheen Greens, *134,* 135
Pumpkin, 51
Sour Orange, 14
Boiled Cassava with Mojo Sauce, 76, *77*
Vinaigrette, Chayote and Watercress Salad with, 81
Spinners, *32,* 33
Split Pea Fritters, *38,* 39
Squash. *See* Calabaza
Star anise, 14
Stews
Chicken and Rice, 192
Meat, 73–75, *74*
Provision, 64–65
Vegetable, 82
White Bean Sauce, 35
Sweet potatoes
Provision Stew, 64–65
Vegetables Stewed in Coconut Milk, 98–100, *99*

T
Tamarind Sauce, 40
Tarte Tatin, Plantain, 170–71, *173*
Thyme, 14–15
Tomatoes, 15
Cassava Hash, 67
Cornmeal with Smoked Herring, 118
Mackerel with Reduced Coconut Milk, 106
Sazón (Dominican Republic), 23
Stewed Okra, 142, *143*
Turmeric, 15

V
Vanilla, 15
Vegetable(s). *See also specific vegetables*
Mash, 148
Stew, 82
Stewed in Coconut Milk, 98–100, *99*
Vinegar, 15

W
Watercress and Chayote Salad with Sour Orange Vinaigrette, 81
Whipped Cream, Coconut, 171
Wok, 19

Text copyright © 2024 by Lesley Enston
Photographs copyright © 2024 by Marc Baptiste, except
as noted below
Cover illustration copyright © 2024 by Nicholas Huggins

All rights reserved.

Published in the United States by Ten Speed Press, an
imprint of Random House, a division of Penguin Random
House LLC, New York.
TenSpeed.com | CrownPublishing.com

Ten Speed Press and the Ten Speed Press colophon are
registered trademarks of Penguin Random House LLC.

Photo credits:
Page iv: Alex—stock.adobe.com
Pages v and 2: saikorn—stock.adobe.com
Pages vii, 24, 42, 60, 78, 92, 114, 130, 150, 174, 194, and 210:
    Natalia Baran—stock.adobe.com
Page vii: kovgabor79—stock.adobe.com
Page xiv: GW3NDOL!N—stock.adobe.com
Pages 2–3: Ken Enston—copyright © 2024 by Ken Enston
Page 9: Piman Khrutmuang—stock.adobe.com
Pages 16–17: cenz07—stock.adobe.com
Page 25: Deanna Wallach
Page 179: gusti—stock.adobe.com
Page 232: Atibon Nazaire
Page 236: Samuel—stock.adobe.com

Typefaces: Brownfox's Gerbera and Hanoded Fonts'
Breakfast Noodles

Library of Congress Cataloging-in-Publication Data
Names: Enston, Lesley, 1980- author. | Baptiste, Marc,
photographer.
Title: Belly full : exploring the Caribbean cuisine through
11 fundamental ingredients / Lesley Enston ; photography
by Marc Baptiste.
Description: California : Ten Speed Press, [2024] | Includes
index. | Identifiers: LCCN 2023037423 (print) | LCCN
2023037424 (ebook) | ISBN 9781984861825 (hardcover) |
ISBN 9781984861832 (ebook)
Subjects: LCSH: Cooking, Caribbean. | LCGFT: Cookbooks.
Classification: LCC TX716.A1 E57 2024 (print) | LCC TX716.
A1 (ebook) | DDC 641.59729—dc23/eng/20230809
LC record available at https://lccn.loc.gov/2023037423
LC ebook record available at https://lccn.loc.
gov/2023037424

ISBN: 978-1-9848-6182-5
Ebook ISBN: 978-1-9848-6183-2

Printed in China

Acquiring editor: Dervla Kelly | Project editor: Claire Yee
Production editors: Natalie Blachere and Abby Oladipo
Editorial assistant: Gabby Ureña Matos
Art director: Emma Campion | Designer: Lizzie Allen
Production designers: Mari Gill and Faith Hague
Production manager: Jane Chinn
Prepress color manager: Nick Patton
Food stylist: Luciana Lamboy (for all photos except
page 5, 161, and 195)
Food stylist assistant: Rosanna Añil
Prop stylist: Gerri Williams (for all photos except
page 5, 161, and 195)
Prop stylist assistant: Sadie Frost
Photo assistants: Paul Storey and Skye Baptiste
Recipe developer: Lesley Enston
Copyeditor: Ivy McFadden
Proofreaders: Hope Clarke and Rachel Holzman
Indexer: Elizabeth Parson
Publicist: Felix Cruz | Marketer: Monica Stanton

10 9 8 7 6 5 4 3 2 1

First Edition